Walter I. Farmer

The Safekeepers

Cultural Property Studies

Schriften zum Kulturgüterschutz

Cultural Property Studies
Schriften zum Kulturgüterschutz

Edited by
Herausgegeben von

Professor Dr. Hans W. Baade, Austin / Texas
Professor Dr. Wilfried Fiedler, Saarbrücken
Professor Dr. Dr. h.c. Erik Jayme, Heidelberg
Professor Dr. Kurt Siehr, Zürich

Walter I. Farmer

The Safekeepers

A Memoir of the Arts at the End of World War II

Revised and prefaced by
Klaus Goldmann

With an introduction by
Margaret Farmer Planton

W DE G Walter de Gruyter · Berlin · New York 2000

Walter I. Farmer, Staff member, U.S. Monuments, Fine Arts & Archives (MFA & A) 1945/46
Dr. Klaus Goldmann, Museum für Vor- und Frühgeschichte, Staatl. Museen zu Berlin, Preußischer Kulturbesitz (Pre- and Early History Museum), Berlin, Germany
Margaret Farmer Planton, Daughter of the late author Walter I. Farmer and Renate Hobirk-Farmer, Chillicothe, Ohio, U.S.A.

♾ Printed on acid-free paper which falls within the guidelines of the ANSI to ensure permanence and durability.

Die Deutsche Bibliothek – CIP Einheitsaufnahme

Farmer, Walter I.:
The Safekeepers : a memoir of the arts at the end of World War II / Walter I. Farmer. Rev. and pref. by Klaus Goldmann. With an introd. by Margaret Farmer Planton. – Berlin ; New York : de Gruyter, 2000
(Cultural property studies)
ISBN 3-11-016897-9

Printed in Germany
Cover: +malsy kommunikation und gestaltung, Bremen
Data Convertion: Werksatz Schmidt & Schulz, Gräfenhainichen
Printing and Binding: Hubert & Co, Göttingen

Preface

German reunification on October 3, 1990, was a historic date for East and West German museums and a turning point for the Berlin State Museums. The Berlin collections had been involved in negotiations during the Cold War. The Soviets and later the German Democratic Republic (GDR) asked for the return of all the art that had been evacuated from Berlin at the end of World War II from the area which had become the U.S. and British Zones of occupation after V-E-Day. After the capitulation these parts of the Berlin collections found their way to Allied Collecting Points for safekeeping and returned to West-Berlin during the fifties. Before WW II most of the State Museums collections had been housed on the Berlin museum island; since 1945 the museum island was in the Soviet sector. Therefore the Berlin collection became 'twins' – one in West Berlin and one in East Berlin. The curators in the East were not allowed to contact their colleagues in the West; in reality they have been good partners, but nobody could speak about this fact, then!

With Germany's reunification the 'reunited' State Museums started intensive research on the post-war history of their collections in the East and the West. At the same time the Soviet Union opened many archives and the world learned that many parts of the State Museum collections remained in Russian strong rooms, when officially 'all' spoils of war had been returned to the GDR in 1955–59.

A lively discussion arose and is going on world wide questioning what happened at the end of WW II when the western Allies found most of the art and archives the Germans had captured during the war. All German owned collections were taken into custody by military law to establish their rightful owner.

The most prominent parts of the Berlin State Museums collections had been transferred from their bomb-proof shelters in Berlin in March and early April 1945 to a saltmine at Merkers/Kaiseroda in Thuringia where they were found by Patton's 3rd Army. They were evacuated from the mine in mid-April and brought to the Reichsbank-building at Frankfurt/Main. In August 1945 they were shipped to the U.S. Central Collecting Point in the former Landes-museum in Wiesbaden. This Collecting Point gave shelter to many German owned collections which had been taken into custody. The architect, organizer, and first director of this institution was U.S. Capt. Walter I. Farmer, MFA&A, who had been given the responsibility for a crucial part of Germany's cultural heritage. His memoirs give a detailed and personal account of this important chapter in the history of the Berlin State Museum collections.

The author, Walter Ings Farmer, wrote the manuscript with the assistance of Dr. Ruth K. Meyer in the early nineties. It was revised later in close cooperation with Walter's daughter, Margaret Farmer Planton, when many new files in German, U.S., and Russian archives could be evaluated. It can be shown that the Berlin State Museums played a major role not only during the cold war but also in world politics at least since 1939.

Berlin, Germany
July 2000

Klaus Goldmann

Contents

Abbreviations

ADHG	American Defense – Harvard Group
Advisory Commitee	Advisory Committee on Post-War Foreign Policy Preparation
AMG	Allied Military Gouverment
CAD	Civil Affairs Division of the War Department
CCCR	Committee on Conservation of Cultural Recources
CORC	Coordinating Committee of the Allied Control Council, Germany
DP	Displaced Person
EAC	European Advisory Commission
ERR	Einsatzstab Reichsleiter Rosenberg
GDR	German Democratic Republic
I. G. Farben	Interessen Gemeinschaft Farben (German Chemical Trust)
JCS	Joint Chiefs of Staff
JDC	Joint Destribution Committee
KFM	Kaiser-Friedrich-Museum (Berlin)
Land	State Government in US Zone of occupation
MFA & A	Monuments, Fine Arts and Archives
NGA	National Gallery of Art (Washington, D.C.)
MacMillan Committee	British Committee on the Preservation and Restitution of Works of Art, Archives, and Other Material in Enemy Hands
MP	Military Police
OCS	Officiers Candidate School
OMGUS	Office of Military Government for Germany (U.S.)
OSS	Office of Strategic Services
RDR	(Division for) Reparations, Deliveries and Restitution
Roberts Commission	American Commission for the Protection and Salvage of Artistic and Historic Monuments in War Areas
SWNCC	State, War, Navy Coordinating Committee
SANACC	State, Army, Navy, and Air Force Coordinating Committee
SHAEF	Supreme Headquarters, Allied Expeditionary Forces
UNICEF	United Nations International Children's Emergency Fund

UNRRA	United Nations Relief and Rehabilitations Administration
USFET	US Forces, European Theater
USNR	US Naval Reserve
USGCC	US Group, Control Council
Vaucher Commission	Inter-Allied Commission for the Protection and Restitution of Cultural Materials
VE	(V-E) Victory in Europe
V 1	Vergeltungswaffe 1 (German V-Weapons, Flying Bomb)
WAC	Women's Army Corps
WCCP	Wiesbaden Central Collecting Point
YIVO	Yiddish Scientific Institut Library (Vilna, Lithuania)

and:

KG	Klaus Goldmann
MFP	Margret Farmer Planton
RKM	Ruth Krueger Meyer
WIF	Walter Ings Farmer

Introduction

When the Russian tanks rolled into Berlin in the Spring of 1945, Germany presented a scene of utter devastation. Years of bombing had destroyed communication and distribution networks, devastated cities, and left urban populations dispossessed. Groups of refugees wandered the roads, seeking food, shelter, and a return to their homes. Allied armies guarded huge numbers of prisoners of war in massive prison camps. The occupying armies faced seemingly insuperable problems of administering the conquered areas, feeding and housing the populace, repairing the devastated infrastructure, and dealing with the ex-rulers of a defeated Germany.

During their thrusts across European territory, all of the armies had encountered cultural and historic properties, sometimes carefully hidden by their German guardians, sometimes in open display. While the Allied armies' primary tasks focused upon daily survival of the German populace in the summer of 1945, they also had to deal with artworks, cultural property, and monuments in the occupied areas. General Eisenhower had laid the foundation for this latter task with his order of 1943 that cultural property not be harmed if at all possible. In the occupying forces small groups of officers were given responsibility for cultural properties as they surfaced in their zone. In the US Army, The Monuments, Fine Arts and Archives group worked under the horrific conditions of a war-flattened Germany to identify and preserve items of cultural significance from further damage. (see Appendix No. I)*

Years later, Germany had not only been rebuilt but had become a NATO ally and an economic powerhouse. In the prosperous 1980's the search for missing cultural properties emerged as a topic in the media. Scholars had been studying aging paper records and were searching for surviving witnesses and staff to find out what might be known about what had happened to some of the greatest treasures of the German and other European museums as Allied armies had followed the bombers through European cities in 1945.

This memoir, *The Safekeepers,* brings my Father's life to the pivotal date of 6 November 1945 when he received a command he could not accept. My Father, then Captain Walter I. Farmer, was Director of the Wiesbaden Collecting Point. He received a telegram from the highest US command to send at least 200 premier German-owned artworks to Washington. The safety and protection of masterpieces had consumed all his energies for months, this order was contrary to everything he and the other 34 Monuments, Fine Arts and Archives officers had been working so hard for. His direct call to action brought 32 Arts officers to his

* See page 121

office on 7 November 1945 to discuss this outrageous order, collectively they wrote a protest to their army orders, a protest for which they could have been subject to court martial. This 'protest' took on new significance in 1987 when Germany's search for missing art treasures led Dr. Klaus Goldmann to interview my Father in Washington D.C. This interview brought the story of the 'protest,' now called the "Wiesbaden Manifesto," forward into international view after years of silence.

Dr. Goldmann was joined by Lynn Nicholas and others in sending Father a stream of questions about the Wiesbaden Collecting Point. I became involved in 1987 in my family's story as I helped Father write, edit and translate various materials. My parents, Walter and Renate Hobirk Farmer, had often shared with me the story of how they met and the love of art and beautiful things they shared. Father was the Director of the Wiesbaden Collecting Point from June 1945 through March 1946. Mother was the Chief of Staff at the Wiesbaden Collecting Point from July 1945 to May 1947. Now, years later, I helped Father organize the extensive archives he had kept. I edited his field notebook, reviewed original documents, created lists, translated articles from Germany, and transcribed the letters he had written home to his first wife Josselyn. The letters show the boundless enthusiasm he had for the work and the gratitude he felt for the opportunity to preserve art masterpieces.

In the 1990's art became a politically heated topic with Russia acknowledging that they had confiscated and had been hiding German and other European museum collections. The publication of Lynn Nicholas's *The Rape of Europa* brought the issues to a wider readership and awareness. In January 1995, Father was one of five US arts officers who spoke at The Bard Graduate Center symposium "The Spoils of War: World War II & Its Aftermath." This decisive international assembly ended with German Ambassador Hagen Graf Lambsdorff acknowledging the Manifesto's importance to Germany when he read the entire document aloud. On February 9, 1996 Father accepted the Grosse Verdienstkreuz, signed by German President Roman Herzog, on behalf of all MFA&A officers from German Vice-Chancellor and Minister for Foreign Affairs Dr. Klaus Kinkel. This honor was followed in May 1997 by the 'Humanitarian of the Year Award' from Die Grossloge der Alten Freien und Angenommenen Maurer von Deutschland.

Before Father passed away in August 1997, I promised to finish working on his memoirs. It is my deepest gratitude, affection and respect that I finish his story. It has been a unique and rewarding time for me as an adult to work so closely with my Father, Mother, other arts officers and Dr. Goldmann to write about my parents' war time work. I was fortunate to be able to accompany Father to New York, Bonn, Berlin and Fürth. The recognition he received from the German government and the Masons meant a great deal to him. The deep friendship with Dr. Goldmann and his family shows the depth of personal commitment to establishing the truth that he has guided all the research.

Father also wished to express his gratitude to Dr. Ruth K. Meyer, former director of the Taft Museum in Cincinnati, Ohio, who prepared the first draft of this memoir in 1994. She interviewed many arts officers and checked archival sources. In 1998 and 1999, Dr. Goldmann, Dr. Martin Albrecht and Renate Farmer have helped me finish the story of the Wiesbaden Manifesto.

Father continued to hope that all missing artworks will be recovered. Now in 2000 it seems likely that some collections will be returned to their pre World War II homes as international legal debates continue. There must always be hope and room for further honorable actions in world history.

Chillicothe, Ohio
June 2000

Margaret Farmer Planton

Chapter one: My Castle

As a child I had constructed an imaginary castle where I could live as I pleased undisturbed by my parents or my siblings who never shared my real world interests. As I grew older the castle became a metaphor of a place for spiritual refuge and a space inside me to which I withdrew for private fantasies of what my life might become. For the period of my military service that will be told later, I forcibly adapted myself as an individual who disguised his interest in the arts and culture so as to survive in the company of men who would not have understood. With my cultivated tastes well hidden I was able to excel in my position as the Colonel's chief administrative officer while embracing the regimental motto *Honest Duty*. I was astonished when Bell called me "the culture of the regiment" in his inscription of the book that preserves the history of our military service. I thought my castle walls had been thicker than that.

I was born on 7 July 1911 in the northern Ohio town of Alliance, 50 miles from Cleveland. As the fourth and last child of a couple who were already in their forties at the time of my birth I entered a well settled household and my coming did little to disturb long established routines. Father was an executive at a steel factory and mother led a moderate social life. Without their noticing I moved with rapidity into a precocious adolescence. I had discovered reading, music and collecting at a very early age and for my interest in these pursuits I was rewarded with adult friendships and encouragement.

From my own pleasant home I had wandered to the house of two maiden ladies, the Vale sisters, who gave me music lessons, showed me how to examine works of art and taught me to cultivate a garden. The Vale sisters also guided me into genealogical research and they began to instruct me in the drawing of a family tree. I plunged early into a lifelong study of genealogy. My uncle, the Honorable David Adams Hollingsworth, a prominent Ohio politician, published his autobiography in 1920. I took his book to school and the teacher read aloud from it to our class. Suddenly, at the age of nine, I discovered the pride of being "somebody." Hollingsworth served as Ohio's attorney general and in the US Congress. From his book I learned that my family came to America with William Penn. A few years later I attended the huge family reunion he hosted and was given a family heirloom. My parents indulged my enthusiasms by buying me a piano and allowing me to expand into my older siblings quarters when they moved away from home. In the top floor of our house I began to shelve and arrange my own collections into a personal museum of carefully chosen family heirlooms, nature specimens and other treasures.

My own father's career provided me with a model for success, although his pursuit of it meant that he was frequently absent during my youth. Father was an executive for the Morgan Engineering Company, the principal industry in Alliance, Ohio. He had been apprenticed as a machinist in Wheeling, West Virginia, and became an expert estimator of fabrication costs for the heavy cranes and other machinery the Morgan company manufactured.

When it became clear that America would intervene in the First World War father's skills were put to the service of the US government as Morgan prepared to manufacture munitions and heavy ordnance weapons. For a hectic period of time father kept residences in New York and Washington as he shuttled between the bureaucrats and the financiers who were preparing the nation for war. Immediately after the war work slowed dramatically at the Morgan factory and father went on the road looking for business, so I saw little of him. Still I have wonderful memories of him when he was at home and especially of his kindness to everyone. He instilled in me the Quaker heritage of responsibility for the welfare of others. Modestly, but not humbly, one offers one's service to humanity by fitting into a community. His death in 1927 when I was sixteen deprived me of his guidance just as I entered young manhood, but I tried always to live by his example.

Continuing my genealogical research I discovered my kinship with Lydia Farmer Painter, a great Victorian explorer who had written a book about her adventures. It was through a search for her book that I gained a new paternal influence in my life. Her son, Kenyon Vickers Painter, lived in Cleveland where his Farmer ancestors had moved to direct the management of the Pittsburgh Cleveland Railroad. There they had prospered and his father had built for Lydia an 80 room mansion that still stands at the corner of Lee Road and Fairmont Boulevard.

Knowing that Lydia was dead, I wrote a letter to Kenyon Painter asking him how to get to see a copy of her book. Impressed with my youthful enthusiasm for family history Painter invited me to visit him in Cleveland. There he took me into his home where I found displayed all the treasures his mother had collected. Kenyon Painter was adding to that accumulation and embellishing their estate with gardens, a zoo and an aviary.

The house was like a museum containing paintings, sculptures, tapestries and masses of rare books. My visits to Cleveland were extended and I took on the task of cataloguing his library. Although Painter was married and had children of his own, they were still too young to share his collector's passion and moreover, he wanted to parent a fatherless boy. Through his mentoring I began to see the future directions that my life could take in the arts and in architecture.

The structural design of the house had been appropriated from Compton Wynates, a Tudor manor house in Warwickshire, England, and Painter was actively importing "gothic" paneling and furniture to complement the exterior. When the paneling arrived I was given the pleasure of arranging the installation of the panels. With Painter I traveled to New York going to see art dealers and attending auctions to buy works to enrich this magnificent setting.

Through this period of time my life in Alliance was that of a typical high school student and I attended my share of parties and entertainments when not in Cleveland. Painter's influence in my life was stronger than that of my classmates and when he offered me a chance to go on a hunting expedition to Africa in 1929 I was ready to leave school and postpone my graduation. Over the summer my trunks were prepared, but the advancing crisis in the stock market led to the cancellation of that trip and I was graduated from high school in January 1930.

Painter had taken over the direction of my education and thought that I should spend a year after high school exploring the world of work before enrolling at Yale University, his alma mater. Among his many enthusiasms, Painter was a wild game hunter and trophy collector. He had sponsored expeditions led by Carl Akeley, a famous taxidermist and the inventor of a motion picture camera who had a studio in New York City. In the summer of 1930 I was given a job with Akeley's firm and on a salary of twenty-five dollars a week took up residence at Sloan House in New York.

The next six months completed the transformation of a precocious small town boy into a worldly young man. First to go was my broad Ohio accent eliminated by means of reading aloud and imitating the vocal tones of my new companions. I enrolled in night school classes at Columbia University, took riding lessons in Central Park and spent money intended for food on feasting my eyes and ears at the opera and at concerts. I was nearly frantic to experience at once everything the city could offer.

When I returned to Alliance for the Christmas holidays I was nearly unrecognizable to my mother, sister and brothers. I was painfully thin and acutely nervous having been virtually electrified by all my new passions. My mother was horrified and would not hear of my returning to New York. My nervous system had long been a concern to my family who had observed my excessive energy and abundant high spirits wondering how my enthusiasms and obsessive interests in the arts were to be channeled into a normal and productive life.

The powerful influence of Kenyon Painter was waning. My mentor was beset with his own problems brought about by the stock market collapse and threats to the Union Trust Bank of Cleveland in which he was a principal stock holder. As the depression worsened, Painter's Cleveland holdings were wiped out and when he died his wife sold the great house to an order of nuns.

Without my father's earning power our family's fortunes had suffered along with everyone else's. I had received a small inheritance from the estate of my uncle D. A. Hollingsworth and this established a college fund of $ 5000. To afford the four years needed to earn a degree I chose Miami University at Oxford, Ohio, where a course in architecture had recently been established. I enrolled for the 1930–1931 winter term and settled once more into a small rural town, albeit with an academic atmosphere.

It wasn't New York, but Oxford did have a cultural life which I embraced by joining the clubs and activities for music and theater students. Shortly after arriving I went to hear a dramatic reading given by Mrs. Wade McMillan and immediately acquired a new mentor. Marian Thayer McMillan was a scholar and an author who gave lectures around the country on the arts and other spiritually motivated topics. She had great dramatic presence and the content of her lectures gently challenged the provincial minds of her audiences. Henry James had been a special mentor and she had published their correspondence. Appropriately mirroring her style, she also wrote a book called *Reflections: the Story of Water.*[1] It is basically a photographic album in which tranquil views of lakes and their shorelines are rotated 180 degrees so that the horizontal becomes vertical and mirrored images can be read like the Rorschach inkblot. Her texts accompanying the images blend Eastern religions, myths and folklore to provoke the viewer's interpretations. Marian's sister-in-law, Mary McMillan, was also a poet who wrote Sapphic verse and enjoyed an equally ardent following. In Oxford, the McMillans held a salon where the arts were debated in a lively fashion.

My decision to study architecture at Miami represented a realistic compromise. I would have vastly preferred a course in museum studies or even the field of interior design since my experience with Kenyon Vickers Painter's house and collections had uncovered a talent for these vocations. But, at this time one could study art history only at the Eastern universities and there were no college programs for interior design in the United States. Only with the Parsons School faculty in Paris could one really take courses and study the historic styles that influenced the practice of decoration internationally. Alliance, Ohio, had produced a Parsons' graduate, Bill Tollerton, near my age and proud to show me the beautiful renderings he had produced in Paris. The Miami program in architecture was in its second year of existence when I joined the class. Our curriculum was dominated by the revival of Classicism promoted by the Ecole des Beaux Arts in Paris and sustained in America by most of the other schools of architecture. The modernism of Le Corbusier and Mies van der Rohe was unknown to us and the International Style to which they contributed was not to be named until the end of our decade when Philip Johnson organized his landmark exhibition at the Museum of Modern Art.

We learned to draw columns in the proper Doric, Ionic and Corinthian orders while studying the mechanics of engineering a building. In addition to these

---

[1] Thayer McMillan, Marian. *Reflections: the Story of Water.* New York, Greenberg, 1936.

courses that demanded a great deal of studio time I studied in the school of liberal arts. When the first summer of my college career arrived I left for the University of Colorado to earn credit for courses missed by my late arrival at Oxford. In Boulder, Colorado, I supported myself by giving English riding lessons, a skill acquired in New York's Central Park.

In my second year I continued the pattern of studies and social life I had quickly established on my arrival in Oxford. In my sophomore year I was consumed with planning for a summer abroad in 1933 with my mother to visit England and look up our Farmer and Ings relatives. We were planning to be gone for four months. We would rent a car and I intended to see every English cathedral and as many stately homes and formal gardens as possible along the way. Old issues of *Country Life* magazine were my guides for an itinerary that would benefit both my architectural education and my genealogical interests.

The trip was an enormous success thanks in part to my advance planning and the years of genealogical research I had done on the Farmer family. Arriving in London I stated my mission to the staff of the English Speaking Union who were delighted to help me write the required letters to owners of the great houses asking for admittance. They also coached me in proper conduct and forms of address used when meeting the landed aristocracy. This help proved invaluable for at each stop we received a wonderful welcome. Our hosts were surprised to meet a young American college student who was already so knowledgeable in English life and customs. During the course of the trip I enlarged my library of books on English architecture and decorative arts and started a collection of prints and drawings.

Returning to Oxford, Ohio, after this glorious excursion I settled down to my junior year and architectural studies. Enriched by my recent travels, I began to draw a project for an Adam style townhouse only to run into conflict with my professor who disputed my designs. Although I knew he had not been to England or seen what I had freshly experienced, I tried to bear his criticisms until his interference provoked me to a towering anger. Fortunately, the head of the School of Architecture, Russell Porter, came to my aid and I was released from my critic's tutelage. Dean Kratt took over as my advisor and my academic performance began to measure up to the high expectations that I nurtured for myself. He encouraged my musical interests and, with his approval, I was able to add courses to my program to graduate with degrees from two colleges, one in architecture and one in mathematics.

With graduation day approaching my classmates were debating what to give the university as our departing gift. I suggested that we raise funds to acquire a base for a statue of George Washington by Jean-Antoine Houdon that needed proper elevation and that we have the schools' modest collections of paintings cleaned and restored. For the second project I went into Cincinnati where picture restorers at the A. B. Closson Company showed me how to remove layers of dirt that were clinging to the varnished surfaces. At the time I never thought that a few months later I would find my first job with this firm.

Although I longed to go east and continue my studies in architecture at Harvard where I had been admitted, the money for my education was gone. By 1935 all of the family members who had prospered before the crash of 1929 were dead and their fortunes had expired with them. Once more I was grateful to Russell Potter, who recognized my situation and introduced me to interior designers in Cincinnati. Potter knew I lacked training in the structural requirements of architecture and that because of the depression there were no apprenticeships in the field. To study interior design had been a part of my original motivation and I might have a better chance immediately in that profession.

The A. B. Closson Company, known familiarly as Clossons, offered me the opportunity to work in a large firm employing many designers and serving a regional clientele. The store had a strong reputation and drew shoppers from the three state area. Their merchandise reflected the broad market they served with departments for gifts, home accessories, prints and paintings as well as furniture and draperies. My architectural training came into use when it was found that I could draw perspective renderings for the decorators' presentations. I earned fifteen dollars a week. The downtown Cincinnati location put me in the heart of things. I started my career with enthusiasm and set about making new friends and continuing my studies and contact with beautiful things in Ohio's second largest city.

When I entered the Clossons work force in the fall of 1935 it provided employment for a team of interior designers who served a wealthy Jewish clientele residing in the suburbs of Clifton, Walnut Hills and Hyde Park, but most notable in Avondale where the crenellated mansions of the German settlers were thickly clustered. Cincinnati's earliest residents had come directly from England and the American colonies at the turn of the Nineteenth century. The German settlers had arrived shortly afterwards and established a tightly knit and rapidly prospering community. There were two aristocracies, Gentile and Jew, and they mingled freely for the purposes of business, government and philanthropic causes, not the least of them the arts. But, social clubs were segregated and neighborhood borders were defined.

Clossons was housed in a five story building on Race Street in the heart of the downtown district with showrooms on the street level for gifts and accessories as well as furniture. The second floor featured the Red Velvet Room where traveling dealers in fine arts and prints would offer showings to local collectors. Next came a floor for the storage and display of the fabrics from which the designers fashioned the draperies and home furnishings for which the store was noted. Another floor displayed Oriental rugs and tapestries and finally there was a top floor of offices. When I arrived after my college graduation my first assignment was to fold and shelve the extensive collection of fine fabric samples which the decorators drew upon when planning for their clients.

Among the decorators were Vashti Cohen, a graduate of the Parsons School in New York, Evelyn Lindahl and other young women of my age. Mrs. Erma Wald was my special mentor for she introduced me to her Jewish clients. As the daughters of these clients married and set up housekeeping I began to build my own clientele from among them and their friends.

After a year or more of widening my social and professional contacts I began to teach at the Cincinnati Art Museum. The museum had an extensive program of lectures and classes for children and adults. Women were particularly interested in courses in interior design and lectures on fields within the decorative arts, such as silver, porcelains, and fabrics and also on the design of gardens. Ernestine Evans, the museum educator, encouraged my teaching and she soon became a frequent social companion.

The art museum classes developed my natural fondness for holding forth on various subjects I had studied and they brought me into contact with potential clients. My world expanded even more when I began to make appearances on the local Ruth Lyons radio program.

As respect for my talents grew I endeavored to maintain the principles which I felt were so necessary to being successful as a designer. I saw myself as a doctor of design called in to minister to an ailing house where the residents had all but given up hope of making a home. Many young wives were struggling to cope with older houses that had been built in the previous century according to contractor plans and without the benefit of an architect. Although located in desirable neighborhoods, these houses always featured awkward arrangements of mantelpieces, bookcases, inglenooks, and columns. With my background in architectural design I did not hesitate to order the removal of these elements when they stood in the way of opening up a room to more light and better circulation.

While enjoying every aspect of my social and professional life along with all the young men of my age group I followed the political events in England and on the Continent where the Nazi party was beginning to menace the freedom of Germany's neighbors. Political sentiments among my friends favored isolationism and non-interventionary measures. But when Adolf Hitler invaded Poland in 1939 the likelihood of the United States staying out of the war diminished. Young men in our group began to talk about enlisting in the Navy, the Army or the Air Force and applying for officer's training.

It seemed I would gain nothing but rejection from a voluntary induction because of poor eyesight and having worn glasses since childhood. Much as I admired the courage of my friends and even envied their opportunities to prove their patriotism, I would have to wait and see if the Army would draft me.

Events in Europe were taking on new importance for me. By 1940 I had formed a friendship with a Polish family, the Liszniewskis, who were connected to the international worlds of both music and diplomacy. Mme. Marguerite Melville-Liszniewska, an American child prodigy, studied in Vienna with the great pianist, Lisezitsky, and there had married Dr. Karol Liszniewski. He found employment in the diplomatic service and Madame became assistant to Lisezitsky. Their daughter Josselyn and her brother John had been born in Vienna. After the First World War the family had moved to London and thereafter came to Cincinnati where Madame Liszniewska was engaged to teach master classes in piano at the College-Conservatory of Music.

Josselyn Liszniewska was outstanding among our circle of friends who were fascinated by her array of continental accomplishments. Of course, she was beautiful in an elegant way that appeared exotic to our Midwestern eyes. Raised in the Middle European milieu, she spoke eight languages and had begun doctoral studies at the University of Cincinnati planning to earn degrees in both French and organic chemistry. I cannot recall exactly when I realized that I was in love with Josselyn.

The entry of the United States into the war in Europe abruptly altered the tempo of our lives as the young men whom I had grown to know professionally and socially started marching off to war. I had to move from the large apartment I'd shared with five friends to a smaller place with a young physician, James Ruegsegger. Soon he too went off to join the Navy.

During 1941 I was called up for military service four times by the Army and four times rejected on account of my eyesight. These rejections were intensely disappointing. In spite of my tastes for beauty and refinement in living, I was no less ready than any man of my age to serve my country and believed it to be my duty. I tried to enlist in the Navy with no success and then an older friend who had connections with officers at a base near Dayton drove me there personally to try to gain my admittance to the Air Force. Once again I passed all the tests and was rejected because I could not read without glasses.

Returning to work at Clossons I was caught up in the bustle of the 1941 holiday shopping season. My courtship of Josselyn was becoming more ardent and she had made a trip to California to make a farewell visit to another admirer. After that trip she said she would marry me and we announced our engagement at an elegant Christmas dance given by Jack and Babs Emery at their Indian Hill estate, Peterloon.

It was difficult to get to know her because she studied all the time and when she wasn't studying we were in the company of her family or out with other couples.

The two months of our engagement did not offer us time to become better acquainted. She had exams and I worked long hours keeping my customers at Clossons happy and to afford to be married. On the day of our wedding I moved to the home of Dr. Liszniewski where I had renovated and furnished a flat for us. I knew I had married a real European princess.

Five weeks later, in March, 1942, I received another Army induction notice. Thirty years old, I was to be drafted into service with the Medical Corps where my eyesight would not be a problem. At the induction center in Ft. Thomas, Kentucky, I found myself among a group of recruits from the hills of that state and West Virginia. We left for Ft. Sam Houston in San Antonio on Good Friday. On Easter Sunday I began my military career quickly resolving to disguise my privileged background. I listed my occupation as "draftsman," for I certainly didn't want anyone in the Army to know I had been an interior designer.

Determined to maintain a protective cover around my personality, I did dare to speak up when one of the sergeants asked if anyone in our unit could use a typewriter. I raised my hand and in that instant I was lifted out of the ranks and suddenly given the opportunity to rise into the Army's bureaucracy. Recognizing my lucky break I concentrated all my efforts to display my attention to detail and willingness to work. The Army rewards such diligence and I was soon promoted from private to 1st class. I became the assistant to the First Sergeant, who was in charge of all the details of personnel management. In this role I processed all the company's paperwork and deepened my knowledge of Army procedures.

From this vantage point I could study how to get myself into Officers Candidate School. First I applied for the Quartermaster Corps. Fortunately, a kindly officer questioned my request and suggested I would do better in the general service engineers where my architectural training would be put to use. Miraculously, I was accepted as officer material and was sent to Ft. Belvoir near Washington to attend Engineers Officers Candidate School.

My chances for a spot in OCS might have ended suddenly when once again I was scheduled for a physical examination. Just as I walked into the medics pyramidal tent for the final procedure, a vision test, the doctor was turning over the eye chart. Before he flipped it to its blank side, I glimpsed it quickly and memorized the first few lines so that when the time came I recited them perfectly. Pass. But, making the grade at Ft. Belvoir didn't mean staying the course and I soon discovered that the training officers would do everything in their power to eliminate older candidates like myself. We were challenged, threatened and intimidated in every conceivable way as we learned army discipline and the futility of questioning orders.

In late fall 1942 we spent our time learning to build bridges on the Potomac River. The barracks were unheated and we were constantly outdoors in cold, rainy weather. If my health had broken at any moment I would have been sent back to the medics. To make myself useful I volunteered to teach reading, writing, and how to decipher maps. Now I would have to learn to fire a gun. I learned to shoot and to perform military drills and even served as company commandant during a particularly rigorous inspection. With good luck and with some covert assistance from the guys in my platoon, I managed to survive the weapons training.

There remained one final physical exam, one more eye test to pass. Another miracle occurred when the exam was canceled because it conflicted with the Christmas holidays. In January 1943 I was graduated and commissioned as a second lieutenant in the Army. After a few days leave spent in Cincinnati, I was ordered to Camp Claiborne in Louisiana where a new regiment of engineers was to be formed.

My new rank entitled me to have Josselyn join me in what she imagined to be the glamorous life of a military post. She drove down from Cincinnati in my car and we rented a small farm house some distance from the base. There we confronted the fact that Josselyn had never learned to keep house. I arrived home for dinner one evening where Josse presented me with a live chicken which she planned to serve for our supper. Neither of us had ever begun preparing a meal quite literally from scratch. Our married life did improve when we were able to move to an apartment closer to the base. But, I was frequently absent on training maneuvers and thoroughly exhausted when I did manage to join her. Josselyn returned to Cincinnati as I boarded the train east. Joss and I had been married for only 100 days.

Many of the officers at Camp Claiborne were being called up from the reserves and most had served in World War I. New battalions were formed as more men arrived and the organization was fluid with possibilities for soldiers to arrive and make their marks through their demonstrated commitment to the regulations and their leadership skills. Naturally, everyone was showing off hoping to earn their superior ratings and receive their own commands. In this atmosphere of strivers I met my training officer, Colonel Frank F. Bell, a World War I retread who had been recalled to active duty from his prosperous career as a civilian engineer in the town of Uvalde, Texas.

Colonel Bell worshipped the army's regulations and adored the fact that every detail of military life could be ordered by the book. It was absolutely clear how one could please this colonel and I quickly adapted myself to his style. When he got his regimental command he requested that I join his headquarters staff as adjutant even though I did not have the rank of Captain that was usually required. But this was wartime and earning the rank was anticipated. As the Colonel's adjutant I would be his office manager handling all the paperwork for the two battalions under his leadership. I was thankful not to be an aide, for that was a servile position requiring all sorts of personal attendance. An adjutant was required to be a manager I learned, and he controlled the destiny of many, many soldiers through the organization of office systems. But one had to be consistently fair and perfectly neutral. These were qualities I admired in others and determined to strengthen in myself.

I had made first lieutenant on my thirty-second birthday, 7 July 1943, and now held a significant appointment, so I felt my military career was proceeding nicely. On 14 October 1943, we got our overseas orders. We were headed for England to train as support troops for the pending Allied invasion. Ten years had passed since my first trip to England with my mother and I hoped to contact my relatives. Our troops gathered at Ft. Miles Standish in Taunton, Massachusetts, from where we would be sent to board the liner *Mauretania,* which was now serving as a troop ship. Sailing on the 31st of October without a convoy we made the crossing in little more than a week and landed at Liverpool on 9 November 1943.

Chapter two: Honest Duty

Throughout our Atlantic crossing Colonel Bell did not slacken his disciplined routine and our regiment continued to drill all the way to England. I never saw the ocean. On the night we arrived the 373rd regiment entrained for transport to Packington Park Camp No. 5 located in the Arden Forest in North Warwickshire.[1] Before daylight we reached the Earl of Aylesworth's estate near Stratford. Our camp was so newly built that the concrete block barracks were still damp from construction. England had become a nation of military encampments as it prepared with its allies to launch an invasion of the continent to free Europe from the tyranny of Adolf Hitler and his Nazi troops.

The Earl of Aylesworth sent word to Colonel Bell that he would like to welcome the Americans personally and I was included in the party that went to the manor house. Packington Park is noted for its chapel where Händel had played a concert and for the Pompeian decor that had been added to a salon in the mid-18th century when that style was all the rage because of the contemporary excavations. Graciously, the Earl showed us around the property including a vast modern kitchen only recently installed and now totally unattended. No food and no help to serve it anyway, the Earl remarked with a shrug.

The 373rd Engineers had been ordered to build camps that would be used by the thousands of American GIs anticipated to arrive in the spring of 1944 before the continental invasion would be launched. To be closer to these work sites the regimental headquarters was immediately relocated from Warwick to Shropshire and situated at Mawley Hall on the estate of Sir Walter Blount near Cleobury-Mortimer. From late November until the end of January 1944 our troops were working on the grounds of a number of beautiful estates in Wales and Scotland building summer tented camps and remodeling existing facilities.

Mawley Hall was built between 1600 and 1700 in the Restoration style associated with Sir Christopher Wren and was noted for outstanding plasterwork done by Italian craftsman in a later period. At first I was thrilled to be sleeping in such surroundings beneath a magnificent crystal chandelier. But with no heat these palatial digs did not promote a particularly joyful 1943 Christmas season.

In mid-January we received orders for one of our two battalions to go to Sully Camp on the Bristol Channel east of Barry, Wales, where the troops would con-

---

1 Following the end of the war as a result of requests and subscriptions from former members of the Regiment a history of the 373rd Engineer General Service Regiment was published in Dallas, Texas. No date of publication. My copy is to be found in with my papers at the National Gallery of Art, Washington, DC.

struct a shipping depot. This would be one of the regiment's most outstanding wartime operations. Open storage facilities, railroads, access roads and a winter tented camp for 250 were required. Regimental headquarters were once again established at a country estate, Clytha Hall, but we officers lived in Cardiff at a local pub with hotel rooms. I found these beer soaked quarters odious, but as it turned out I did not spend much time there. In mid-February I wound up in a hospital. On the way to Clytha Hall I was in command from the lead jeep of a convoy moving under fire from German aircraft. The jeep skidded off the road throwing everyone clear, but then it rolled over on top of me. My back was broken and I would now spend four months in a plaster cast.

For long term care I was sent to a hospital in Bristol. Because of my convalescence I had been transferred out of my regiment and did not know where I would be assigned upon return to regular duty. Before my accident Colonel Bell had initiated the paperwork for my promotion to Captain and I received this advancement in rank while in the Bristol hospital. Even so it seemed my bright future in the military had suddenly ended.

To avoid falling into depression and to keep myself active when I had recovered enough, I took advantage of the situation and started visiting the local antique shops and bookstores. Desperately, I struggled into my uniform and pulling it over my body cast set out with an American orderly as my escort. We went to Bristol cathedral and farther on to the beautiful town of Bath. We explored the nearby excavations of Roman ruins and took in the popular vaudeville shows that continued to provide people with entertainment and relief from wartime shortages and hardships. In the depressed economy I found the shopkeepers eager to deal generously and the art and book collecting opportunities were too good to pass up. We soldiers could send home our purchases in our empty ration boxes without paying shipping charges until the packages reached the United States. When I returned to Cincinnati after the war an entire room at Clossons had been set aside for my storage.

On 15 April 1944, while I was still in the hospital, the Regiment had begun operations on "Overlord," the invasion of France. Eleven camps, all in South Wales, had to be rehabilitated and operated by the 373rd. The purpose of this mission was to feed, clothe, supply, house and process certain tactical troops passing through these marshaling camps on their way to board ships for the invasion of Normandy.

When I was released from the hospital and ready for reassignment I was pleased to learn that Colonel Bell had asked for my return to his regiment and had sent his command car to bring me back. I rejoined the 373rd Engineers who were still encamped in Wales. Once again I would be his adjutant, but Bell also had a new assignment for me. He had decided that our regiment must have a band and I was to be its commander. To organize his band he had to overcome the fact that back in the States our regiment had been activated without a band as a wartime economy so of course it had no instruments. That did not deter the Colonel who now revealed that he was spiritually addicted to the wail of bagpipes.

Bell had seen an ad in a London newspaper offering a set of bagpipes for sale. He sent for them and paid for them personally, then let it be known that if anyone wanted to learn to play the bagpipes, they would receive special "perks." Of course I knew that Bell's notion of "perks" meant you got to work double duty. Nevertheless, the Colonel's band immediately began to grow as more and more soldiers with musical talent showed up to claim a place in the group.

In no time at all, the idea of a band gained great popularity and Bell was able to requisition or commandeer enough other traditional instruments to outfit the unit. The men were soon trying to emulate the rhythms of Glenn Miller and Tommy Dorsey while also sounding the morning reveille. Sometime later when we were in France, our band was made official as the 425th Army Service Force Band. While we were stationed at Le Havre, they were traveling about entertaining other troops. They found it hard to make the morning call at 4:45 a.m. that our colonel enjoyed.

It wasn't easy serving under Colonel Bell, but gradually I learned the advantages of the tremendous power that the position of his adjutant conferred on me. Bell was hot-tempered, full of profanity and intolerant of mistakes. Realizing that no one could do anything about these personality traits, I positioned myself centrally in a buffer zone that I created between him and the other officers. By anticipating problems and by being scrupulously faithful to my duties I became his "fair-haired boy," but never lost the respect of the other men. The largely administrative duties of the headquarters company required me to serve as his personnel representative, the only one who could sign all official papers and delegate work to others. As his trust in my integrity grew I began to represent him to other company commanders and moved freely among other echelons of army brass. So while missing ordinary friendships and the opportunity to express my artistic nature I was gaining leadership skills and self-confidence that would be useful in the future.

During my hospitalization, the regiment had moved to St. Donat's Castle near Glamorganshire, Wales, on 7 June 1944. Now the invasion of Normandy was underway and when I rejoined them we were concentrating forces for our final move to staging areas and adding final touches to our training. St. Donat's Castle was all that this confirmed castle dweller could desire and I responded to these surroundings with passionate enthusiasm. Dating from the time of Cromwell, St. Donat's had crenellated towers, a moat and a drawbridge as well as beautiful rose garden and a grand view of Bristol harbor. At that time it was owned by the American millionaire William Randolph Hearst. Here our troops celebrated the 4th of July, with drills and sports to unify and raise our spirits as we anticipated our orders to cross the English channel. On this occasion "my" band acquitted itself magnificently and our patriotic feelings were deeply stirred.

Once again it turned out that our time in wondrous surroundings would be brief. On 14 July we were ordered to Winchester to prepare to cross the English Channel and participate in the conquest of Normandy.

Although we thought that our departure for France was imminent, it turned out that our regiment was detained in England in order to provide additional engineering services. Conditions had deteriorated at the temporary breakwater protection for landing and docking at the "Omaha" and "Utah" invasion beaches. Unusually heavy storms had broken up the artificial harbors which had been hastily constructed by massing the hulks of sunken ships. A sort of landing platform, called a Phoenix, also known as a Mulberry, had to be built in the River Thames and floated across the channel to enable the unloading of thousands of men and their tons of equipment. Immediate replacements for these landing facilities were given the highest priority by Supreme Headquarters Allied Expeditionary Forces (SHAEF). British contractors who were assigned to build the Phoenix landing platforms were finding it difficult to meet their commitments on schedule. They were encountering labor difficulties because the construction sites were in the path of German V-1 bombardments aimed at London and installations along the Thames. Additional British troops were unavailable, therefore, the British Ministry of War had requested aid from the US Corps of Engineers.

In order to supervise the building of the Phoenix units at the Tilbury Docks on the Thames near London our regimental headquarters were relocated there and the troops were barracked at a British camp at Purfleet, Essex, seven miles closer to the city. During the thirty-five days of this assignment the 373rd worked under constant alert as the German V-1 flying bombs, also called robot bombs or buzz bombs, targeted for London and this vicinity in general, passed over or fell in the area. We called our area Buzz-Bomb Boulevard and counted ourselves fortunate that no casualties occurred.

The Phoenix units were turned over to the British troops who would float them to France and our regiment finally departed on 24 August 1944 for the marshaling area near Southampton from which it would make its channel crossing. It took two days before we boarded a ship and sailed for "Utah" Beach where we landed at four in the morning. From the landing site we were taken to Vezin, near Rennes, about 255 kilometers (160 miles) into the Brittany Peninsula. We bivouacked there to await further orders.

The devastation of the countryside through which we had driven was immense. Since I did not have the opportunity to make extensive notes at that time I would like to quote here from the account written by James Rorimer who had passed through the area a month or so before we did. Rorimer was the Monuments, Fine Arts and Archives officer with the Advance Section, Communications Zone, in Normandy, with Seine Section, in Paris and with the Seventh Army/Western Military District, US Zone in Germany. As part of his far-flung duties he was to be my supervisor at the Wiesbaden Collecting Point beginning in June of the following year.

When drafted for military service, Rorimer was the curator of the Medieval Department of the Metropolitan Museum of Art and he had created the Cloisters under an endowment from John D. Rockefeller, Jr. The sense of outrage he experienced when confronted with war-ravaged Normandy emerges from the opening pages of his memoir, *Survival,* published in 1950. In the opening paragraph Rorimer indites the Germans for disregarding once again the Rule of Land Warfare, as they had in the First World War. "Before and during battle a historic monument was no more sacred to the Germans than a military installation. Again and again they used church towers as observation posts and snipers fired from them at our advancing troops."

From his perspective as the recent guardian of the Cloisters, Rorimer observed the ghost-like towns of the Norman coast line:

> The mere recording of the damage that had been done to the monuments and other art treasures would be a thankless task, trying in the extreme even to the hardened archaeologist whose life is devoted to gathering fragments and attempting to piece them together in the effort to restore a semblance of the past. The attempt to record this damage amid the many gaping craters and fire-swept hulks of building would be like trying to scoop up wine from a broken keg. The hardy Normans would need encouragement and direction almost as much as building supplies and transportation. An architect or inspector who had tenderly protected and reinforced a hundred decaying buildings in peace time would now be confronted with countless problems which centuries to come would not be able to solve. Where a few roof tiles on a cathedral used to need repair each year, now all of these tiles might be dislodged by shell blasts and be piled almost beyond salvage on the floor of the nave or on the pavements of adjoining streets. As the armies pressed on more quickly, the destruction became less irreparable but more widespread.[2]

A week after our encampment at Vezin, near Rennes, the 373rd Engineers received its orders to repair and maintain some 425 kilometers (265 miles) of the French National Highway System from Lamballe on the West to the sea on the North. We were further ordered to send companies to remove debris from three points along the canal in the vicinity of Dinan. This debris, caused by enemy action at three bridge sites, was blocking navigation.

---

2 Rorimer, James J. and Gilbert Rabin, *Survival,* New York: Abelard Press, 1950, 2–3.

Inevitably, our units encountered situations similar to those that Rorimer described in which the purpose of the monuments officer was tested by the dilemmas of a field command. Although only a second lieutenant Rorimer was charged with trying to prevent combat officers from sheltering their troops in the abandoned chateaux of the French countryside and allowing the mens' negligence or vandalism to hasten a building's deterioration. Officers of the MFA & A were empowered to post notices advising allied troops that the rubble of a modest parish church no less than that of a cathedral should not be scavenged for paving stones or filling materials.

Many commanders were sensitive to these notices and moreover knew that they bore the full authority of General Dwight Eisenhower. Others pressed by the circumstances of war-time dismissed the monuments officers as interfering nuisances. When our regimental headquarters was transferred to Brest at the beginning of September 1944 we were quartered on the grounds of a burned-out chateau near the village of Le Fôret. I was impressed with the way that Colonel Bell emphatically lectured all our officers on the need to instruct their men about the significance of preservation activities. At the same time these men faced daily threats of personal destruction by the mines that the Germans had placed near all the transportation lines and facilities. We were not far from the front line of the Battle of Brest and directly under surrounding artillery fire.

The larger mission of our regiment had been to follow the battle into Brest and eventually to clear its harbor so that the delivery of supplies for the military forces could be accelerated. However, after the surrender of German troops, it became apparent that the harbor was far too clogged and damaged to permit speedy opening and repair. Our orders were changed and we were sent to Le Havre to enter behind the British-Canadians who had captured the city on September 15th.

Le Havre being some 570 kilometers (350 miles) from Brest and bridges on the Seine having been destroyed, the river had to be crossed on a Bailey Bridge laid by the British at Rouen. Passing through that great city would offer me my first glimpse of a French Gothic cathedral and I was eager for that opportunity however brief. It was a tragic event. At Rouen the cathedral towers still stood, but beneath them there were mounds of stone as elements of the cathedral's fabric and its sculptures had fallen under bombardment; the entire medieval quarter nearby had been leveled. Now I fully grasped what this war would mean to the continued existence of everything I cared about and found ennobling in European culture. Deep within me a sense of dedication to some future role in preservation must have formed.

For about seven months, with the exception of approximately a month's time out for the "Ardennes Bulge" the 373rd Engineers camped in and around Le Havre, France, its largest assignment since activation. As a prelude to capture of the

Port of Le Havre by British-Canadian troops, Allied airfleets poured a tremendous weight of explosives upon the German garrison sheltered in the innumerable blockhouses and pillboxes during the four years of occupancy by the enemy. Le Havre would have been a formidable citadel to storm from the sea as all vantage points upon the beach approaches were welded into an intricate system of concrete and steel and guns. The mouth of the Seine was one of the most heavily fortified areas of the entire French invasion coast and the Allies came upon it like waves, first from the sky and then from the land.

The raining bombs of the 5th and 6th of September 1944 numbed the Nazi defenders and tore apart their chain of forts. The Germans had so integrated their bastions with the city itself that a large section of the port business and residential sectors were smashed by the air blow and many civilians were killed. Huge fires were kindled and there was no water in the broken mains to counter the flames. When the 373rd Engineers arrived upon the scene, the first US Army troop unit in Le Havre, vast areas were burning and smoldering. Streets were twisted and pitted and filled with fallen buildings. A dreadful stench hung in the early fall air almost discouraging one from drawing breath. Before we could begin to help rebuild the town and its all important harbor regimental units were fully engaged in checking for and removing mines and booby traps.

Restoration of the city's sewers and road system were our next priorities. By October 1944 work could commence on clearing the dock and beach sectors of Le Havre. Many of these missions required our headquarters to make liaisons with the British Navy operating minesweepers nearby in the English Channel. At Le Havre, Colonel Bell outranked all the other commanding officers so everyone in our military area, which covered most of north eastern France, reported to him. This meant that he had 10,000 men under his command and increased the scope of my own work enormously since I was directly responsible for supervising all personnel and discipline matters ranging from promotions to court-martials.

Through these contacts I became acquainted with a group of British officers at the minesweeping base with whom I could share my off-duty hours. As part of his strict discipline, Colonel Bell would not permit our regiment to have an officers club and socialization among us was sternly frowned upon. By contrast, the British Navy prided itself upon its conviviality and warmly welcomed me as an expatriate. My friendships with the British naval officers became important as a source of relaxation and diversion from the daily grind of existing as a member of an occupation army. I remember most vividly the New Year's Eve party that these British officers staged to usher in 1945 with magnificent style.

By the New Year the campaign code-named "Rhineland" was underway and our missions multiplied with the first being that of providing support facilities at the Quartermaster Depot between Charleroi and Namur. Other units then became involved in the rapidly expanding process of rounding up Germans who were being captured and needed to be contained. In addition to dealing with these prisoners we were also put to work helping to provide for the handling of large numbers of displaced persons (DPs) including Russians, Poles, Italians, and French who were being set free as the Allies advanced. If all of this were not enough, just at this time came another order to move troops in position to build a bridge across the Rhine at Cologne.

Now the regimental headquarters was moved ahead to Andernach on the west bank of the Rhine between Bonn and Coblenz. Those units not engaged in bridge building were ordered to accelerate construction of two 50,000 men prisoner of war camps. As soon as one had been finished regimental headquarters moved deeper into Germany to Aschaffenburg between Frankfurt and Würzburg in Bavaria. The rear party of the regiment left behind in Le Havre now moved in to join us at the end of April.

With victory in sight, Colonel Bell became the Group Commander of Engineer Construction Group E. Our headquarters was now responsible for a geographic area that included the greater part of the upper Rhine Valley in Southern Germany to Czechoslovakia on the East, Switzerland on the South and France and Luxembourg on the West. Coupled with the problem of the physical size of the area to be administered was the fact that after VE Day many units were scheduled for immediate and direct redeployment to the Pacific Theater. Others were being returned to the United States for indirect redeployment so we were constantly involved in revising plans for units and projects.

From my position as the Colonel's adjutant I could anticipate what the coming weeks would bring as the army shifted from the mode of invasion and conquest to that of military governance. The frantic and dangerous period of combat support had passed and increasingly our tasks revolved around management of the enclosures we had built to hold the hundreds of thousands of prisoners of war captured by the Allied Army. While some work was being done by our units to rebuild elements of the German infrastructure we were not slated to be involved in the future Army of Occupation. Rumor had it that we would return to the States for retraining and outfitting and then be sent to the Pacific Theater to continue the war with Japan.

Regimental headquarters had once more been established at a country estate, the Schönbusch summer palace near Aschaffenburg. Gradually, the pace of my military work was slackening and I began to find time to indulge some of my former interests. At Schönbusch I instinctively took up the role of preservationist and went about the grounds gathering up the furniture and possessions of this once lovely home which had been scattered by marauding troops and DPs. With the aid of a faithful caretaker we stored away what remained in the hope that the owners would one day be able to undertake restoration. It seemed that everywhere I looked there was work of this kind to be done if anything was to be salvaged of the beautiful Germany that had existed before the Nazis.

It must have been in this mood that I became aware of the existence of the cadre of Monuments Specialist officers and the Monuments, Fine Arts and Archives (MFA & A) branch of the Army. Nearly every issue of the service newspaper, *The Stars and Stripes,* carried a story of the increasing American efforts to safeguard the treasures which were being uncovered through military intelligence. The discovery of collections from the Berlin museums in the Kaiseroda mine at Merkers had been much discussed in April and now in May there were daily stories about the art which the Nazis had looted in France, Holland and elsewhere.

Our regiment was under the command of the 12th Army headquartered in Frankfurt and my routine duties took me to the SHAEF headquarters there frequently. On 10 June 1945 we received official notice that we were to return to the States within that month. Colonel Bell assigned me to supervise the preparations for our departure. On the very next day while seeing to that business I found out that there was an office for the MFA & A in Frankfurt. I searched out the unit to inquire how I might join them. It was a beautiful day and since it was lunchtime, no one was around to talk with so I waited in the sunshine out in front of the IG Farben factory building where SHAEF was located.

Ever since our regiment had landed in Normandy almost a year earlier I had seen nothing but destruction on the continent of Europe. I had seen with what carelessness and even viciousness the troops, ours and theirs, behaved when confronted with beautiful objects and when quartered in wonderful historic surroundings. Frequently horror stricken, I had restrained all my impulses to lecture, preach, plead or even intervene and this restraint had gnawed at my guts. But I was a Captain in the Engineers and as the Regimental Adjutant my duties had been clear. As an officer my leadership credibility and my effectiveness would have been utterly compromised by any display of sentimentality or even sympathy for the cultural environment of the conquered enemy.

Affiliation with the MFA & A would afford me a kind of personal redemption. If I were selected I would have an opportunity to work for something I believed in and to make a positive rather than a negative contribution to society. With thoughts such as these swirling through my brain I returned that afternoon to the MFA & A office and met British Colonel Geoffrey Webb and American Lieutenant Charles Kuhn who interviewed me. Under their questioning, I described for them my education in architecture and my work in interior design. I told them of my training with the general service engineers and my rise to Regimental Adjutant. Again and again Kuhn brought the conversation back to what I had been able to do to assist Colonel Bell's command.

Slowly it dawned on me that I outranked this brilliant Harvard graduate and director of its *Germanic Art Museum* and that I knew far more about how the army worked than he did. Lt. Kuhn was looking for someone to rebuild a former museum in Wiesbaden that had until recently seen service as the headquarters of the western division of the Luftwaffe. Allied bombing raids aimed at destroying this Luftwaffe headquarters had targeted the Wiesbaden area, but miraculously the *Landesmuseum* had survived with moderate damages to the roof and a lot of blownout windows. Now the German airmen were all prisoners of war and the building had become a refuge for DPs who were hastening its internal deterioration. But the 12th US Army who had jurisdiction over the city had requisitioned the building. The *Landesmuseum* suggested itself as the obvious repository for the collections of art that were piling up in the *Reichsbank* of Frankfurt as more and more of the hidden Nazi repositories were uncovered. But before the art could be moved the MFA & A wanted a building that had been made secure and would offer adequate storage for the indefinite period during which the art collections would be under American protection.

Kuhn had been around the army long enough to know that its regulations and procedures would tangle his project in red tape and could jeopardize the mission of the MFA & A. He'd been around SHAEF long enough to see that cultural preservation was definitely not a high military priority and he probably reasoned that his corps of highly educated art experts weren't going to be able to speak the army's language. I, on the other hand, was an army man adept at negotiating my way through the chain of command and capable of circumventing its policies should the need arise. I left Kuhn's office with the understanding that if I could secure my transfer out of the 373rd he would make a place for me in the MFA & A.

I returned to our regimental headquarters to learn that our orders to depart from Germany were being processed rapidly and I had no time to lose in securing my release. I wrote that night to Kuhn to explain the need to move quickly on my transfer. Now I had to confront Colonel Bell and seek his approval for my wishes. To my great joy, he assented to my request stipulating only that I should remain with the regiment to organize its departure and accompany the troops to Le Havre where they would board a ship for their return to the States. This I was glad to do and went with them to Camp Lucky Strike on 15 June 1945. By 19 June the Regiment had completely assembled and I was free to leave. As a parting gift, an officer gave me a jeep. From the port in France I raced to Frankfurt to await the orders that would transfer me to the new occupation government and a new military career as a Monuments Officer.

Chapter three: Museum Man

Beginning in Wiesbaden

Upon my return from Le Havre, it did not take more than a few meetings with the officers assigned to the MFA & A unit to convince me that I had found myself among an elite group. Once again by great and accidental fortune I was poised to enter upon an exceptional adventure. Lt. Charles Kuhn had interviewed me 11 June 1945 without revealing that he was a native Cincinnatian and knew perfectly well where I'd gone to school and what I'd been doing before the war as an interior designer at Clossons. What he had seen in my eager presentation of my talents was the organizational ability I had acquired with the Colonel as the regimental adjutant. Luckily he also perceived that this ability overlaid skills in architectural engineering, a profound appreciation of the arts and a sincere understanding of the preservation theology.

I say theology for I had found myself among the high priesthood of the American museum profession. My colleagues in MFA & A were *museum men* and they said that phrase with a reverence which awed everyone, but especially themselves. They were graduates in art history from leading American universities and if they had not all gone to Harvard to attend the course in museum management given by Paul Sachs they were not about to let that handicap stand in the way of the careers which they envisioned resuming upon their reentry into civilian life. I do not mean disrespect to these colleagues; indeed I longed to join their exalted ranks and secretly cherished the notion that, by excelling in whatever role I was to play with the MFA & A, I too would become a *museum man*. I had certainly observed the career of the Cincinnati Art Museum director, Walter Siple, Harvard graduate, Paul Sachs student and museum man, so I had not the slightest difficulty in fantasizing how this amazing opportunity might lead me into greater museum service than the classes which I had given at the Cincinnati Art Museum in the education department a decade earlier. I knew I had talents for connoisseurship and for the social role of a museum director. What I lacked was a Ph.D. and the experience of working as a curator in a great museum. And languages – it would have been a great help in the months ahead if I had ever studied German or French.[1]

---

1 At the conclusion of my service I submitted a report, a "History of the Wiesbaden Collecting Point, 13th of July 1945–5th of March 1946," which covers the period of my directorship. See National Archives RG 260, Box 127, Activity Reports and my papers at the National Gallery of Art (NGA), Washington, D.C.

The Wiesbaden *Landesmuseum,* which would now hold the national art collections, had been designed by Theodor Fischer and completed in 1915 to serve as a cultural facility displaying three civic collections of fine arts, natural sciences and archaeology.[2] Magnificently proportioned, it was E shaped in plan. Perhaps from regard for the city's origins, the design represented a climatic moment in the period of Romanesque revivalism that had influenced civic architecture in Germany at the turn of the century. The entrance featured an astonishing two-storied octagonally planned domed foyer reminiscent of the Cathedral of Aachen decorated with gilded mosaics. The visitor next proceeded into an Early Christian basilican hall where once a fountain played, but it had long since been clogged with refuse. I never saw the famous Mithraic Shrine to be seen today in Wiesbaden for it had been stored away along with other treasures of the city's Roman past. Once one went beyond these antiquarian features the museum's planning became quite advanced in its strategic use of light sources and the flow of its galleries. So as to be illuminated by skylights, galleries for the three museum departments were quartered on the top floor of this multi-stored municipal building.

Before the war each of the museum departments had had its own director and staff and the upper floor had been divided up so that the archaeological collections occupied the south wing, the fine arts occupied the center and the natural sciences collections were displayed in the north end of the building. A lavish central hall served as a foyer for the paintings gallery where there had been some relatively significant works. But, the finest works had been removed from Wiesbaden by the former director Hermann Voss when Hitler appointed him director of the Linz Commission. In March 1943 Voss succeeded Hans Posse who had run the Commission from his post as Director of the Dresden *Gemäldegalerie.*[3] He moved the best seventy-seven paintings to Dresden for protection from bombing. When the Russians occupied Dresden after the war they sent seventy-seven paintings from the Wiesbaden collection to Moscow. Sixty-four of these paintings were returned from the USSR to the German Democratic Republic (GDR) in the year 1955. In 1988 these sixty-four paintings were returned from the Government of the GDR to the Wiesbaden Museum in the Federal Republic of Germany and shown for the first time again in 1992/3. One of the remaining missing paintings was shown at the Moscow Pushkin Museum in 1995. Their saga is not finished yet.[4]

---

2 Schmidt, Ulrich. *The Art Collections in the Museum of Wiesbaden.* Munich: Schnell & Steiner, 1982.

3 Nicholas, Lynn H. *The Rape of Europa,* New York: Knopf 1994, 44. Posse received his assignment as the head of Hitler's museum in Linz on 26 June 1939. He died of cancer of the mouth in 1943, (*Ibid.*, 171).

4 RKM, interview with Arnulf Herbst, former director of the Wiesbaden Museum, Frankfurt, April 28, 1994. Audiotape with the WIF papers. MFP received an updated letter dated September 17, 1996 from Dr. Ingrid Koszinowski of the Museum Wiesbaden. Letter in WIF papers.

Because they contained a wealth of Roman materials the archaeological collections of Wiesbaden in advance of the bombings had been packed and put into storage. The natural sciences collections had not been so fortunate, that wing of the building was in total chaos. Shattered glass from the panes of the specimen cases that lined the room and from the windows was heaped to a depth of two feet as if to make a crystalline habitat for this unique collection of stuffed zoological and botanical specimens. It was some time before, as I remember, a former director, *Dr. Schmitt,* returned to reclaim his post.

After the removal and storage of the fine arts and archaeological collections the museum building had been turned over to the German air force, the *Luftwaffe,* who had used it as their barracks and for a machine shop. One of the *Luftwaffe's* western command was based in Wiesbaden on account of the vast size of its local airport facilities and it was from that airport that many of the air strikes on France and England had originated. During the chaotic final days of Hitler even the *Luftwaffe* must have lost their discipline and they had simply abandoned their supplies. Next, the *Landesmuseum* had become the refuge of DPs seeking any kind of shelter. To make room for themselves the DPs had dumped everything that was of no use to them out the windows so that trash in the courtyards reached the second story. In addition to the DPs, the US Army moved in a quartermaster's supply unit that had used the building as a warehouse and center for the distribution of soldiers' uniforms and rations. Evicting this unit was one of the early responsibilities of the MFA & A officers stationed at Frankfurt and it had not made them popular with the Army.

Fortunately, the building was so strongly built that it had sustained a minimum of external damages from the Allied bombardments. At the time of our occupation the below-ground levels were used as offices for public works administrations such as the water department and the pumping station. There were more than 300 rooms in the building and it had 2000 broken windows; all of them had been blown out in the bombing. Only its roofline was marred by installations of anti-aircraft guns that had been emplaced in the eaves at the corners of the building by hacking away portions of the roof. Broken windows and the pierced eaves were letting in moisture, and the sandbags which weighted down the guns were putting unnecessary stress on the roof trusses, but otherwise the building seemed sound. We later discovered that some interior walls had been weakened by the bombing and shored them up until more permanent repairs could be made. By the time we took over the building none of its systems were operational. There was no heat, no running water and no electricity. Still the place was crowded with people who had no where else to go. The stench in the building was obnoxious for, although the plumbing no longer functioned, the lavatories were still in use. Moving the DPs out and then beginning the repairs that would make the building a museum once again would be first priorities.

Initially I did not know what role the MFA & A strategists had in mind for me. At first I thought that I had been selected for the MFA & A primarily because they urgently needed someone to organize the rehabilitation of a museum building in Wiesbaden and to prepare it for the shipments of art it was to receive from the *Reichsbank* in Frankfurt. Rapidly, Kuhn filled me in on the developments. On 22 June he and Jim Rorimer had requisitioned the *Landesmuseum* building. He told me that the US Third Army had been led through a variety of intelligence reports to a mine at Merkers in central Germany. There, in the potash mines of the Kaiseroda works, German curators had stored thousands of crates filled with works of art that had been evacuated from the State Museums of Berlin. From the mines these crates had been taken by twenty-six ten-ton truck loads to the *Reichsbank* in Frankfurt on April 17, 1945.[5] Three truck loads had been shipped just earlier on April 15.[6] When I learned of the immense importance of the works to be transferred to Wiesbaden, I assumed I would be working in a supportive role with Lt. Kuhn or another of the museum men once the building had been secured.

I began my work in Wiesbaden in the latter half of June 1945 thinking that I was to be a building engineer and additionally responsible to survey and protect other cultural properties in the *Regierungsbezirk,* a governmental district which included the *Land,* or county, of Hesse and the immediate area of Nassau. While I was overseeing the rehabilitation of a building I was also expected to be moving around the countryside in a 100 mile vicinity visiting the temporary repositories where other significant collections had been stored and checking on reports of looting at the great houses of our region. I was given no job instructions.

The first few weeks I spent in Wiesbaden remain a blur in my memory because I was working eighteen hour days and even when sleeping my mind continued to turn over the tasks and the challenges of the assignment. I vaguely recall I was surprised that the town was not as ravaged by bombing as Frankfurt had been. Here the Allies had concentrated their attacks on the vicinity of the *Landesmuseum* where the *Luftwaffe* had their headquarters and on the airfield outside

---

[5] Report of the American Commission for the Protection and Salvage of Artistic and Historic Monuments in War Areas, Washington, D.C., 1946, 132–133.

[6] See Supreme Headquarters, Allied Expeditionary Force, G-4 Division: "Report covering the discovery, removal, transporting and storage of gold, silver, platinum and currency, fine art treasures and German patent records from salt mines in the Merkers and Heringen area to the Frankfurt area in Germany. 26. April 1945." National Archives, Washington, D.C., Record Group RG 331, Records of Allied Operational and Occupation Headquarters, World War II, SHAEF, G-5, Monuments, Fine Arts and Archives Section, Subject File, MFA & A Reports, AMG 290. Copy see: Staatliche Museen zu Berlin, Zentralarchiv, No. V. 4.3.2. GA-LN 79.

of town. Wiesbaden had some nicer hotels in which the American military now were quartered. My own lodgings were on the third floor of a third class hotel and I suppose I ate, but I cannot now say where.

Vividly I recall my first visit to the Wiesbaden *Landesmuseum* which appeared damaged, but salvageable if only one could triumph over Army bureaucracy and German paralysis. To make it functional I was going to have to do battle with the US Army that only reluctantly approved of the MFA & A's mission within the Military Government. My troops would be drawn from among our former enemies, the recently conquered soldiers who were starving, exhausted and demoralized. My mind whirled as I contemplated my first priority: a program to ensure the building's security.

Lt. Kuhn had informed me fully of the enormous value of the works of art that were headed our way. As a part of my indoctrination for my new position I had gone to Frankfurt with him to see the collections that were in storage at the *Reichsbank.* The crates from the *Kaiser Friedrich Museum* and others lined the hallways of the bank leaving only the narrowest passages. In rooms off these corridors leaning against the walls were the uncrated 19 and 20 century pictures from the *Nationalgalerie* in Berlin which also had been stored in the mine of Kaiseroda-Merkers.

Along with these artistic treasures lining the halls I was shown the cases of eyeglasses, false teeth, wedding rings and other bits of personal property that had been confiscated from the Jews and other persecuted people at the concentration camps. It was a gruesome experience to see these human relics side by side with the cultural relics of a great country.

Above all else was the restoration of the building's systems and maintenance of its security perimeter. The enormous value of the collections that would be stored in the Collecting Point would warrant nothing short of the establishment of a fortress and the adoption of a siege mentality. Moreover, the building had to be completely weatherproofed, fully cleaned and ready to be heated during the winter. And there had to be a competent, well-trained staff. I was given less than two months for these accomplishments.

Immediately, I began to put up a tall barbed wire fence around the museum which I requisitioned from American supplies. The lower story of windows had been covered by roughly made brick walls as a protection against air raids. But there was no alternative to the security fence because the building had never been designed to store collections of the extraordinary value that were now anticipated.

To find a staff for my museum I had to go immediately to the office of the *Arbeitsamt,* the Wiesbaden employment agency, and submit requests for qualified people. I needed sappers, as the former European army engineers were called, since they were skilled workmen who could repair and maintain the building. I needed guards, cleaners and secretaries to staff the offices which would soon be coping with the paperwork that the military even in civilian government guise was sure to demand.

Nothing could be accomplished until I had found somebody who could direct the workers since I did not speak a word of German. On Day One when my workers arrived from the *Arbeitsamt* I had frantically pantomimed the gestures of setting posts for the fencing and other immediate jobs I wanted done, but these dumb shows could not continue.

Frau Renate Hobirk was the ideal applicant for the position of translator. Her father was an international businessman and he had provided her a modern education. Frau Hobirk had studied languages in Switzerland and had learned English and French living in those countries. She had married a banker and was living in Berlin. At the end of the war Frau Hobirk was assigned to service as a general's secretary with a German army unit in the Harz Mountain area some hundred miles southwest of Berlin. The officers fled as American forces approached. The American Army unit was delighted to meet Frau Hobirk who could speak with them and help them find their way around the region. In exchange for her assistance they offered her transport out of the east Harz area which was to be given over to the Russians. Wearing a pair of Army coveralls she rode on a truck with the troops as far as Wiesbaden where she knew an old family friend resided.

Arriving in Wiesbaden in the early weeks of July 1945 Frau Hobirk discovered her friend living in a tiny apartment so modest that she could only offer her guest a bed on the floor. She went to the *Arbeitsamt* to register and found my request for a translator waiting to be filled. A job at the *Landesmuseum* was the ideal solution. I was overjoyed because in addition to her efficiency as an office worker and her skills as a linguist she was also familiar with the forms of protocol still beloved by the older German citizens who soon came calling to present their respects to the new museum director. With all her accomplishments she took over as my chief of staff and moved into the building living in the apartment of the caretaker who also remained there with his family.

Fortunately, I soon located Professor Doctor Engineer Otto F. Seeler, an architect of Cuban birth who had been living in Wiesbaden.[7] Born of German parents he had also lived in Florida as a child where he had learned English. Seeler had received all his training in Germany and then married the daughter of a promi-

---

7 Dr. Seeler graciously agreed to be interviewed for this book. The audiotape of his conversation with RKM will be found with the WIF papers.

nent Wiesbaden family. He was a wonderful colleague who went on to become a Professor at Notre Dame University in Indiana and director of their program in Rome.

Next I found Joseph ("Joe") Kohlmaier, a mechanical engineer with considerable experience. Kohlmaier served as our foreman and Seeler consulted with me on the ways and means to repair the building. In July and early August the sappers got the heating system, the elevator and the plumbing working. Slate and tar paper for the roof were high on my list. The roof tiles had slipped and many lay broken in the gutters. Since the building was relatively new I was told that obtaining similar slates would not be a problem and these did arrive without difficulty. Taking over the daily supervision of our crews, Kohlmaier and Seeler freed me to continue planning.

Lt. Kuhn, Capt. La Farge, and Lt. Edith Standen from headquarters made frequent visits to the museum to inspect how the work was going so that they could determine when the shipments from Frankfurt could begin. They were my most ardent supporters and did much to encourage me.

In mid July, I asked for a meeting with local contractors because glass was so desperately needed. Every single window in the building had been blown out during the air raid. There were windowless buildings all over Germany and I had tried to requisition glass through Army supply channels. Luckily, one of the tradesmen recalled that the *Luftwaffe* had been erecting barracks near the Wiesbaden airfield and that his firm had delivered tons of wire impregnated glass to the building site not long before the surrender.

Moving on this tip immediately, I went out to the airfield where next to the nearly completed barracks the glass still awaited its installation. This treasure was buried under a mountain of trash so it had never attracted the notice of the American Air Force that now controlled the airfield. Without telling anyone or asking for approval I intended to seize that glass shipment, bring it back to the *Landesmuseum* and set the glaziers to work. From the motor pool I requisitioned a truck with a boom and went with our trucks and workers to begin loading our prize; twenty-five tons of glass.

I might have made my raid without detection except that the boom of the crane needed to hoist the glass became entangled in overhead Signal Corps' wires at the gate and pulled them down. Immediately I ordered my men to begin restoring the wires, but already the base had erupted into confusion. The MPs arrived and asserting my rank (but not explaining why I was there) I showed them that the situation was under control and they left without challenging me. Over the next few days the trucks returned repeatedly for the glass without being halted. Later on, I heard that Bancel La Farge, while in command of the MFA & A office in Berlin, had boasted of my feat to some Air Force officers who were furious to learn that such a vast quantity of glass had disappeared beneath their noses when they too had many windows to replace.

Reglazing the windows was a lengthy operation. I set up a brigade system so that one crew removed the sash, the second cleaned out the broken glass and walked it down to the glaziers. Then the same crew returned the sash and put it in place. If there was no sash, the space was filled directly with glass. The Germans had never seen this sort of assembly line technique and marveled at my Yankee ingenuity. Meanwhile, new slates for the roof had been found and installed making the building weather-proof again. Only the skylights resisted our advances. It appeared to me that they were not well designed. Their angle of emplacement caused drainage problems and the putty we could obtain was so inferior that these overhead windows continued to leak.

While these relatively clean tasks were going on other crews were removing five years worth of accumulated trash from inside the building and its courtyards. If ever there had been a stable fit for Hercules this was it.

Flood lights were next on my list. Over a period of weeks in July and August I sent out search parties to scavenge headlights from the wrecked jeeps and army trucks that were littering the local landscape so that these lights could be installed around the building to illuminate it at night.

I also wanted to rehire former members of the museum staff who were trained as curators and conservators so that the shipments of collections could be managed according to standard museum practices. Once these people learned that restoration of the *Landesmuseum* had become an American priority they began to return to the building from which they had been driven by the wartime circumstances, *Luftwaffe* invasion and the occupation from DPs'. But after I rehired some of them, I encountered a problem that was to plague many of the German museums the MFA & A was trying to put back into order. After 1933 as the Nazi bureaucracy took on greater power many civil employees became members of the party. Some, like Dr. Ferdinand Kutsch and *Dr. Schmitt,* refused and resigned. Others who joined simply had no choice as they feared they could not find other jobs. Now shortly after their reinstatement, the US Military Government had ordered that no former Nazi party members could be employed and I had to fire all of the former fine arts staff members including an older woman who was the sole supporter of her aged mother. This pained me deeply.

Gradually, through the *Arbeitsamt* I found the people needed for the work ahead and by their employment I was able to return to them some measure of the dignity that years of wartime hardship had stripped away. The *Arbeitsamt* also issued ration cards, and for those who took employment rations were a bit higher than for unemployed, but nevertheless by far insufficient for men who had to accomplish the hard work I demanded. Some of my workers had no clothing other than the German army uniforms they had been wearing through the general mobilization of their country and at the moment of their defeat. Now, in order to continue to employ them I would have to outfit them, because the US Military Government had suddenly forbidden the Germans to wear their former uniforms. I had to go to the Army supply depots and get cast-off US garments for them to wear.

My new employees had been living on a starvation diet and I soon realized that they were in no shape to work at the tasks I had planned for them. Moreover they were attempting to reunite with their families and as their wives and children returned to the city they too would have to be cared for. Our Military Government was not prepared for this obligation, nor was the struggling German government which was still in formation. Needing these workers desperately I would have to find a way to get them food and so turned to UNRRA, the United Nations Relief and Rehabilitation Administration, to barter for nutritional staples for these families. UNRRA could use the salvaged *Luftwaffe* cots and stoves in exchange for food. It was a dreadful situation, so full of hopelessness and despair that I shudder remembering how hard I had to drive these frail people in order to accomplish the work according to the timetable I'd been given.

Never in my life had I had so much responsibility for the welfare of others. Even my service with Colonel Frank F. Bell had not been so personally demanding. There was no one else but me to whom these people could turn for help. Actually, at this point I was glad not to know German because I could not hear their pitiable stories first hand. Many of my letters home to my wife, Josselyn, describe the two poles of my experience during this time: exhilaration at the thought of the work I was accomplishing and anxiety over the conditions under which it was being done. Describing the chaotic circumstances I wrote to her in June that, "we have to go the labor office everyday since it seems that someone always fails to show up." During the summer Josselyn began sending me packages with treats she thought I might enjoy. Since I had been spending my own pay to buy food for the men I wrote back asking instead for staples such as cooking oil, canned goods and bouillon cubes to stock the mess kitchen which I set up for lunch.

Each morning I conducted a staff meeting to grapple with the daily challenges of procuring supplies and establishing museum policies. The director of the archaeological collection, Dr. Ferdinand Kutsch, participated enthusiastically. He was grateful that we were planning to assist him to reinstall his collections and his library as part of our mission. In the beginning of my appointment at Wiesbaden while my official status had been unclear I had felt it appropriate that Kutsch sign receipts for works of art, antiquities and objects of cultural value that were then coming under our protective custody. I felt we were fortunate that he was so eager to work with us and I enjoyed his company.

Dr. Kutsch had connections with the remnants of the German museum profession and its academic circles. He also knew the local collectors who now came searching for objects that were missing from their homes and might have been reclaimed in the investigatory net that the MFA & A had thrown out all over Europe. At this early stage there was little we could do except listen to their laments and assure them that our procedures were being designed to effect the restitution of as much as possible of the art that had been looted. By July the full extent of the looting and pillaging as well as the destruction by bombardment had been documented in the international press and everyone who had lost something had hopes for its return. For the time being, I asked Frau Hobirk to record the losses claimed by our visitors.

The Regierungsbezirk

I continued with the external responsibilities for the *Regierungsbezirk,* our district of Hesse Nassau. This meant traveling to check out reports of German art repositories and making inventories so that works in storage could be transferred to the Collecting Point for identification of their ownership. The primary goal was to prevent any further deterioration of monuments and deposites. From storage at the Collecting Point the art would eventually be "restituted," that is to say, returned to the owners provided they had accurate documentation.

I recall that my comrade on the first of my repository excursions was another MFA & A officer stationed nearby in Höchst, Lt. Edith Standen. Before the war Edith, who was of Anglo-American parents, had studied at Oxford and found a job as the secretary to the Joseph Widener Collection near Philadelphia. In 1944, she had assisted in the transfer of the paintings in the Widener collection to the National Gallery of Art in Washington. That done, she had joined the Women's Army Corps (WAC) out of patriotism and hoped to be sent to England where her mother resided. A WAC officer noticed her interests and career and sent her to Mason Hammond who was then running the MFA & A office in Barbizon outside Paris. From there she had come to the MFA & A office at Höchst, a town near Frankfurt, where she joined our colleagues in preservation work. Throughout the later months of my service in MFA & A we worked together in Wiesbaden and she eventually succeeded me as director of the Collecting Point in March 1946. Edith remained in Wiesbaden until early 1947 when she was transferred to the MFA & A office in Stuttgart to continue working in the field of preservation until she left the Army late that year. Returning to the States, Edith became an associate curator at the Metropolitan Museum of Art during the administrations of directors Francis Henry Taylor and James Rorimer. Retiring from a distinguished career, she was Curator Emeritus and remained a valued friend who helped me and all her other MFA & A colleagues enormously.[8]

MFA & A headquarters at Höchst served as a clearinghouse for reports coming in from military intelligence sources, civilians, and MFA & A officers who had been in the field since April 1945, so Edith and I were in frequent communication during the month of July regarding repositories in my area. Typically these repositories were located in castles, churches or civic buildings that had been presumed to be safe by the German collectors and museum officials because they were remote from the battlelines and bombing targets. Sometimes the repositories contained only local collections of sentimental value, but frequently we did find some extraordinary things so these tours took on the nature of adventures which our MFA & A group thoroughly enjoyed. I was particularly lucky to have my own jeep. Adding to our adventures we got to drive on the *Autobahn,* Hitler's new superhighway which certainly was the most glorious road I'd ever seen.

I recall making my first trip to a repository with Edith on the Fourth of July weekend when we drove north to Hachenburg. There we were met by the Most Reverend Abbot of Marienstatt who was in charge of the Hachenburg repository. An assortment of provincial archives and libraries as well as paintings from museums in Bonn had been stored there. When a local official or trusted member of the community like the Abbot was nearby to keep watch over a repository and if it was weatherproof we might decided to leave it undisturbed. But if a repository contained extremely valuable items or if its security was in question we would arrange to transport the collections back to the *Landesmuseum* in Wiesbaden.

I was pleased to be able to take action to prevent further deterioration of Schloss Biebrich, Schloss Wiesbaden and Schloss Weilburg. Schloss Biebrich had not been damaged but was suffering from various tenants. I had it cleaned out, boarded up, and surrounded by a fence. At Schloss Wiesbaden further damage was prevented by boarding up the windows, and putting it off limits. At Schloss Weilburg it was necessary for me to go after an American Army outfit that had helped themselves to the antique furniture for their own quarters. The furniture was returned and the building was made weathertight. Schloss Weilburg's roof was patched to protect the library of the Mining Union of Essen and a teachers college; we also shored up the Orangerie at this wonderful place.

After learning of the deteriorating condition of the *Staatsarchiv* building in Wiesbaden, I arranged for temporary glazing. There too, all the windows had been blown out and the valuable documents were scattered all over the floors. We

---

8 RKM interview with Edith Standen, New York, February 17, 1994.

could not obtain real glass, but there was an opaque plastic material called "Besella" which would serve to block out the windows until the city could find the means to restore them.

The partitioning of Germany into four zones of occupation, US, British, French and Russian, provided the MFA & A officers with some additional challenges. At the time when the German museum officials had stored their collections they had not foreseen the cataclysmic failure of the Third Reich nor that the storage places they had picked could be under one of four different Military Governments. As usual the British and the Americans worked well together and shipments passed between the cooperating MFA & A facilities established by both countries. It was a different matter with the French and the Russians.

It had been learned that the libraries of our own *Landesmuseum* in Wiesbaden had been stored in a castle located within the French zone of occupation. Arriving there we encountered frustrating delays in completing the formalities to remove the cases. The French had never been enthusiastic about the mission of the MFA & A and although forced by treaties to comply with Military Government Law No. 52 which defined the Allied policy on the restitution of cultural objects in war areas they gave their cooperation grudgingly when required to release treasures found in their zone. In the absence of any other agreements on cultural reparations, it was to be MFA & A practice to restitute German art to German museums eventually provided they could demonstrate ownership prior to 1933 through inventories, accession books and other documentation. Knowing what the Germans had done to the works of art and collections in their country the French had little liking for the policies of restitution that determined Law No. 52.

In his book *Survival,* James Rorimer wrote that by the end of 1945, 384 repositories were reported in the Western Military District, the Seventh Army area. This count did not include those turned over to Third Army at the time of the Allied invasion. Of these 296 were inspected and 86 were evacuated.[9] My letters and notes remind me that I visited more than a dozen repositories in the first two months of my administration before late August when I felt required to remain on duty full time at the *Landesmuseum.*

On 8 July 1945 I took a truck to Schloss Langenau where part of the treasures from the *Wallraf-Richartz Museum* of Cologne had been stored. The trip led us through a range of mountains and glorious forests. When we arrived we found that there was much too much to move in one load and that the measures for storing the paintings were adequate, we left the paintings under guard.

[9] Rorimer, James J. and Gilbert Rabin: *Survival.* New York: Abelard Press, 1950, 227.

Wisely, the Cologne curators had scattered their collections among different repositories. Another trip took us to a riverside water castle at Runkel where we felt it wisest to remove the works on paper that could be harmed by continued exposure to damp conditions. This was another of the Wallraf-Richartz repositories and among the paintings stored there was the marvelous *Madonna in the Rose Bower* by Stephan Lochner. Long one of my favorites, it was a thrill to see it even in a storeroom. The destruction of the center city of Cologne was so complete that it would be many years before the Wallraf-Richartz collection was reassembled under one roof.

Another of our trips took us to Ramsthal where the collection of Dr. Richard von Kühlmann was discovered in a building occupied by American troops. Von Kühlmann had lived in Berlin and had served 1909–14 as a counselor of embassy (Botschaftsrat) in England. He was also reported to have been moving in high circles of Nazi Germany before getting involved in the 20 July attempt on the life of Hitler. The contents of the repository including paintings, rugs and furniture were brought back to the Collecting Point for storage to await restitution to him or members of his family. Our policies required fair treatment of members of the government of our former enemies for had such treasures not been protected they might have been looted or abused by our troops or others. Now we were an Army of occupation in Germany with a reputation to protect from international criticism.

While we were moving around inspecting repositories in our district of Greater Hesse I had the chance to visit Marburg where the first Collecting Point in the Western Military District had been established under the direction of MFA & A officer Walker Hancock. Hancock had explored the Siegen mine in April before his assignment to Marburg, where a subsidiary Collecting Point was set up in the modern Archives Building of Marburg University. It was one of the few buildings in Marburg to suffer from bombing but, as it was the second largest institution of its kind before the war and was fireproof, it was eventually possible to concentrate 3,457 works of art and the National stamp collection there. Hancock and I had a lot to talk about as we were sharing the challenge of setting up a collecting point. Of his early days in Marburg Hancock wrote that, "Even the problem of getting a broom with which to make a start required days of patience and plotting."[10] Among the objects in the Marburg Collecting Point were paintings from the *Folkwang Museum* in Essen, from the *Suermondt Museum* in Aachen, and the *Wallraf-Richartz Museum* in Cologne. Seven hundred and sixty-six objects representing the finest paintings, sculptures and decorative arts from the Rhineland were evacuated to Marburg from the copper mine

---

[10] Hancock, Walker. "Experiences of a Monuments Officer in Germany," *College Art Journal*, (Vol. V, No. 4, May 1946): 308.

in Siegen. When Hancock had visited the mine in April he had found it dripping with moisture. Mold had developed on paintings and sculptures, and nothing was being done to counteract the humidity. During the summer, assisted by Monuments Specialist Lt. Lamont Moore assigned to the US Ninth Army, Hancock evacuated the Siegen mine.

While the organization of the Collecting Point facility was progressing I was still responsible for the inspection of monuments and other restitution efforts in the *Regierungsbezirk.* It became clear to me that this external duty was likely to interfere with my performance and I was most eager to do my best at the *Landesmuseum.* Luckily, through my contacts with German cultural officials, I had discovered that a former cultural minister in the pre-Nazi days was living in Marburg. Dr. Friedrich Bleibaum was well suited to take over the duties of visiting the ruined schlosses and other public buildings and reporting back to me. I was able to obtain a truck, tar paper, and other supplies for his work.

Assistence to Artists

For weeks an artist had been visiting the Military Government offices trying to explain his predicament, but no one seemed to understand him. With the help of a fellow officer, I interviewed him and learned that his request was quite simple. He felt he had been cursed by the Nazis and wanted to be given official permission to resume his career. Alo Altripp had been among the artists whom the Nazis had labeled as degenerates. In 1933 at the beginning of their campaign against international modern art, an exhibition of his paintings in Essen had been invaded by troops who had closed down his show. Gestapo enforcers had ordered him not to paint. Of course, he had never ceased to make his art in secret and had risked his life to buy his supplies. Going to visit his studio I went up the stairs as one man and came down as quite another.

Until that time I had been a classicist who scorned contemporary art and rejected the modern art movements of the twentieth century. When the Cincinnati Art Museum had displayed Picasso's great mural *Guernica* in 1940, my dear friend the art educator Ernestine Evans had tried in vain to make me see and feel the power of its statement. Five years later in his studio Altripp showed me the paintings he had made with common house paint and brushes fashioned from rubber hose. Using an expressive language of gestures and exclamations he showed me how these abstract paintings conveyed both the despair and the hopefulness he felt as he had labored in secrecy. Even though he was a "degenerate artist" he was required to do military service and had entered the lowest ranks of the *Wehrmacht.* For them he worked as a stable boy. This duty gave him some cover from their frequent inspections and in the horse barns he continued to paint. Somehow he procured good paper and used gasoline as a solvent. The realization came over me that if this man had ever been caught painting he would have been sent to a concentration camp and shot. Alo's sincerity and the beauty of his painting permanently altered my view of the modern artist and at last made me receptive to contemporary art.

Confronted with the authenticity of Alo's emotions and the strength of his commitment I knew that I had been wrong to think that modern artists were charlatans. Quite literally, the scales fell from my eyes as together we studied art books from the library of the museum. Using illustrations in catalogues of art exhibitions Altripp patiently introduced me to everything I had failed to appreciate about cubism, expressionism and abstraction, the international movements which he had studied in the schools and academies of Mainz, Munich and Dresden. After the Gestapo had closed his show he sought out another "degenerate," Paul Klee, who lived in exile in Switzerland after the Nazis had closed down Germany's greatest modern art school, the *Bauhaus*, where Klee was a faculty member.

During the months I would spend in Wiesbaden, Altripp became a valued friend and teacher. I bought several paintings from him which still hang in my living room both to humble and instruct me. After my service in Wiesbaden I was able to assist him by bringing some of his work to the Museum of Modern Art and to a dealer in New York on my return to the States. Later on I arranged an exhibition of his paintings in Houston, Texas, and helped him gain a fellowship to come to America and work at the Barnes Foundation in Pennsylvania. We maintained a friendship until his death in 1991. It is my great hope that one day he will receive the greater recognition that his career deserves.

Earlier I described how vast the *Landesmuseum* was with its many subterranean floors and how it had embraced many civic functions. Among them I discovered that the building had for some time provided studios for local artists. As our new regime became established these artists came forward to introduce themselves and seek whatever favors the new US Military Government might be ready to bestow. Those who had clearly been party members had to be evicted, among them Barth Marks who was quite well known as a sculptor for the Nazis and who had frequently exhibited in Berlin. In their place I was able to give studios to Altripp and others who had not embraced the party.

One artist who never would have made the cut for Hitler's collection was the Russian born Expressionist painter Alexej Jawlensky. Jawlensky had studied at the Academy in St. Petersburg while also serving in the Russian Army. He left the Army in 1896 and moved to Munich where he met Wassily Kandinsky who introduced him to the avant-garde artistic circles of the city. In the first decade of this century he traveled and lived in Russia, Italy and France where he met Matisse. Jawlensky became recognized as the artist who most successfully imported the style of Matisse and *Les Fauves* into Germany before World War I. When he was in Munich Jawlensky participated in the vibrant art life of the city as a member of *Der Blaue Reiter,* The Blue Rider group dominated by Kandinsky. After a wartime exile in Switzerland, Jawlensky lived in Italy until 1921 when he moved to Wiesbaden. Back in Germany he joined Lionel Feininger, Paul Klee and Kandinsky to form *Die Blauen Vier* in 1929. Despite his international reputation his last years in Wiesbaden were overshadowed by a paralyzing illness and his condemnation by the Nazis. Like Alo Altripp, Jawlensky had been forbidden to paint by the Nazis and three of his works had been included in the 1937 exhibition of "Degenerate Art."[11]

Jawlensky shared his years in Wiesbaden with a woman whom he married once she had born his child. After his death 15 March 1941, Madame Jawlensky had endeavored to keep the contents of his studio hidden from the Nazis who she knew would destroy it. Clearly she hoped to perpetuate his memory but also to use the painter's estate to support herself and her child. Needing a better hiding place she appealed to the Henkell family, famous as champagne makers who had been friends of the painter. Their large home offered secure basement storage. However, when the war was over this grand house attracted the attention of members of the US Air Corps who wanted a central city headquarters for their general. Frau Jawlensky was alarmed to learn from German servants of the General that the Henkell house had been requisitioned for his use and the basement would be cleared out because in the view of the Air Force its contents posed a fire hazard.

Frau Jawlensky began her frantic appeals with a visit to the office of the *Bürgermeister* of Wiesbaden. He could not help her but sent her to the US Military Government. Running between offices she eventually learned of the existence of my Collecting Point and came to see me. Gladly, I was able to intercede on her behalf and went at once in our truck to remove the paintings for her. Seventy-seven canvases were received at the Collecting Point on 21 September where we held then for a few weeks until Frau Jawlensky could make arrangements to store them herself.[12]

For the time being the Jawlensky canvases brought a breath of fresh air into the museum. As there was no need to hold them indefinitely we stored them in and around my office and planned to photograph them for our records. First to rush and see them was our resident artist Alo Altripp who had known and deeply

[11] Rattemeyer, Volker. *Alexej von Jawlensky.* Wiesbaden 1991; in general: Haftmann, Werner. *Banned and Persecuted. Dictatorship of Art under Hitler.* Cologne 1986.

[12] Many of these paintings have now entered the permanent collection of the Wiesbaden Museum.

admired Jawlensky and his art. Excitedly he pointed out to me the elements of Jawlensky's style. He had used brilliant colors and exaggerated facial proportions at one point in his career and then had developed an abstract style of greater harmony and elegance based on his appreciation of Paul Klee. I wrote to Josselyn that I wanted to do a show of Jawlensky's paintings and I certainly wanted to buy one. I had already purchased several of Alo's paintings and hung them in my office which I had also filled with plants. The office certainly bore no resemblance to the office of Colonel Bell's adjutant and I exulted in the pleasure of being able to surround myself with so much fine art.

The joy I found in the museum work constantly mitigated against the threatening atmosphere that otherwise pervaded our times. It turned out that Frau Jawlensky had been right to be concerned about the safety of her husband's art. While in the Henkell's basement I had noticed a portrait bust of a member of the Henkell family by Georg Kolbe, a famous German sculptor. I recognized the quality of the work, but as we had had no communications with the Henkell family I decided to leave it behind hoping that they would take steps to protect their own collections. I later regretted that decision when we learned from the same German house staff that the basement had been totally emptied by US airmen and the bust had probably been destroyed along with other art objects. It saddened me to learn that despite the work of the Roberts Commission and the presence of the MFA & A branch of Military Government we had not influenced general military conduct significantly.

Ready!

It was not until almost two months had passed and a great deal had been accomplished that I learned that I was to be in charge of the Wiesbaden Central Collecting Point and responsible for all of its internal and external activities. My lack of museum credentials had been discounted. As a Captain in the Army and as a former regimental adjutant I knew how to get things done. Like my fellow officers I was eager to put everything into the job and openly thrived on the excitement of seeing marvelous works of art and knowing that I had a part in preserving them. My work in Wiesbaden began to assume the aspect of a personal crusade that had increasing focus and meaning. I was exhilarated by the authority to implement the vision I had for the Collecting Point facilities and felt well compensated by the praise I was earning from my colleagues. Jim Rorimer and Charles Kuhn were amazed at the progress we were making with the rehabilitation of the building and they were impressed by my intuitive grasp of museum practices and procedures. I was enormously elated to be made director, I had been quite resigned to working for one of the experienced museum men.

By mid-July we knew that the bulk of the artwork stored in Frankfurt would be coming to Wiesbaden starting on 20 August 1945. The building was coming together and the daily work was well in hand under the supervision of Frau Hobirk who was now my Chief of Staff. Anticipating that we would be needing more personnel, the MFA & A headquarters sent me another American art historian, a young corporal named Kenneth Lindsay. Today Dr. Kenneth Lindsay is a professor emeritus of art history at the State University of New York in Binghamton, where he founded that department.[13] He was in Paris with a Signal Intelligence unit decoding messages and read in *Stars and Stripes* about James Rorimer's search for staff to protect the treasures of Germany. Lt. Kuhn was able to assign him to Wiesbaden despite the fact that he was an enlisted man. By August in addition to Lindsay I had added two other Germans to my administrative staff. Fräulein Lore Hengstenberg was our secretary and Herr Richard van Pilgrim was the receptionist. Pilgrim's job was going to become very significant once the art shipments had arrived and we would be expecting a stream of visitors and inspectors, not to mention curiosity-seekers who were sure to learn how important the *Landesmuseum* had become in the recovery of Germany.

In my capacity as cultural officer for the district I had also had the true pleasure of capturing one of the arch-Nazis. Although before the war he had not been known to sympathize with their policies, once he had succeeded Hans Posse as head of the Linz Commission, Hermann Voss enthusiastically carried out the plans for building Hitler's art collection.[14] Together Posse and Voss had been responsible for a great deal of the looting activity and forced sales by Jewish collectors that created a mountain of treasures in Bavaria that were now finding their way to Craig Smyth's Collecting Point in Munich. One day in August, Dr. Voss had called my office and politely asked for an appointment. I guess he was hoping to get back into his old job as director of the Wiesbaden paintings collection, but when he arrived I welcomed him with a detachment of military police who took him away to prison where he awaited trial for his war crimes.

Let me digress briefly to mention the second Central Collecting Point located at Munich in the Eastern Military District. On a reconnaissance trip to the area James Rorimer had inspected and then recommended the use of two buildings, the *Führerbau* and the *Verwaltungsbau,* to be collecting points for the art that the Nazis had looted from other European countries. There were no other buildings so well suited to house the Göring Collection, the Rosenberg and Hitler confiscations and other looted items. Lieutenant (USNR) Craig Smyth arrived in Munich 4 June 1945 to take charge of the buildings and the myriad details which

---

13 Interview and text supplied by Lindsay to RKM will be with the WIF papers at NGA.

14 Nicholas, see note 3, 171–172, provides an illuminating profile of Voss and his activities.

attended the operation. By October this Collecting Point housed books, documents and 13,619 cases and uncrated works of art. In a lecture given at the University of Groningen 13 March 1986 Craig Smyth recounted his activities and this lecture was later published in The Netherlands.[15] In *The Rape of Europa* by Lynn Nicholas the Munich Collecting Point is extensively discussed.[16] Since I never had the opportunity of visiting Munich during this period I refer my readers to these authors.

The Wiesbaden Museum was not quite secure yet. The *Luftwaffe* had had their headquarters in a group of buildings across the street from the *Landesmuseum* and a tunnel had been dug to facilitate movement between an officers' house and our building. The house had been flattened by the bombings, but the entrance to the tunnel had been blocked off. However, no one pointed out to me that the residue of the Wiesbaden collection of paintings, that had not been taken to Dresden, were stored in rooms reached through the tunnel. Some American soldiers discovered the tunnel, opened it and by scattering its floor with hay were able to turn it into a tunnel of love for their rendezvous with artloving WACs. It seems that for their favors a few of the girls got to choose paintings with which they decorated their quarters until one of their commanding officers became suspicious and had the good sense to notify me. We immediately reinforced the tunnel barriers and reclaimed the purloined paintings. That story always gets a laugh, but of course there was nothing very laughable about it.

As August 20th came closer our intense work began to show results. The roof did not leak and there was glass in the windows. The electrical and plumbing systems were functioning again. We knew the heating system would work, but we had no luck with the humidification system. The fire alarms had been reconnected to the City Fire Department. Steps could now be taken to prepare for the arrival of the shipment. I had seen the collections stacked in Frankfurt so I knew the types of materials we would be storing. The carpentry shop built racks for the uncrated paintings of the Berlin *Nationalgalerie.* Frau Hobirk and her secretaries were ready to begin creating inventory lists.

Final preparations also included hightened security of the building. It took a lot of maneuvering through Army channels to obtain tanks at three corners of the building sighting along the fence. The entrance to the building had a sentry station manned by the Army. Both courtyards and the inside of the fence were also patrolled by GIs. There was a growing staff of guards consisting of American GIs and German regular and secret policemen. I trusted no one. I was the guard who guarded the guards.

---

15 Smyth, Craig Hugh. *Repatriation of Art from the Collecting Point in Munich after World War II.* The Hague, Gary Schwartz/SDU Publishers 1988.

16 Nicholas, see note 3, 358.

20 August 1945

At last the day we had been working toward had come. I was off making some last minute inspection of the building when the trucks from Frankfurt arrived. When I ran down to the courtyard, Jim Rorimer was already out of his jeep and pacing about anxious to begin the work of unloading the first of fifty-seven truck loads of art. At that moment we had seventy-six rooms ready to receive these shipments and work was continuing on others that we anticipated needing since more repositories were scheduled to be emptied and their contents were also to be transferred to Wiesbaden. On the day the shipments began the Army blockaded all the intersections to the road between Frankfurt and Wiesbaden so that the heavily armed convoy could roll without interruption from the *Reichsbank* to the museum. Everything was recorded as it entered the building by Frau Hobirk and her staff. Absolutely no lists came with the shipment.

It is hard to say who was most excited. The German staff gave shouts of joy – the "Bunte Königin" *(Nefertiti)* is here – she's safe! The *Welfenschatz* (Guelph Treasure) is here! All gave a collective sigh that these collections were arriving safely. They had been stored away and out of sight for so many years.

From 20 August until the end of the month the bumper-to-bumper trucks went back and forth to the *Reichsbank* ferrying the crated collections of the Berlin State Museums and 393 loosely wrapped paintings of the Berlin *Nationalgalerie.* These were a sensitive responsibility for should anything have happened to a canvas the blame now would fall upon the MFA & A and especially on me. Immediately I realized how very fortunate I was that most of this shipment was coming in *crated* and that that work had been done by German museum officials. There and then I decided that my policy would be that we would never uncrate works of art unless ordered to do so. Of course the temptation to open up these boxes and display their marvelous contents was overwhelming for all the MFA & A officers and my staff. But I judged that the risks of damage or worse yet of theft were too great to permit us to gratify our appetites for visual pleasures. Later rounding the corner into my office I got a private thrill each time I patted the crate that contained the painting of *Venus* by Botticelli.

Unable to see such masterpieces I took quiet satisfaction in the pleasure of reading over and over the list of collections we had under our roof.[17] We started

---

[17] The list of collections was recorded and prepared by Frau Hobirk and the final list in the Appendix IIb, pages 153–171 was created under Edith Standen. Original copies will be found with my papers at the NGA.

Only in January of 1997 did Dr. Klaus Goldmann give me a copy of a list created in Frankfurt at the Reichsbank dated 22 June 1945 signed by Mason Hammond – why had I never seen that list?

asking everyone for shipping and accession lists to help us inventory the cases holding these collections. For starters, there were the collections of the state museums beginning with 89 cases of classical antiquities; 163 cases of Egyptian art; 49 cases of Islamic ceramics, sculpture and carpets; and cases holding 1188 paintings of the *Gemäldegalerie (Kaiser Friedrich Museum)*. The sculpture collection filled 350 cases and there were 2300 portfolios of prints, drawings and other works on paper forming the contents of the famous Berlin *Kupferstichkabinett*. The Early Christian and Byzantine collection filled seven cases with paintings, sculptures, ceramics and jewelry. From the National Gallery in addition to their 393 canvases there were 288 cases of decorative arts and from the *Kunstgewerbe Museum* there were 45 cases containing similar materials. We had the Zeughaus collection of arms and uniforms of 39 cases and 51 cases of flags. Thirty cases of folk art belonged to the *Museum für Deutsche Volkskunde* and there were 92 cases holding the ethnological collection of the *Völkerkunde Museum*. There were four cases from the Asian Art department and six cases of prehistoric art from the *Museum für Vor- und Frühgeschichte*. Concluding the shipment were the 14 cases and 742 portfolios containing books and plates from the State Art Library.

In addition to these collections from the Berlin state museums we received from the *Reichsbank* during this same time two collections of loot from Poland. The Nazis had gathered up 13 cases of archaeological materials and 773 liturgical objects looted from the treasuries of the Polish churches. Custodianship of these materials posed special problems that led to one of our most secure installations at the Collecting Point. There were no inventories for the uncrated church treasures which had been randomly gathered by the Nazis as spoils that they intended to melt down for currency. That was why they had been taken to the *Reichsbank*. We anticipated the need to arrange these objects so that delegations from Poland would be able to survey them and identify the things they had lost. We chose a remote corner room on the second floor in the region of the former archaeological department because it had only one doorway. Shelving was installed in an E-shape from floor to ceiling and the windows were covered with barbed wire outside and boarded up inside. These marvelous Polish works of art were then unpacked and put on shelved three and four deep in the Treasure Room which soon would hold other spectacular national treasures.

The story of the Hungarian Coronation Regalia belongs to Jim Rorimer for he was the MFA & A officer who first received it and eventually conveyed it to the *Reichsbank* and then to Wiesbaden.[18] For months Jim had been hearing rumors concerning the whereabouts of the Holy Crown of Hungary. Hungarians believe that so long as the Crown is safe, Hungary is safe. Members of an elite group of

---

18 Rorimer, see note 9, 154–157.

guards began an elaborate sequence of movements to keep the Crown hidden until the fate of their country was determined and a new government established. When their country was occupied by the Russians at the end of the war the Hungarians who were charged with the protection of the Crown decided to place it with the United States government for safekeeping.

In his book *Survival* Rorimer recounted that in the early part of June he had been in the quarters of Major Paul Kubala at Augsburg. Kubala was in charge of the Seventh Army Interrogation Center and he told Rorimer he thought he knew the whereabouts of the Crown. Rorimer had a hunch that the iron strong box he had just been sitting on might have held the Hungarian regalia. Back at his headquarters Rorimer began an investigation that eventually encouraged Kubala to turn in a report to headquarters in which he described his efforts to obtain the Royal Crown. Kubala told how at the time of the German surrender he had received an ancient box from Colonel Pajtas and twelve guards of the Hungarian Army. Pajtas said the box contained the Crown, but he could not open it because all of the keys had been taken by the Prime Minister of Hungary.[19]

A series of attempts was made to turn the box over to other authorities who would not accept it without knowledge of its contents. Meanwhile interrogations of all Hungarian nationals continued until the keys were obtained. On or about the 24th of July the box was opened but only the sword of St. Stephen was found in it. Now Pajtas explained that he had removed its contents according to his instructions and had hidden the Crown, the scepter and the Holy Apple. Kubala then told Pajtas that the Hungarians had put him in an exceedingly difficult position inasmuch as the whole world knew the box was in the possession of the Seventh Army. Pajtas returned the following day with an old mud-covered gasoline drum. The drum was chiseled open by Colonel Pajtas and three very muddy and deteriorated leather-covered boxes appeared. Kubala and Pajtas took the Crown, scepter and Holy Apple into Kubala's bathroom and washed them off before repacking them in the original box where the sword of St. Stephen had remained all the while.

On 3 August the strong-box was opened again in the presence of the Commanding General of the Seventh Army, other interested officials and representatives of the press. Rorimer was there to receive the regalia and supervise its transfer to the Reichsbank in Frankfurt. Six weeks later the Crown, the scepter, and the Holy Apple arrived in Wiesbaden on the 17th of September to be stored in our Treasure Room. These Hungarian treasures remained in Wiesbaden until 17 April 1946 when they were sent to Munich. From there they were eventually transported to the United States where they remained at Fort Knox until they

---

[19] See note 18.

were returned to Hungary during the administration of President Jimmy Carter in 1977.[20]

Our responsibility for these collections did not stop with providing them a safe repose. By early September inquiries were being received from curators and museum officials in Berlin who were anxious to know if their treasures were all right. Now I realized that despite my cautious assessment of the risks certain cases containing paintings would have to be opened in order to check on the condition of canvases and wood panels that had been too long in storage. To conduct these inspections we would need a trained conservator on the staff as well as the services of expert curators. Our staff was enlarged to include Frau Dr. Wulfhild Schoppa, an art historian who was appointed Acting Director of the Wiesbaden *Gemäldegalerie.* Two photographers came from Photo Marburg who would document the condition of the greatest works that were in our care. In October I was able to hire Frau Flinsch as the museum's conservator so that she could carry out the temporary conservation procedures that would stabilize a panel that developed a crack or a canvas with a blister on its surface.

I also wanted to hire someone who had known the condition of these great paintings before the war and so was happy to engage Dr. Ernst Holzinger, director of the *Städelsches Kunstinstitut* in Frankfurt who would come one or two days a week to attend the opening of the paintings cases and assist in our inspections. Dr. Holzinger proved to be a great asset to our operations for his reputation as a museum director in Germany was outstanding. He had survived the Nazi period without capitulation and guarded his museum's collections with care and integrity. It was a great pleasure and privilege to work with him.

Now the place was really humming with activity. By October an additional typist joined our work force. Under the supervision of Joe Kohlmaier, our foreman, the building was in excellent condition with the exception of continuing problems with the elevator. Full electrical power was still not available in Wiesbaden and this had hampered its repair. There was also a shortage of light bulbs which prevented illuminating the security fence to the degree I felt was necessary. My greatest concern was that with our first winter approaching we had not yet received the coal we had requisitioned. But I felt confident that with perseverance these problems would be overcome and continued my work with the greatest enthusiasm.

We began to receive visitors as early as September when we were requested to provide overnight hospitality for very special guests. The sculpture of the *Madonna and Child* by Michelangelo was being escorted back to Belgium by a

---

20 Simontsits, Attila L. *The Last Battle of St. Stephen's Crown.* Cambridge: University Press. 1991.

group of Belgian and American officials and guards. The removal of this work from Brugge in 1944 was a major incident in the history of the Nazis war-time art confiscation policies and its discovery in the Austrian mine of Altaussee indicated that it had probably been intended for Hitler's planned museum in Linz. MFA & A officers had been successful in transporting the work from its hiding place and restoring it to the grateful Belgians.

Once we had put the art from the Berlin museums in place we were open for business and other collections began to arrive at our doors. Most of these materials were "displaced art." Their owners had hidden them in hopes of returning to retrieve them and were prevented from doing so for any number of reasons. Some works came to us from the repositories discovered in British and French zones of occupation, such as works belonging to museums in Cologne, Kassel, Karlsruhe and Mainz. Additional works of art arrived from Walker Hancock's Collecting Point in Marburg in order to consolidate certain important Berlin collections. A number of tapestries from Prussian palace collections had been stored at Marburg and after we received them we decided that they and all our organic materials such as the other textiles, Egyptian papyrus and the taxidermy of the Wiesbaden natural sciences collection should be fumigated. Everything was gathered together in rooms of the Natural Science Department and given a good dose of cyanide gas by a Hamburg shipping firm.

As our store rooms filled I had more and more reason to be fearful that our security could be breached and something would be stolen. Feeling increasingly nervous I distrusted everyone, both the Americans and the Germans, for there had simply been too much evidence as documented in the press that acts of looting continued. The Treasure Room made me particularly anxious since everything had arrived uncrated and had been put into open storage on the shelves that lined the room. I ordered safes and strong boxes in the fervent hope that they would arrive and be filled before something disappeared. As a means of control I had begun a systematic program of photography documenting the most valuable objects. Photo Marburg became our official photographic company. But photographic supplies, paper, chemicals and equipment were so scarce that this project had been stalled until mid-September.

With winter approaching we anticipated future shortages of food and I continued the employee's canteen in the museum so that our staff could have hot lunches. In my letters I constantly urged Joss to send me kitchen supplies so that our work could continue. The German government was far from ready to resume caring for its population and the American occupation government deferred this responsibility to UNRRA, the United Nations Relief and Rehabilitation Administration. The future of our occupation was unclear at the time and rumors circulated widely since all of our positions had been frozen for the next six months. Although perfectly thrilled to be here doing this vital work, others were sick and tired of fighting endless bureaucratic skirmishes amongst the ruins of the German nation and they longed to leave for home. Daily we were pleading for requisitioned supplies and attempting communications without reliable phone service while being endlessly confronted with a ravaged landscape and a destitute civilian population that looked to us for help.

The Military Government soon recognized that the German people were desperately in need of firewood for cooking and for some time had been denuding the Wiesbaden parks of their trees. An order was passed that every German was entitled to one tree from the forests beyond the town, but how were they supposed to get there? There was no reliable public transportation so knowing I would lose the precious time and energy of my workers to this activity I sent my truck into the forest to harvest these trees and then distributed the sawn logs in the museum's courtyard.

It was in this climate that my Collecting Point took on the aspect of a refuge for the other MFA & A officers who were stationed nearby. Because they were frozen in their duty they could not leave for home even though the work that they had been brought together to do was almost finished. By October the repositories were nearly emptied of their precious contents and the Collecting Points were filled with art works awaiting their fate through the slow process of restitution. Now it was the time for official visits from the governments whose art collections had been looted. Escorted by MFA & A officers they came in search of their missing treasures.

My colleagues loved these visits since it gave them the opportunity to visit our storerooms and see great works of art that had been inaccessible to them for almost a decade. As he was now the commander of our branch at Frankfurt, Major Bancel La Farge was a frequent visitor. In peacetime La Farge had been an architect with an active practice in New York. I had grown to admire and respect him for he had wisely counseled me during the first weeks in Wiesbaden when we began the repairs to the *Landesmuseum* building.

Another Höchst based officer, Lt. Thomas Carr Howe, Jr. who served as Deputy Chief of the MFA & A section under La Farge wrote a wonderful book about his experiences, *Salt Mines and Castles,* that was published immediately after his return to the States in 1946. Howe had served with the Special Evacuation Team that had explored the mines at Altaussee, emptied the castle of Neuschwanstein and found the great altarpiece of Veit Stoss in an underground bunker in Nuremberg. In the same location the team had found the coronation regalia of the Holy Roman Empire including the Crown dating from the eleventh century, a shield, two swords and the orb. Accompanied by Edith Standen, Howe enjoyed driving over from headquarters at Höchst for the weekend. There was little entertainment available elsewhere and after a tour of our Collecting Point and several hours in the Treasure Room I would invite the group back to my office to share a glass of Tokay wine and hours of stories concerning the now legendary exploits of the MFA & A.

James Rorimer was a frequent guest with many official reasons to journey out to Wiesbaden and always enough time to spare examining the contents of the Treasure Room. As a medievalist Rorimer found much to admire among the intricately wrought and bejewelled chalices and reliquaries that filled the shelves. We particularly enjoyed examining the Guelph treasure from Berlin which I had first seen on display in Cleveland in 1930 as a boy. I felt particularly honored when Rorimer suggested that I might want to write a book about the confiscation of the Polish church treasures and by means of this publication assist in restoring them to the former owners. Other MFA & A officers would use the opportunity of their close contacts with this amazing accumulation of riches to further their scholarly interests. On his return to the States, Sgt. Ken Lindsay wrote a master's thesis on the Hungarian crown and a latecomer to the group, Captain Joseph Kelleher, used the same work of art as the topic for a Ph.D. dissertation at Princeton.

I am not certain when Kelleher arrived on the scene in Wiesbaden, but I do remember he had made a great impression on everyone. In his book Howe described him vividly as a "black Irishman" and said that Kelleher had "interrupted his brilliant career in the Fine Arts department at Princeton" to join the MFA & A.[21] When I knew him he was hospitalized and wore a cast on his leg as a result of an accident. Seeing him took me back to the days when I had been hospitalized in England and I felt pity for him in his confinement. Knowing how bored he must be, I invited him over to the Collecting Point where he spent his days looking on and occasionally assisting in our work. Kelleher had been assigned to the local Military Government for Greater Hesse and was looking for something to do so as to make his mark as others had done. Though they found him witty and amusing, instinctively I distrusted him and later found out I had been right to do so. He wanted my job as director of the Collecting Point and would soon set about trying to discredit me.[22]

Naively, I played into his hands. By the first week of November I was feeling exhausted by the pace since arriving in Wiesbaden four months earlier. I had begun to think about taking a leave and wrote to Josselyn on 3 November 1945 that this might be possible since Captain Kelleher would be here for a while. I was hoping to travel to England to see friends made during my tour of duty there and

---

21 Howe, Thomas Carr. *Salt Mines and Castles.* Indianapolis, New York: Bobbs-Merrill 1946, 285.

22 The papers of Thomas Carr Howe in the Archives of American Art, Washington, D.C., contain a number of letters from Kelleher to Howe that reveal his personality.

to escape the growing depression of winter in desolated Germany. To add to our difficulties electrical power was now rationed and in our offices we worked in the half light descending from overcast skies.

This was an ideal spot from which I too would further my career. To the praise I received from my fellow officers and especially from my boss, Jim Rorimer, were added good words of encouragement received from the New Yorker writer Janet Flanner. Under the pseudonym Genêt she had authored her "Letter from Paris" since October 1925. Now she had come to Frankfurt and Wiesbaden to do research for a lengthy article about the Nazi's systematic program of looting European art collections and the American response to the challenge of restitution.[23] She was eager to learn all about the MFA & A and stayed with us for several days. I gave her a tour of the Collecting Point and did not neglect to show her that our activities also included helping to revive the contemporary arts in Germany. She saw Alo Altripp's work and gave me a note to enclose with a letter to Monroe Wheeler, director of the Museum of Modern Art in New York. I was dreaming of organizing an exhibition of Alo's work to send to the States and saw this as an opportunity to launch my own career as a curator. A whole world of possibilities had opened up for me in Wiesbaden and I was eager to make the most of it.

23 "The Beautiful Spoils: The Monuments Men." Reprinted in Flanner, Janet. *Men and Monuments.* New York: Da Capo Press, republished 1990, 220–290.

Chapter four: Westward Ho, Watteau!

The telegram was hand delivered to me from the Military Government Office in Wiesbaden. Reading over it quickly I saw my world turn dark with malevolence and treachery. On 6 November 1945 I was ordered to prepare a shipment of at least 200 German museum owned paintings from the Collecting Point for transport to the United States. Now I understood the uneasy manner of my MFA & A colleagues over the past few weeks. They knew, but I did not, that representatives of our government had been planning for some time to help themselves to the greatest treasures of the German people that were stored in the Wiesbaden Collecting Point under my care. It seemed a pretext for their removal had been found. Within the last days of October or early November I had received a VIP from Washington whose attitude towards my efforts contrasted strikingly to that of other guests. He was critical when they had been full of praise. He was suspicious when they had been overflowing with gratitude for a job well done.

He was Harry A. McBride, a colonel in the Army and administrator at the National Gallery of Art (NGA).[1] When he had toured the Collecting Point with me he had pointedly questioned the damp Army blankets that were hanging in the doorways and the pools of water on the linoleum floor. He thought the roof had been leaking. But the puddles on the floor were nothing more than a primitive attempt to add badly needed moisture to the air of the *Landesmuseum* since its proper humidification system was inoperable. Parts for sensitive equipment installed in the pre-War decades were impossible to come by in the months immediately after the end of World War II. It was out of the question to replace the system. We were lucky to have heat, lucky to have brickettes to burn in the furnace, lucky that the floors were covered with linoleum and not hardwoods which would have buckled if we had poured water out on them. The air in the Collecting Point was bone dry and this environment threatened the safety of the paintings and sculpture. Moist air is critical to the preservation of centuries-old panel paintings and we had a significant number of them among the crates that held the collection of the *Kaiser Friedrich Museum.* Moreover, our improvised system had been endorsed by all the museum professionals, American and German, who had visited the Collecting Point.

---

1 Nicholas, Lynn H. *The Rape of Europa.* New York: Knopf 1994, 394, misdates McBride's arrival at the Wiesbaden Collecting Point and our confrontation, which I believe took place several days or even a week before I received the telegram ordering the shipment of the paintings to America.

But McBride had to file a report that would be critical of my stewardship in order to implement the plan to remove German paintings to America for safekeeping and return them if and when the German nation had earned the right to their return.[2] This was the conditional phrase that had found its way into circulation and which came to haunt us all for it insulted everyone from the MFA & A to the German museum community to the cultured populations of Germany who had been no fonder of Hitler and the Nazis than we were. To have introduced this scheme of blatant looting just when our operation was running so smoothly and our relations with the German people were beginning to be mended was an outrage that I found intolerable.

Why had I not been told of the rumors that such a plot was being hatched? My only answer is that I was not in regular attendance for the bull sessions at MFA & A headquarters in Höchst or the office in Frankfurt where solid information and sprightly gossip were routinely exchanged. Immersed in my work at the Collecting Point I took little notice of the office politics in which the others participated. And I was not one of them, not one of the museum men who knew personally those in the orbit of the Roberts Commission and the State Department in Washington who could have been instrumental in the decision that the United States would plunder the collections of the *Kaiser Friedrich Museum* and the Berlin *Nationalgalerie.*

Plunder is the only word. Better yet, make that systematic plunder. The list of works I saw when it arrived could only have been drawn up by trained art historians. Who had consulted on the drafting of this list and what exactly were their future plans for this exotic and unique accumulation of masterpieces?[3] I will point out only a few of the headliners as I continue to tell the story of the Wiesbaden Manifesto from my point of view. Here are the orders that I received.

> From 7th US Army
> To office mil Govt for Stadtkreis Wiesbaden
> BT
> Higher headquarters desiges (sic) that immediate preparations be made for prompt shipment to the unitek of a selection of at least two zero zero German works of art of greatest importance X most of these are now in art collecting point Wiesbaden X selections will be made by personnel from headquarters CMA US Forces CMA European theater who will assist in packing and shipment by motor transport to Bremen X from CG seventh Army to Director CMA office of Military Government for Stadtkreis Wiesbaden CMA ref no able three three zero two seven X you will provide sufficient material and personnel X this headquarter is to be

---

2 Howe, Thomas Carr. *Salt Mines and Castles.* Indianapolis, New York: Bobbs-Merrill 1946, 230.

3 A full list of the 202 paintings ultimately selected is given in the Appendix II d, page 180–193 of this book.

> informed by telephone of progress and anticipated requirements X operation to be completed by two zero November X Transportation and military security during transit will be provided by this headquarters X.

Reading the telegram I collapsed in my chair and broke into tears. Nervous exhaustion that I had been holding at bay overtook me. Was it only that I was the last to know? Not at all. My outrage was so personal because in the last month I had been developing such good relations with Dr. Ernst Holzinger, Frau Schoppa, Frau Flinsch and other German museum professionals who were profoundly grateful for the work that was being done to preserve their national heritage. How could I look them in the eye? How could I ask them to make the condition reports and pack for shipment this star-studded list of treasures? A mockery was being made of our entire operation. Not only was there no need to "safeguard" these paintings in the United States, but in transporting them on the open seas in the dead of winter these panel paintings and canvases would be exposed to the most pernicious climatic conditions that one could imagine. You must recall that this was before the days of the blockbuster exhibition. Now great treasures fly back and forth across the Atlantic Ocean routinely. Hermetically sealed and flown at jetspeed their crate environments can be controlled "from wall to wall," as the museum folks say, without turning a hair. But this was 1945 and who knew yet if the shipping channels were completely safe and free from mines? And what did the military know about transporting art anyway. Wasn't that why we, the MFA & A had come into existence?

My fury was intense but it burned itself out quickly and I began to think. I decided I would call every last one of the Monuments Specialist Officers, even those as far away as Paris and Berlin, and ask them to meet the following day in Wiesbaden so that we could organize a protest to this order. Even with all my training-by-the-book as a regimental adjutant I was ready to lead an action that could result in a court martial and the end of my military career. But then I had never planned a military career in the first place. It had happened by chance and I had made the most of every opportunity. I felt I had nothing to lose.

This attitude was markedly different from that of some of my colleagues. Although on hearing my call they assembled with the same sense of purpose which had driven me to summon them, many had private reservations about our proposed action. They wanted to return to the United States and resume careers in the top American museums especially the National Gallery of Art in Washington and the Metropolitan Museum of Art. As our discussions progressed on the following day it became clear that they all felt they could see the fingerprints of highly placed officials of both institutions on the order for the shipment of the 202. If they sided with me, if they signed the protest that we were about to draft what would be their fate? Would they ever get to use those hard-earned degrees? Would their career ladders still accomodate them if they protested the directive of their commanders?

I found work for the museum staff in other parts of the building so that they would not overhear what I knew would be a lively proceeding. I asked only Frau Hobirk to stay and serve as stenographer for the meeting. Thirty-two of the thirty-five Monuments Specialist Officers then stationed in Germany attended the meeting and many vocally contributed ideas for the protest document which was written by Captain Everett P. (Bill) Lesley with editorial assistance from Lt. Charles Parkhurst and others.[4] The words were carefully chosen. They were much better than I at articulating the pain we all felt over the loss of moral purpose which was about to befall the MFA & A. They knew how to temper outrage with factual data and raise the ethical implications of the pending action to the level of an international crisis of conscience for the United States of America. At the end of the day I recall Bill Lesley made the only light-hearted statement of the session when he said, "I feel like Thomas Jefferson when he wrote the Declaration of Independence."

> U.S. Forces, European Theater Germany
>
> 7 November 1945
>
> 1. We, the undersigned, Monuments, Fine Arts and Archives Specialist Officers of the Armed Forces of the United States, wish to make known our convictions regarding the transportation to the United States of works of art, the property of German institutions or Nationals, for purposes of protective custody.
>
> 2.a. We are unanimously agreed that the transportation of these works of art, undertaken by the United States Army, upon direction from the highest national authority, establishes a precedent which is neither morally tenable nor trustworthy.
>
> b. Since the beginning of United States participation in the war, it has been the declared policy of the Allied Forces, so far as military necessity would permit, to protect and preserve from deterioration consequent upon the processes of war, all monuments, documents or other objects of historic, artistic, cultural or archaeological value. The war is at an end, and no doctrine of "military necessity" can now be invoked for the further protection of the objects to be moved, for the reason that depots and personnel, both fully competent for their protection, have been inaugurated and are functioning.
>
> c. The Allied Nations are at present preparing to prosecute individuals for the crime of sequestering, under pretext of "protective custody," the cultural treasures

---

[4] Thomas Carr Howe, Jr. Papers, Archives of American Art, Washington, D.C, contain a letter from Lesley to Howe dated 30 December 1946 following the publication of Howe's *Salt Mines.* It concludes:

> If on the other hand, you were led – as I am sure you were – by niceness of feeling and a prudent desire to protect, not to connect me with the Wiesbaden Manifesto, that is the one thing which might do me tangible harm which I am willing to stand behind for the rest of my life and would welcome as an individual responsibility. That document was not "drafted" – it was written of a piece, and, despite the highfalutin' Jeffersonian diction, it was written by your fretful but still mordantly pleased E.P.L.

of German-occupied countries. A major part of the indictment follows upon the reasoning that, even though these individuals were acting under military orders, the dictates of a higher ethical law made it encumbent upon them to refuse to take part in, or countenance, the fulfillment of these orders. We, the undersigned, feel it is our duty to point out that, though as members of the Armed Forces we will carry out the orders we receive, we are thus put before any candid eyes as no less culpable than those whose prosecution we affect to sanction.

3. We wish to state that from our own knowledge, no historical grievance will rankle so long, or be the cause of so much justified bitterness, as the removal, for any reason, of a part of the heritage of any nation, even if that heritage may be interpreted as a prize of war. And though this removal may be done with every intention of altruism, we are none the less convinced that it is our duty, individually and collectively, to protest against it, and state that though our obligations are to the nation to which we owe allegiance, there are yet further obligation to common justice, decency and the establishment of the power of right, not of expediency or might, among civilized nations.

Twenty-four officers agreed to sign the protest: three stated that they agreed with its sentiments but did not feel at liberty to sign. Five others including Lt. Craig H. Smyth, director of the Munich Collecting Point, expressed similar sentiments by means of separate letters to Major La Farge.[5]

It is only now that the story is a half-century old that the details of the plot behind the shipment of the 202 can be discerned thanks to the patient scholarship of Lynn Nicholas and others. But before we turn to her very recent account we should consider the story as told by Tom Howe in his book published in 1946 while the 202 were stored in the vaults of the National Gallery of Art in Washington.[6]

For most of the summer of 1945 Howe had been assigned to the Munich Collecting Point where he had worked with evacuation teams bringing works of art out of the Austrian mines and Bavarian castles where they had been hidden by the Nazis. At the end of September he was reassigned to the MFA & A section at Höchst which was part of the Military Government's Restitution Control Branch of the Economics Division headquartered there. Major Bancel La Farge was in charge assisted by my friend Captain Edith Standen, Corporal James Reeds and a German civilian stenographer. When Howe arrived this group was involved in arranging token restitutions of looted works of art to France, Belgium and Holland in accordance with proposals made by General Clay at the time of the Potsdam Conference.[7]

Howe already knew of the proposed removal of German-owned art to the United States, an idea which he thought had been under discussion since the

---

5 Appendix IIa, page 147–152.

6 Howe, see note 2. See also: Kopper, Philip. *America's National Gallery of Art: A gift to the nation.* New York: Abrams, 1991, 217–235.

7 Howe, see note 2, 230.

Potsdam Conference held near Berlin from 17 July until 2 August 1945. It was at that time that the document which proposed categorization of works of art (see "The Roberts Commission", Appendix I) had emerged from General Lucius Clay's headquarters and become known to many conference participants and to the top Monuments Specialist Officers.[8] Howe asked Edith if there had been any new developments. She replied that there had. She knew of a cable from General Clay to the War Department early in September. Howe wrote:

> The cable spoke of 'holding German objects of art in trust for eventual return to the German people.' But it didn't contain the clause 'if and when the German nation had earned the right to their return' which had appeared in the original document. Besides the cable there had been a communication from Berlin asking (Höchst) for an estimate of the cubic footage in art repositories of the American Zone.[9]

Charles Kuhn had still been at Frankfurt in September and together with Bancel they figured out a reply although the question was impossible to answer with accuracy. The Monuments Officers were stunned: would anyone seriously be considering moving everything we had placed under our protection to the United States? Knowing the immense quantities of German treasure it is no wonder that the crowd at Höchst had been alarmed.

Howe had offered Standen the hope that since at that moment Kuhn was back in the States along with John Nicholas Brown, General Eisenhower's cultural advisor who had toured Germany during the summer, the two might be able to discourage the projected removal. Howe continued.

> I had only one piece of information to contribute on the subject: a letter from George Stout saying that he had been asked by the Roberts Commission to give an opinion, based on purely technical grounds, of the risk involved in sending paintings to America. He did so, stating that to remove them would cube the risk of leaving them in Germany.[10]

Before the end of October Bancel, Tom and Edith prepared a staff study on the purely technical, not the moral, objections to a shipment of art from Germany. It was delivered to Colonel Hayden Smith, Chief of Staff to Major General C. L. Adcock, Deputy Director of the Office of Military Government, US Zone, headquartered in Frankfurt. Howe continued:

> Nothing came of our recommendations. Within two weeks, Colonel Harry McBride, administrator of the National Gallery in Washington, arrived in Berlin to expedite the first shipment. He flew down to Frankfurt two days later to discuss

---

[8] John Nicholas Brown, 9. August 1945, in Appendix App. III a, page 199–202.

[9] Howe, see note 2, 262; see also note 1 and *College Art Journal,* Jan. 46 (Ch. Kuhn).

[10] Howe, see note 2, 262.

> ways and means with Major La Farge. We learned from him that General Clay's recommendation for immediate removal had been approved by the highest national authority. The General was now in Washington. The futility of protest was obvious.[11]

According to Howe, La Farge told McBride that the Monuments Officers were strongly opposed to the project and some might request transfer rather than comply with the order. McBride said any such request would probably be refused and outright defiance would only lead to a court-martial. Even then, the order would still be carried out. The Quartermaster Corps would be called in to do the work. Now Howe said, "Bancel realized that his primary duty was the 'protection and salvage' of art works. If he deliberately left them at the mercy of whatever troops might be available to do the packing, then he would be guilty of dereliction of duty."[12] At this point in his story Howe inserted the text of the Wiesbaden Manifesto, as the protest that was written in my office at the Collecting Point came to be known. Although Army regulations forbade the publication of such a statement, copies were widely distributed and in the new year the Manifesto appeared in an article by Charles Kuhn in *College Art Journal* in January, in the *Magazine of Art,* in February, and in the New York *Times,* 7 February 1946.[13]

According to Howe, since the subjects of morality and the safety of the works intended for transport had been dismissed as non-issues by our superiors, the debate now focused on which paintings to send. Howe outlined the discussion. Now that the cat was out of the bag, so to speak, everything had to be speeded up. It would be most efficient to take works from one Collecting Point. Wiesbaden was close to hand and besides it seems that Lt. Craig H. Smyth, director of the Munich Collecting Point, put up a strong defense against a raid on his operation. "He said that his entire staff of non-Nazi museum specialists would walk out. This would seriously impede the restitution program in the Eastern Military District."[14] Smyth's Collecting Point had become the refuge of enormous quantities of looted art from France, Holland and Belgium. At that time, to the best of my knowledge there were no German-owned collections stored there from which selections could have been made.[15]

---

11 Howe, see note 2, 273.

12 Howe, see note 2, 273.

13 Howe, see note 2, 274–75.

14 Howe, see note 2, 276.

15 "The Munich pictures were still where the Germans had left them, in the rural repositories of Dietramzell, Ettal and Raitenhaslach, and despite (John) Walker's advice during his July visit, had not yet been brought to the Collecting Point." Nicholas, see note 1, 392.

Walker Hancock had an even more profound reaction to the news that works from the Collecting Points were being selected for a trip to the United States. Howe was present when Bancel La Farge broke the news to him. Hancock said, "In that case I can't go back to Marburg. Everything that we were able to accomplish was possible because I had the confidence of certain people. I can't go back and tell them that I have betrayed them."[16] In 1994 he writes me that he can never forget, was John Brown's remark: "If they take those pictures we'll never again be able to raise our heads from the pillow!"[17] When Hancock published his own story "Experiences of a Monuments Officer in Germany" in the May 1946 issue of the *College Art Journal* he omitted all mention of the shipment of German art to the US. He did return to Marburg, but only long enough to pack and say goodbye to Professor Richard Hamann, the distinguished old German scholar with whom he had been consulting. "I quoted the official statement", Hancock said, "about the paintings being held in trust for the German people and added that there was no reason to doubt it. Very slowly he said, 'If they take our old art, we must try to create a fine new art.' Then, after a long pause he added, 'I never thought they would take them.'"[18]

And what of my friend Captain James Rorimer, still attached as Monuments Specialist to the Third Army at their headquarters? I looked up to Jim, my boss, out of respect for the professionalism he had displayed to me and my appreciation for his great scholarly knowledge. I remember on the day of our meeting in my office while the Manifesto was being written Jim paced nervously in the corridor. He sympathized with us, but he could not bring himself to join us in our common protest. His former boss, director of the Metropolitan Museum of Art, Francis Henry Taylor, was a member of the Roberts Commission and was said to favor bringing works from German collections to the US for safekeeping.

In the January 1945 issue of *The Atlantic Monthly* was published Taylor's account of a recent trip he had made to Europe. As background to his report on the current status of well-loved tourist destinations, European capital cities and their monuments, he outlined the insane goals of the Nazis cultural policies and the great devastation to museums, religious institutions and private collections that their looting had caused. The title of his article, "The Rape of Europa," makes clear the deep, righteous, animosity that he held for the Nazis.[19] On the concluding page he groped to bring his views of the situation into a calmer perspective saying,

---

16 Howe, see note 2, 276.

17 Letter Hancock to WIF, Nov. 5, 1994 (WIF papers).

18 Howe, see note 2, 277. Hancock repeated this story to RKM in an interview in August, 1993.

19 Taylor, Francis Henry. "The Rape of Europa," *Atlantic Monthly*, (vol. 175, January, 1945), 52–58.

> As we approach the final settlement with the filthy beasts who have done their utmost to destroy the European civilization which we cherish, there must necessarily be a period of soul-searching and calm reflection before justice can be dispensed and retribution made …
>
> If one recognizes that the Teutonic disease may lie dormant for half a century and suddenly break out with virulence because of social, economic and political circumstances, one sees immediately the danger of reducing Germany to the same kind of cultural desert that she has made of Poland. For in the arid soil of such a desert the germs of future wars may breed. With this in mind the committees which have been meeting in London, composed of representatives of the United Nations governments, many of whom have had a tragic personal stake in the discussions, have tried to arrive at an intelligent and just program for settling the artistic problems of the peace, rather than a vindictive one.
>
> General Eisenhower has already made public the policy of Military Government in Germany and has issued orders and directives to his officers in regard to property control in general. All forms of property, including cultural material, works of art, books, scientific speciments, will be subject to the same general seizure and "freezing" restrictions. Stolen or looted objects recovered will be held for disposition by the proper international bodies appointed under the terms of the peace settlement.

Taylor's tirade continued with a cannonade of alarming statistics and concluded with a statement that seems most characteristic of his state of mind.

> War crimes must be punished and those who have been pillaged compensated, for Germany must learn that the rape of Europe, however scientifically and ruthlessly carried out, did not pay. German scholarship and Germany's claims to intellectual equality can never again be entertained until the slate is clean.

After reading Taylor's article one can understand why those in the MFA & A who knew him would have had no difficulty in believing that he strongly supported the American seizure of works of art from the German museum collections. While peace negotiations were still continuing Taylor and others probably thought it would not hurt to make a display of American power even if it would wound those Germans who had had no more liking for Hitler than we did.

At the time of the writing of the protest James Rorimer told us that he agreed with its sentiments, but felt he could not sign. On the following day he wrote to his commanding officer asking to be relieved, but the request was refused.[20] In his book *Survival,* published in 1950, Jim Rorimer treats the shipment of the 202 and the protest summarily saying that:

> Neither we nor the Germans knew of President Truman's promise to return the paintings when they could be more adequately housed in German museums … After three years in America, involving a stay at the National Gallery in Washington and later a grand tour of other American museums, the paintings were all safely returned to Germany.[21]

---

20 Rorimer papers, Archives of American Art, Rorimer to Edwards, November 8, 1945.

21 Rorimer James J., and Gilbert Rabin. *Survival.* NewYork: Abelard Press 1950, 232.

James Rorimer succeeded Francis Henry Taylor as director of the Metropolitan Museum of Art in 1955.

Among our leadership it fell to the former lieutenant and at that time Harvard Professor, Charles Kuhn, to explain the reasoning behind our protest and the chain of events that had led to it. His article for the January 1946 *College Art Journal* said:

> In March 1945, about the time of the Remagen bridge-head, the newly appointed cultural advisor to General Eisenhower succeeded in obtaining an interview with his deputy, Lieutenant General Lucius B. Clay. During the course of their conversation, General Clay revealed his desire to send German owned works of art to the United States. The General could have had but little information regarding the condition of the museum collections in Germany. The only reports from the field that had been received were from the Aachen salient. There were only vague rumors regarding the number of repositories and no knowledge as to the conditions of storage. But the General knew what all the world knew – these repositories contained 'damned good pictures.'
>
> The cultural advisor expressed his disapproval of the proposal and nothing further was heard of it at the Frankfurt headquarters until after V-E Day, during the Potsdam Conference. Early in August an unsigned and undated document was received by the Monuments, Fine Arts and Archives Section, having the letterhead of the 'Headquarters, U.S. Group Control Council' and the subject 'Art Objects in U.S. Zone.' The paper referred to the great number and the value of art objects stored in emergency repositories in the U.S. Zone of occupation and divided the objects into three categories or classes according to ownership. 'Class C' was described as 'works of art placed in the U.S. Zone by Germany for safe keeping which are bona fide property of the German nation.' Regarding the disposition of this category, the following statement was made, 'It is believed that the U.S. would desire the works of art in Class C to be made available for reparations and to be divided among a number of nations. Even if this is to be done, these works of art should be placed in facilities equipped for proper care. These works of art might well be returned to the U.S. to be inventoried, and cared for by our leading Museums. They could be held in trusteeship for return, many years from now to the German people *if and when the German nation had earned the right to their return.*' Attached to the document was a note dated July 29, 1945, signed by Clay's chief of staff, which said in part, 'General Clay states that this paper has been approved by the President for implementation after the close of the current Big 3 conference.'[22]

Kuhn pointed out that General Clay's proposal had been written without full knowledge of the situation and contrary to the advice of the Monuments Specialist Officers in his command and that when it met with a cool reaction it was modified. Kuhn said: "In a cable to the Civil Affairs Division of the War Department dated September 4, the general speaks of holding German objects

---

22 "German Paintings in the National Gallery: A Protest," *College Art Journal*, (Vol. V, No. 2, January 1946), 78–79, emphasizing by Charles Kuhn. (Cultural Adviser was John Nicholas Brown).

of art in trust for eventual return to the German people. He omitted the qualifying clause that appeared in his original paper."[23]

The next event according to Kuhn was the issuing of a press release by the White House on 26 September. Kuhn said that the text had been written in General Clay's office and was cabeled to the public relations office of the War Department over the General's signature on 15 September: "(the) United States Government will retain [the paintings] only as long as necessary to insure their physical safety ... When the objects of art are definitely established as being bona fide German ownership they will be returned to Germany when conditions there warrant. The reason for bringing these perishable art objects to the United States is that expert personnel is not available within the American Zone to assure their safety. At present these perishable objects are being stored under conditions which would bring about their deterioration. For many of these objects there are not adequate housing facilities in Germany."[24]

Before his return to the States to resume his career as an art historian at Harvard, Kuhn had been in charge of the MFA & A sections at Frankfurt and Höchst. It had been he who had selected the *Landesmuseum* at Wiesbaden as a Collecting Point and appointed me to be its director as I described in the last chapter. Kuhn had overseen and praised the restoration of the building and the institution of proper museum practices. With a rising tone his article continued:

> This building was placed in charge of Captain Walter I. Farmer, a Monuments Specialist Officer, a trained architect with museum experience and a man wise in the ways of the army. For two months, Captain Farmer worked night and day preparing the building to receive the objects. The roof was repaired, broken glass was replaced, special shelving was constructed, accession cards were printed, engineering and janitorial labor was procured, a highly trained German curatorial staff, a restorer, photographer, librarian, and secretaries were engaged. Captain Farmer even succeeded in obtaining the two most sought after items in the German theater – sufficient coal to keep the building warm and dry during the impending winter and a guard detail of U.S. troops to police the premises twenty-four hours a day.[25]

After refuting and rejecting other insulting clauses in the White House press release Kuhn also published the text of the Wiesbaden Manifesto. He ruefully concluded his article by saying, "It is useless to speculate as to the true reason for this act. Perhaps it was nothing more than a token shipment – a face-saving device that high authorities are sometimes forced to indulge in, once they find themselves committed to an unwise policy. Perhaps it was only because they are 'damned good pictures.'"[26]

---

[23] See note 22, 79.

[24] See note 22, 80.

[25] See note 22, 80/81.

[26] See note 22, 82.

Kuhn's article was preceded by an official statement from Gladys E. Hamlin speaking for the Roberts Commission. The statement quoted the White House press release of September 26 and added that, "It is not contemplated that any of these works of art will be exhibited to the public at present." The statement was followed by a list of the 202 paintings.[27]

I would not see Kuhn's stout defense of the management of our Collecting Point until months later when I too had left the Army and returned to the States. Following the writing of the manifesto my days would be occupied with preparations for the shipment.

Throughout the ten days before the departure of the shipment of the 202 I had been kept busy as a sort of traffic cop for all the activities. VIPs came and went, supplies had to be procured and order maintained so that Lamont Moore could carry out his mission. I confided my deepest feelings to my wife, Josselyn, in a letter written on 8 November. In part it said:

> No doubt it is difficult for anyone at home to know the truth about what is going on over here but you expect intelligent people to figure it out. You are probably sure you have the correct picture and it's probably wrong as hell.
>
> We are up in arms about a movement of pictures to the States. I'll disown anyone who says it is the thing to do. We are protesting collectively. God knows if we will get anywhere but we must – it is a matter of morals. We are trying Germans as war criminals for what we are now ordered to do. One thing I know, we match every other country in being rotten, disgusting, petty and dishonest. Now don't be smug and get your back up – come on over and see for your self.
>
> Everyone met here on Tuesday and it was on of the (most) spiritually wonderful things that has ever come into my life. Many people with widely different backgrounds meeting as at a funeral agreeing and acting as one in a matter of great importance to us for our entire lives. We probably could be court martialed. These are great days in my life, but it is probably dull to you. However, I will say again – if I should die at the end of this I shall have lived to the fullest and done my duty to civilization. That is more than 99 and 44/100 of the men alive can say.[28]

Shortly before the shipment departed I wrote to Josse again and could not disguise the depression I felt. I started the letter on 14 November, broke it off and began again on the 17th. I said:

> This dishonor that is forced upon us rests illy on our bones. We are no worse and no better than the Germans – the fact is we have learned a lot from them – on how to be dishonorable. Oh yes, we are doing our duty – that is carrying out orders but we are going to do what we can to let the people back home know what we think about this wretched deal. It stinks to high heaven.

---

[27] Hamlin, Gladys E. "German Paintings in the National Gallery: Official Statement." *College Art Journal,* January 1946, 75–77.

[28] WIF papers.

> These days slip into one another and are gone. Our deadline is Monday. I nearly blush when I see my staff – they are just beginning to realize what is going on. My last illusion is just about shot. My very nature will keep me going but there is nothing now that bears any of the gilding of youth. I suppose I must admit it – I am getting middle-aged. You can't imagine how hard it is to try to justify in the eyes of other people something that you think horrible. Fortunately; those working with me hold me in sufficient esteem that I hope to get by with it.[29]

One might well ask at this point what had been on General Clay's mind when he initiated the proposal to send German works of art to the United States for safe-keeping. Was he an art lover, a connoisseur or a collector with a deep appreciation for European old master paintings? Not at all. In her 1990 biography, Lucius D. Clay: An American Life, Jean Edward Smith devotes a chapter to Clay's involvement with the MFA & A branch and the restitution program for looted and stored works of art. Drawing upon her interviews with the General in which he had additionally shared recollections of a Georgia boyhood Smith summarized his attitude toward the art that had suddenly become his responsibility. "Clay's sense of military rectitude bristled at the prospect of taking the German collection for others. As a soldier he could not condone it, and as a Southerner raised on recollections of Reconstruction he was appalled."[30]

According to Smith, on receiving his command Clay had immediately realized the significance of the situation of German art and Nazi loot at the end of the war and had told Secretary of War Henry Stimson that the US Army had become the custodian of "the greatest single art collection in the world."[31] Clay had expanded the MFA & A and instructed them "to identify, salvage and restore everything worth saving."[32] Further "Clay told Stimson he hoped to get immediate approval to return to their original owners the works the Nazis had looted throughout Europe and to preserve the prewar German art collections in trust for the German people."[33] In Smith's account of events Stimson recommended Clay's plan to Secretary of State James Byrnes, who was then at Potsdam. "Stimson suggested to Clay that he raise the matter immediately with President Truman, and Byrnes concurred."[34]

Smith says that Clay's concern with the protection of Germany's own public art collections such as that of the *Kaiser Friedrich Museum* in Berlin proceeded from

---

29 WIF papers.

30 Smith, Jean Edward. *Lucius D. Clay: An American Life.* New York: Henry Holt and Company, 1990, 313.

31 See note 30, 309.

32 See note 30, 310.

33 See note 30, 310.

34 See note 30, 310.

the fact that the museum was located in the heart of downtown Berlin which was now in the Soviet sector. The building had been severely damaged during the war. "The massive dome was shattered, most of the roof demolished, the lower floor piled high with rubble and the museum's stone walls so cracked that the cellars were flooded with several feet of water. It clearly was in no condition to receive the collection back. Clay was afraid that if he were ordered to return the paintings, they would likely be shipped off to the Soviet Union."[35]

The tide of revenge and retribution sweeping Europe worried Clay. "If he retained the collection in the American Zone, he feared that the German masterpieces might become trading fodder in a struggle for reparations that could see them shipped off to Allied countries as restitution for paintings looted by the Nazis that had not been recovered."[36] This was the restitution policy that the French were advocating.

Clay told his biographer that he was also concerned about the condition of the paintings and was confident that if they could be removed to the United States they would be more properly cared for and more importantly, by shipping them to the US, Clay was ensuring the collection could be preserved intact for the German people.

It was mid-summer at this time and I had only just begun to direct the work of renovating the *Landesmuseum* in Wiesbaden. During the entire 10 months of my tenure General Clay never came near the Collecting Point. He was mired in the problems of governance for our sector of Berlin which lay within the Russian zone of occupation and was many miles away. It appears that he was unaware of the advances toward proper museum management that were being made by the MFA & A officers in the distant American Zone of Occupation.

In the midst of the Potsdam Conference, 19 July 1945, Clay met with President Truman and secured the President's oral approval to send the Kaiser Friedrich collection to the United States "as rapidly as arrangements can be effected."[37] Clay suggested that they be placed on exhibit, "but that an announcement be made to the public, to include the German people, that these works of art will be held in trusteeship for return to the German nation when it has re-earned the right to be considered as a nation."[38] Did Clay have any idea of how large or how diverse these collections were? According to my records we had well over a thousand paintings from the *Kaiser Friedrich Museum* and nearly four hundred from

---

[35] See note 30, 311.

[36] See note 30, 311–312.

[37] See note 30, 312.

[38] See note 30, 312.

the Berlin *Nationalgalerie* not to mention cases and cases of other works of art belonging to the German people.

Now Clay found himself boxed in between the Departments of War and State who as earlier described were wrangling over the issues of restitution and reparations with the Allies. Eventually, Robert Murphy confirmed to Clay that the State Department wanted to use the collection as "replacements in kind" for articles that the Nazis had looted from elsewhere in Europe.[39] Clay protested and in due course the press release was issued in September from the White House and his Berlin headquarters. It drew a range of negative press responses and caused John Nicholas Brown to protest to the State Department. Brown had visited the Munich Collecting Point and knew much about the MFA & A operations so he had confidence in our abilities as safekeepers, but he did not know of Clay's fear that the paintings might be used for reparations. When Clay was asked to comment on Brown's protest to State Department's John McCloy, Clay also told him that he thought the American public was entitled to see the paintings and that "they will certainly not be available for anyone to see for some time in Germany."[40]

What is puzzling about Jean Edward Smith's narration of Clay's involvement in the shipment of the 202 is the omission of any mention of the Wiesbaden Collecting Point and the Protest Manifesto written on 7 November. No less mystifying is the confusion that she injects concerning the number of works actually in storage. Consistently she speaks of the 202 as if these were the only works from the *Kaiser Friedrich Museum* on deposit with us. She states that on 12 November the War Department once again asked Clay's opinion on the use of German masterpieces as restitution items for other countries and she quotes a lengthy reply of 14 November in which Clay rejected this proposal.[41] By this date my staff assisted by the MFA & A officers at Höchst were concentrating all our efforts on the complex arrangements for the shipment. Smith received a very different impression from her conversations with the General. She reports:

> On November 15, 1945, the War Department authorized (Clay) to proceed as he desired. Immediately thereafter, German cameramen painstakingly photographed the paintings to record their condition. Then, using packaging materials scrounged from Army stockpiles, they were carefully packed and loaded onto two German Red Cross railway coaches for shipment to Le Havre. At the French seaport, the paintings were unloaded under tight security and carried aboard the Army transport *James Parker*.[42]

---

[39] See note 30, 312, Appendix IIIa, page 203.

[40] See note 30, 314.

[41] See note 30, 315.

[42] See note 30, 315.

Smith's account is highly inaccurate and demonstrates yet again how little Clay really knew about the activities and the procedures that the Monuments Specialists carried out to safeguard the shipment of the 202. In her research Lynn Nicholas learned that Clay only heard about the Manifesto when months later Eleanor Roosevelt made a trip to Berlin and asked him what the fuss in the press had been about.[43] Although Bancel La Farge caught a lot of heat for not squelching the distribution of the protest document nothing more was said about court martials.

By means of letters to friends and colleagues who had served or were still serving word of the events got around. One provocative response was that of George Stout who wrote a letter to Tom Howe dated 6 January 1946 shortly after he received his copy of the Wiesbaden Manifesto. It had been sent to him in the Far East where he was attempting to set up an MFA & A operation for that theater using once more his considerable skills and reputation as a conservator. His letter reads in part:

> Just how much courtesy those blokes are due is more than I am able to figure out. You could have pushed me over with a feather from a spring chicken when I read in a clipping sheet about two months ago that a selected lot of German-owned works was due to arrive in the States. This was not the first I'd heard about the idea, but I'd left Washington with the notion that the wild scheme dreampt up by some lubber, had been chucked out for the idiocy that it obviously was. Then here comes this.
>
> In Washington I'd had the proposition suggested to me with a lot of bated breath. The impression I got was that some big shot like a cabinet member had cooked it up and that all the lesser dignitaries were a good deal embarassed and sneaking around back stairways in the scared way everybody in Washington has got, trying to figure out who was going to tell him that he was out of order. In a guarded way I was asked to make a comment. So I said nuts to it as far as conservation and safeguard were concerned. I was told that a brief statement on the strictly technical aspects of the question would be accepted. But strictly, they said, technical. So I did. I wrote a little primer about two pages long and gave it out that as far as conservation was concerned, even if they froze, the things ran less risk where they were than hauled and shipped all hell and gone over the globe. Jim Plaut wrote them a piece that was not technical, and one of the commissioners who had his breath going in short pants asked Jim as a personal favor to withdraw it. Since they could easily stuff it anywhere they wanted to, Jim told them to do as they liked.
>
> Now you go and drop a sentence which says, Col. McBride came over from the National Gallery and the infamous project got under way. I don't know quite how to figure that one. Did these fellows in Washington actually wangle the thing? And then use the commission to cover themselves up? You put terrible thoughts in a young boy's head. I never thought that some of those big brass museum directors were anything more than a first-class job of taxidermy, but gaudamighty I thought they would manage to keep on looking like men. I'll think about that until I get some more facts. Meanwhile the manifesto is a noble and sustaining document.[44]

---

[43] Nicholas, see note 1, 399.

[44] Thomas Carr Howe Jr., Papers, see note 4.

When I received the telegram ordering the shipment of the paintings the transport date had been set for ten days later, November 16th. Staggered by the prospect of the work that lay ahead I had immediately called headquarters at Höchst and asked for help. Bancel and the other officers stationed there had to begin planning at once for the shipment which they felt had to be escorted by MFA & A personnel. No one in our section could be spared. Lt. Charles Parkhurst had been asked by his friend McBride to prepare and accompany the shipment but refused in outrage. In 1996 there is still anger in his voice over this episode. It was providential that at this time Lt. Lamont Moore, then stationed in Munich, telephoned Tom Howe to say that he would be dropping by Frankfurt before going on leave. Bancel pressed him into duty as the officer in charge of packing and escorting the 202 on their trip to Washington. According to Howe, Moore and Colonel McBride were old friends from the NGA where Lamont had been director of the educational program.[45] Even so Lamont was willing to sign the Wiesbaden Manifesto.

In his book Howe says that he and Lamont Moore "spent an evening together studying a list of the pictures stored at Wiesbaden. He typed out a tentative selection."[46] What list did they study? My staff had not yet opened all the crates while doing their conservation inspections so an itemized crate list simply did not exist in Wiesbaden. Was this a list which had been prepared at the NGA and presented by Colonel McBride on his arrival?

In *The Rape of Europa,* Lynn Nicholas has described the preparation of this list:

> At the National Gallery, in response to the Army's decision, Chief Curator Walker now ordered a list of Germany's top masterpieces to be prepared by Hanns Swarzenski, a German exile who had been given temporary employment at the Gallery's repository at Biltmore. From memory, prewar catalogues, and a microfilmed copy of the Berlin evacuation documents, he compiled a list of 254 paintings, 73 sculptures, and 39 objets. Swarzenski wrote to Walker that if he, 'had listed more than these, there would be no limit where to stop … but probably I have forgotten a lot from the smaller museums like Stuttgart and Karlsruhe.'
>
> On the list, made without any reference to the present locations of the works, were 102 works from the Kaiser Friedrich Museum in Berlin, Watteau's Gersaint's Shopsign from Charlottenburg, Daumier's Don Quixote from the Nationalgalerie, 2 Chardins from Potsdam, 43 pictures from the Städel in Frankfurt, Manet's Execution of Maximilian I from Mannheim, 26 works from the Alte Pinakothek in Munich – including Dürer's Saints with the note 'probably too fragile' – 9 from Nuremberg, and more from Dresden, Vienna, Karlsruhe, Stuttgart and Kassel.[47]

---

[45] Howe, see note 2, 278.

[46] See note 45.

[47] Nicholas, see note 1, 392. This undated letter was received by NGA on October 15, 1945.

Hanns Swarzenski was well equipped with knowledge of these collections for his father had been the director of the *Städelsches Kunstinstitut* in Frankfurt prior to taking refuge in the United States. John Walker, Curator of the National Gallery of Art, had recent experience of the situation in Germany since he had toured Europe in the summer of 1945. An account of his expedition published under the title, "Europe's Looted Art," in the January 1946 issue of the *National Geographic,* demonstrates that he was almost as vengeful toward the Germans as his colleague in New York, Francis Henry Taylor.

The operation had been code named "Westward Ho" to which our team added the name of Watteau in honor of the inclusion among the 202 of three of his most charming canvases, a *Fête Champetre,* the *French Comedians,* and the *Italian Comedians.* Included in the group were fifteen paintings by Rembrandt, six by Rubens and six by Frans Hals. Three paintings by Raphael, five by Botticelli, and five by Titian, led a large contingent of Italian old masters. Four works by Albrecht Altdorfer stood out among the group by German artists. Two hundred paintings of which *one hundred and fifty were on wooden panels* had been pulled from the Kaiser Friedrich Museum cases. Two works belonging to the Berlin *Nationalgalerie* joined them. The modern master Edouard Manet's *In the Conservatory,* painted in 1879 was included because, we were told, it would please General Eisenhower and the brass of the Third Army whose troops had been photographed with the painting when it was discovered along with the others in the Merkers mine 7 April 1945. The Manet canvas had become emblematic of the Army's rescue of the German art collections in the final days of the war against the Nazis.[48] Inclusion of the *Nationalgalerie* painting of *Don Quixote* by Daumier seemed a quixotic choice to say the least.

When the selection had been confirmed Moore and Captain Kelleher went through the crates in which the *Kaiser Friedrich Museum* paintings were stored looking for each painting. Because there were dozens of cases to search through and no lists of the cases' contents this was a lengthy process. Once a particular work of art was located our staff photographed as it came out of its crate in order to document its condition. Next Lamont Moore examined both the paint surface and its support of wood or canvas and dictated his minute observations on each painting's state of preservation to Frau Hobirk who served as the registrar for the shipment.

Many of the paintings were found to be in urgent need of conservation procedures due to their months of confinement in the salt mines, the *Reichsbank* and

---

[48] See illustrations in Walker, John. "Europe's Looted Art," *National Geographic,* (v. LXXXIX n. 1, January, 1946) 39–52.

the Wiesbaden Collecting Point. But, because of our orders, there was no time for the leisurely process of cleaning and consolidation that great works require before they go on tour. Frau Flinsch, our conservator, removed dust and evidence of salt accumulations. She also secured special tissues to a painting's surface with a light wax. This precautionary measure would hold in place the blisters of paint that were lifting off the panels. These were temporary procedures that we hoped would hold until the paintings arrived at the National Gallery in Washington where we had been told they would be given conservation treatments. Next each painting was passed on for wrapping and packing.

These paintings had been given the most thorough-going scrutiny and were handled with all the delicacy which their age and fragility warranted. Some of the paintings that had been requested proved to be ineligible for travel because they were too large to fit into the railway cars that had been procured for their transport to the harbor. Those that went were crated for shipment in forty-five of the cases originally built at the Kaiser Friedrich Museum which were retrofitted for this purpose and lined with waterproof paper.

Colonel McBride published his account of the transport of the 202 in the *National Geographic,* December, 1948.[49] It said in part:

> Boxcars were out of the question; baggage cars were unheated and often windowless. But in the severely blasted railroad yards at Frankfurt, amid twisted rails grotesquely shattered locomotives, burned-out freight and passenger cars, we found two German hospital cars bearing large red crosses.
>
> From these the interior equipment had been removed. They could be heated and the windows were intact – perfect parlor cars for the 45 cases of paintings, with room to spare for 10 Army cots for the armed guard which was to accompany the shipment.
>
> Convoyed by truck from Wiesbaden, the paintings were carefully loaded and the two cars were shunted around the city to the passenger station, where they were attached to the "Main-Seiner," the night express to Paris. Thus started on November 20, 1945, the most important transatlantic voyage of art![50]

From Paris the shipment went on by rail to Le Havre where the train pulled in alongside the Army transport *James Parker.* McBride continued:

> After an uneventful crossing, the ship passed the Statue of Liberty at 5 p.m. on December 6, with no visible impression upon Botticelli's "Saint Sebastian" or Van Eyck's "The Man with the Pink" or upon the other German-owned masterpieces. Though America was still a wilderness when many of them were painted, they were to discover here an amazingly art-conscious nation.[51]

---

49 McBride, Harry A. "Masterpieces on Tour," *The National Geographic Magazine,* December, 1948, 717–750.

50 See note 49, 745.

51 See note 49, 745.

Word of the sailing of the *James Parker* with its extraordinary contents had been received in New York in advance of its arrival. Janet Flanner, the writer for The *New Yorker* who had been visiting the Collecting Point to research her story, "The Beautiful Spoils," cabled her scoop back to the magazine who ran a short column over her by-line, Genêt, in their 17 November 1945 issue. Despite a few inaccuracies it still makes good reading.

> In Frankfurt am Main, there is an important relic of the badly damaged principal art museum – three now ironic words carved above its portico: 'Wahr, Schön, Gut.' Wiesbaden, Marburg and Frankfurt are the Rhineland's three most important centers for our Army's small Monuments, Fine Arts and Archives Sub-Commission, whose war-and-peace duty it has been to save beauty from destruction and disinterestedly to guard art works until they have been restored to their correct owner, whether the owner is Germany or looted Poland or France. A couple of days ago the Monuments men at Wiesbaden received official word to ship from their depository to the United States four hundred (sic) of its finest German-owned pictures. This export project, casually suggested by American officials at Potsdam, perhaps as a well-meaning attempt to keep the pictures warm this winter in the steam-heated United States, is already regarded in liberated Europe as shockingly similar to the practice of the Einsatzstab Rosenberg, or Minister of Nazi Kultur Rosenberg's Foreign Art Loot Bureau. It has been precisely the task of our Monuments men to undo what we Americans had disdained Rosenberg and his Nazis for doing, and what it was supposedly our policy never to imitate. Of the many errors in occupation we have committed in Germany, nabbing German art à la Nazi will most certainly make the emptiness of the battered museum's slogan, "The True, the Beautiful, the Good" as applicable to us as it is to the citizens of Frankfurt.[52]

The docking of the *James Parker* did not go unnoticed. According to a story in the New York *Times* 7 December 1945 datelined on the day before,

> A valuable store of art, said to consist entirely of paintings worth upward of $ 80,000,000 arrived here last night from Europe in the holds of the army transport James Parker.
>
> Where the paintings came from and where they are going was a mystery. No Army officer on the pier at 44 Street and North River, where the Parker docked with 2483 service passengers, would discuss the shipment, or even admit it was on board.
>
> It was learned elsewhere that a special detail of Army officers was on the ship during the night to take charge of the consignment, which will be unloaded today.
>
> Unusual precautions were taken to keep the arrival of the paintings secret. The canvases were included in more than 40 crates and were left untouched during the night under lock and key.
>
> Presumably the shipment was gathered at sites in Europe where priceless stores of paintings and art objects stolen by the Nazis from the countries they overran were discovered when Allied forces broke through into Germany and the dominated countries.

---

[52] Genêt, "The Beautiful Spoils," *The New Yorker,* 17 November, 1945 v. XXI, n. 40, 71.

The writer of this story quoted the White House announcement of 26 September 1945 when it was reported that paintings would be brought to the US for safekeeping and would be stored at the National Gallery of Art in Washington. During the month of December press reports on the German paintings at the National Gallery continued while our colleagues gathered their forces to add their voices of protest to ours.

On 9 May 1946 Frederick Mortimer Clapp, director of the Frick Collection, and Mrs. Juliana Force, director of the Whitney Museum, sent President Truman the following resolution.

Resolution

> Whereas in all civilized countries one of the most significant public reactions during the recent war was the horrified indignation caused by the surreptitious or brazen looting of works of art by German officials in countries they had conquered;
>
> And whereas that indignation and abhorrence on the part of free peoples was a powerful ingredient in the ardor and unanimity of their support of the war effort of democratically governed states in which the private opinions of citizens are the source and controlling directive of official action;
>
> And whereas two hundred important and valuable pictures belonging to the Kaiser Friedrich and other Berlin museums have been removed from Germany and sent to this country on the still unestablished ground of ensuring their safety;
>
> And whereas it is apparent that disinterested and intelligent people believe that this action cannot be justified on technical, political or moral grounds and that many, including the Germans themselves, may find it had to distinguish between the resultant situation and the 'protective custody' used by the Nazis as a camouflage for the sequestration of the artistic treasures of other countries;
>
> Be it therefore resolved that we, the undersigned, respectfully request the President to order the immediate safe return to Germany of the aforesaid paintings, the cancellation of any plans that may have been made to exhibit them in this country and the countermanding without delay of an further shipments of the kind that may have been contemplated.[53]

This resolution was signed by ninety-five museum and academic colleagues. Their protest was carried on through the summer of 1946 by Letters to the Editor in newspapers and art publications. But these and other efforts did not produce any results that would lead to the immediate return of the 202. Instead, the paintings languished in the storerooms of the National Gallery while debates continued over their fate. Temporary retention of the paintings in the United States had found its champions both in the press and in the Congress where

---

[53] Published in Howe, see note 2, Appendix, 305.

Representative Frances Bolton read all previous government statements guaranteeing return of the paintings into the Congressional Record.

The American Commission for the Protection and Salvage of Artistic and Historic Monuments in War Areas, known as the Roberts Commission, concluded its assignment and went out of business on 30 June 1946.[54] By this time the Cold War between the US and the Russians had begun. When queried in October by the Army, General Clay expressed reluctance to receive the paintings back into his care. He anticipated a protest from the Soviets if the paintings were returned to the Wiesbaden Collecting Point and feared they would be seized by them if the paintings were taken to the *Kaiser Friedrich Museum* in the Russian Sector of Berlin.

Almost a year and a half later, early in 1948, General Clay was preparing to turn over his command of the US Zone to the State Department who would now provide the occupation government. The 202 were a lingering concern and Clay felt compelled to make another recommendation on behalf of the paintings that were still in Washington. On 6 February 1948 Clay informed the Department of the Army that conditions at Wiesbaden and Munich were now sufficiently good to permit return of these paintings. He also pointed out the excellent public relations value of a prompt restoration of these paintings to Germany in the face of the unbridled looting of art treasures by the Soviets.[55] Now the State Department reversed its previous stand against a public showing of the 202 in Washington, before returning them, a showing that Clay had long recommended essentially for its propaganda value.

Captain Edith Standen had returned to America late in 1947 and had continued to speak out against the removal of the 202 and any other removals or exchanges. She quotes prominent Germans' expressions of the significance of art: "We do not want to go without works of art in our ruins. They are our mainstay and foundation, here we can start again – they explain to us consolatory space, temporal existence, age and peacefulness. Even more: They make us happy in a philosophical sense."[56]

The exhibition of the 202 opened with scant fanfare at the National Gallery on 17 March 1948. Careful to distance itself from the long simmering controversy

---

[54] This is the date of the publication of their report which was transmitted to President Truman.

[55] Colonel Theodore S. Riggs, Civil Affairs Division, Department of the Army speaking at Hearings before a subcommittee of the committee on Armed Services, United States Senate on S. 2439. A bill to provide for the temporary retention in the United States of certain German paintings, March 4, April 16, 1948, 3.

[56] Standen, Edith. "Report on Germany," *College Art Journal,* 7, no. 3, 1948, 212–13.

over its stewardship, the National Gallery published a checklist modestly entitled "Paintings from the Berlin Museums Exhibited at the Request of the Department of the Army." But, motivated by an outburst of press coverage the public took an intense interest in the show. From an opening day crowd of more than eight thousand attendance swelled on the weekend to a horde of thirty-five thousand visitors. In two weeks attendance had passed the quarter million mark and art lovers all over the nation were clamoring for a chance to see the exhibition. The showing was extended for a week and upon its closing in Washington almost one million people had seen it.[57]

Through the efforts of the press the exhibition of the 202 in Washington once again brought national attention to the circumstances that had led to their export from Germany. Before the National Gallery exhibition had opened Senator Wayne Morse, chairman of the Subcommittee of the Committee on Armed Services, had held a hearing 4 March 1948 to review the reasons why the paintings had been retained in the United States and to make it perfectly clear that the paintings were going to be returned to Germany immediately after the Washington showing. Then on 2 April 1948 Senator J. William Fulbright introduced a bill, S. 2439, which provided for the temporary retention of the paintings and provided further that they be sent on "tour."[58]

In light of the newly introduced bill Senator Morse reconvened his subcommittee on Friday 16 April for further hearings. There was a sense of urgency because the exhibition at the National Gallery had been scheduled to close after the approaching weekend. Senator Fulbright referred the subcommitte to the contents of his statement on the Senate floor given 2 April which said in part:

> I want to make it clear that I do not question the ownership of these paintings under the Hague Convention. However, I doubt the advisability of their return to Germany at this time. I do not believe that the conditions in Germany are near enough to normal to assume that the people of Germany are interested to any great extent in return of the paintings in order that they may be put on exhibition.[59]

Fulbright's statement continued with his assertion that the paintings should be returned upon the recognition of a national government for Germany. His bill provided that the Director and Chief Curator of the National Gallery should chose the paintings to be shown and that they would select the exhibition venues. Admission fees were to be charged with the net proceeds to be paid to the Unit-

---

[57] Kopper, see note 6, 230–235.

[58] See note 55, 6.

[59] See note 55, 6–7.

ed Nations International Children's Emergency Fund (UNICEF). At this time UNICEF was preparing to carry out a mass innoculation against tuberculosis for 50 million children in eleven European countries. The plight of the children and UNICEF's involvement had been described in a New York *Times* editorial in the 29 March 1948 edition. Several days later Fulbright who had recently visited the exhibition was moved by another press article in the *Washington Post* of 2 April 1948 in which Erik Reger, a newspaper editor in Berlin, currently on a visit to the States had proposed that the 202 should be exhibited in a dozen other American cities. Reger also suggested that eight or ten German art curators and experts come to the United States and take charge of the exhibit as it went from city to city.[60]

Senator Morse introduced comments which had been gathered on the pending legislation from the Department of the Army, Department of State, Internal Revenue Bureau and the National Gallery of Art. The Secretary of the Army backed up the opinions of General Clay who recommended the immediate return of the paintings at the close of the NGA show. Clay had consistently counseled return of the paintings to avoid giving a propaganda issue to the Russians that would allow them to distort the views of the German people.

Huntington Cairns, Secretary of the NGA, speaking on behalf of its trustees declined to comment on the policy of retaining the works of art for exhibition at various places. He did point out that so far the exhibition had been a financial burden to the NGA and that it would need an additional appropriation to meet expenses which would occur with retention of the paintings.

It was then revealed that the Secretary of the Army had been advised by Senator Chan Gurney, Chairman of the Senate Armed Service Committee, that the Army should cancel its plans for returning the 202 and seek an extension of the NGA showing until the Senate had reached its decision on the Fulbright bill.

Next it was Senator Fulbright's turn to testify and he reiterated most of the issues raised in his original senate statement. He felt that conditions in Germany threatened the preservation of the paintings and that, "The American people whether they like it or not have the responsibility to preserve these paintings until order is restored and there is a German government in existence that can reasonably be expected to protect them."[61] With many eloquent phrases concerning the "very great contribution to better relations among the peoples of the Western World," that the 202 could make through their retention and exhibition, Fulbright moved on to read into the record some of the letters of support for his

---

[60] See note 55, 7.

[61] See note 55, 15.

bill. New Yorkers were clamoring for the exhibition to come to the Metropolitan Museum of Art and its director, Francis Henry Taylor, former member of the Roberts Commission, had made it clear that the Met stood read to assist the Army with its cultural burdens.

As a further justification for his actions in submitting his bill Senator Fulbright then produced another newspaper article datelined Paris, March 29, which described the travels of the Austrian state collections which had been removed from Vienna museums, "for an indefinite road tour abroad" until "its sovereignty is restored by treaty and fear of foreign encroachment is dispelled."[62] Two and a half million Parisians had paid $ 350,000 in admissions through the winter long show of Austrian treasures in the French capital, "a handsome source of revenue" for the country from "the exhibition in exile." The Soviet menace to Germany was in Fulbright's view as great as that to Austria.

Cold War politics were now shown to be in alliance with America's thirst for European culture. No peace treaty had been signed to end World War II and in March 1948 no one could say when peace would be established. This was the statement of the next to testify, General William H. Draper Jr., representing the Department of the Army. Draper upheld General Clay's view that the paintings should be returned to Germany immeditately and stored at one of the Collecting Points in the American zone, pending the establishment of a German government that would make provisions for their care.

Next it was the turn of the Department of State. Assistant Secretary of State Charles E. Saltzman opened his statement by saying that State was in full agreement with the Army that the collection should be sent back promptly, "because we feel that the most compelling thing is the importance of our doing with these pictures what we have said we would do and announced we would do."[63]

At the sub-committee hearings Charles Saltzman was followed by the director and the curator of the National Gallery of Art where the 202 were currently on view. David E. Finley, the director, had been a member of the Roberts Commission and was thoroughly familiar with the background of this extraordinary collection and the circumstances that had brought it to the United States. He only reiterated the Gallery's position, previously stated at the 4 March hearings, that the Gallery would do whatever it could to accomodate the wishes of the Army, but could not be responsible for the potential of losses from the collection nor for the additional expenses of retaining it without an additional appropriation.

---

62 See note 55, 23.

63 See note 55, 37.

Curator John Walker addressed his remarks primarily to the issue of the conservation of works of art observing that the majority were paintings on wooden panels and that these works had not benefited from their earlier sojourn in the salt mine at Merkers. The panels had been given conservation treatments at the NGA and "They have had a beneficial convalescence with temperature and humidity carefully controlled in our storage room. They have dried out slowly and got rid of the excessive moisture of the salt mine."[64] Still, Walker admitted that the NGA itself had a firm policy against the loan of panel paintings for touring exhibitions and he felt obligated to point out the risks involved in further circulation of the 202 exhibition.

Now it fell to the director of the St. Louis Art Museum to make the case for a national tour. Casting himself as a representative of the midwest, Perry T. Rathbone endorsed the idea with enthusiasm citing previous international art exhibitions at various Worlds' Fairs that had benefited the American public. In broad terms he laid out the logistics for a touring exhibition under questioning from Senator Morse. Rathbone's testimony was given additional support by a quartet of spokesmen from the Metropolitan Museum of Art representing the administration and departments of conservation and registration that would all be involved in bringing the exhibition to New York and preparing it for further shipment to other American cities, a responsibility they were eager to bear.

The remaining speakers before the subcommittee endorsed Senator Fulbright's bill to retain the 202 and to organize a selection for tour in the United States. The Senator had rounded up a group of prominent art critics and academics who shared his views and had gathered letters of support from citizens across the nation. The great publicity that had thus far attended the shipment and the exhibition seemed to guarantee that there was no likelihood that the paintings would remain forever in the United States, but that at present their retention seemed a wise precaution in light of the Cold War stalemate between us and the Russians in Berlin. The *Kaiser Friedrich Museum* where the paintings had historically resided was sited in the Russian Sector of Berlin.

Only the State Department continued to press for prompt return of the shipment. On 21 April, almost a week after the Morse subcommittee hearings, Charles E. Bohlen, Counselor for the Acting Secretary of State wrote to Senator Chan Gurney, chairman of the Committee of Armed Services, that General Clay was still of the opinion that the paintings should be returned and that State support-

---

64 See note 55, 43. This statement is not true in any way. Salt and potash mines were chosen as repositories because there was no abundant moisture, so that the pictures could not suffer any harm. Before depositing the pictures these mines were carefully checked by German experts concerning temperature and moisture.

ed him. He said in part that, "... any action disturbing to German trust in American good faith strikes a blow at the successful launching of the European Recovery program ... Each concrete act demonstrating American fair dealing and performance in accord with promises can contribute significantly to wholehearted German participation in the great task of recovery."[65]

The copy of the proceedings of Senator Morse hearings on S. 2439, the Fulbright bill, was sent to me along with a letter dated 15 May 1948 from Ardelia R. Hall, a State Department employee, who had been engaged with putting in order the files of the Roberts Commission. A second protest by MFA & A officers against the tour of the 202 was under discussion even though planning for the future exhibitions was well advanced. In compliance with the provisions of the Fulbright bill a German Conservator, Mrs. Irene Kühnel-Kunze, had been in Washington since the end of April studying the condition of the paintings and pleading for their return to Germany. She had the support of Ted Heinrich who had succeeded Edith Standen as director of the Wiesbaden Collecting Point. I had not known Ted when I was in Germany, but understood from Edith who had trained him in our procedures that he was doing an excellent job.

Another protest was now contemplated by former MFA & A officers Bancel La Farge, who had resumed the practice of architecture in New York, and Calvin Hathaway, who had become director of the Cooper Union School and Museum. They had joined forces with our old allies Frederick Mortimer Clapp, director of the Frick Collection and Juliana Force, director of the Whitney Museum to circulate a letter dated 23 May 1948 inviting signatures for to a resolution to be addressed to the President. Against the compelling case that had been made on behalf of the touring exhibition the resolution concluded:

> We believe that it is unethical and undignified, to say the least, to use other people's property without their assent, for any reason whatsoever, even if the risks are few. When the risks are considerable, all interested testimony to the contrary notwithstanding, and the objects are the art inheritance of another people, the implications of such a highhanded undertaking are distressing to contemplate. The reprecussions will be far-reaching.[66]

Once again protest proved futile and a worsening political climate in Berlin where the Russians were staging a blockade only added evidence to Fulbright's claim that conditions were not right for the return of the paintings to the *Kaiser Friedrich Museum.* Eventually fifty-two of the panel paintings were removed and sent back to Germany while the rest moved on to a triumphant reception in New York. From there the show moved on to Philadelphia, Chicago, Boston, Detroit,

---

[65] See note 55, 88–89.

[66] A copy of this letter will be found with my papers at the NGA Washington.

Cleveland, Minneapolis, San Francisco, Los Angeles, St. Louis, Pittsburgh and Toledo. Fifty-four more paintings were removed and returned after the Boston exhibition and the rest returned to Wiesbaden on 22 April 1949.[67]

[67] For a comprehensive study of the physical handling of the 202 see Birkmeyer, Karl M. "Report on the 202 Paintings Belonging to the Berlin Museums in the United States of America," New York, April 22, 1949. A copy of this report is in the Thomas Carr Howe, Jr. Papers, Archives of American Art, Washington, D.C. Copy also in WIF papers in English and German.

Chapter five: Fine Arts and Archives

Once the shipment of the 202 had departed from the Collecting Point I hoped that I would regain my normal enthusiasm for life, but I was wrong. A few days later I received a letter from Josselyn, that classic wartime "Dear John", saying that she wanted a divorce. Among other things she accused me of desertion, of not wishing to return to her to resume our marriage and of putting my career with the Army and now the MFA & A before her. During all the months that I had been writing to her of my pleasure in this branch of service she had been resenting my success and rejecting my need to make a life in the arts. Her denunciations of my conduct were so final and so absolute that I could not imagine trying to patch things up. Still I made the attempt. I wrote her a final letter trying to explain myself, but at heart I knew our life together was over.

Having received that letter I felt more than ever the need for a leave with time to get away and think things through in a different environment. There was no hope of returning to the States. Our job status remained frozen while the Military Government and the Army attempted to come to terms with their responsibilities for the occupation of the American zone. Once again I submitted a request for a leave and this time it was granted. I departed for England on 4 December 1945 for ten days.

Although the evidence of wartime bombardments still lingered in London the city offered me its treasures and the trip refreshed my spirits. The booksellers' storerooms were overflowing with personal libraries that had been forfited by their owners who could no longer house them. I was able to expand my collection of titles in architecture, interiors, furniture and gardening filling box after box to ship home to Cincinnati. Before setting off to visit friends and relatives in the country I dropped in at the headquarters of the English Speaking Union where I had found such a friendly reception twelve years earlier on my student trip. To my delight I was remembered by name by Helena Mills-St. John of the staff and was relieved to see that the sculpture of the founder carved by my mother's cousin, Cecil Thomas, had escaped destruction during the bombardments. I enjoyed visiting cousins and English friends.

Returning to Wiesbaden I felt ready to go on with my work and to plan for a career in the arts once I was discharged from the service. During the time Lamont Moore had spent in Frankfurt and Wiesbaden before leaving as the officer in charge of the 202, I had gotten to know him rather well and had introduced him to the work of Alo Altripp. Lamont shared my enthusiasm for Alo's talent and felt as I did that his work should receive greater international recognition. When he departed with the shipment of paintings, he carried with him to New York two packages of drawings by Alo. Lamont planned to show them to art dealers and museum curators who we hoped would want to offer an exhibition that Alo and I would organize from Wiesbaden. Although this particular dream was never fulfilled in New York, Lamont's delivery did set in motion a chain of events that benefited Alo. Eventually, Alo was given a fellowship at the Barnes Foundation and came to the United States. By this time I was living in Houston, Texas, and organized an exhibition for him there.

Back at the Collecting Point I was confronted with an outrageous act of disobedience by a fellow officer. During my leave of absence Captain Patrick J. Kelleher, the MFA & A officer attached to the Military Government headquarters in Wiesbaden, had opened the case containing Queen *Nefertiti.* Even today I have no clear explanation of what happened. One story is that Joe Kelleher had arranged a dinner party and afterwards for entertainment had offered his guests a thrilling experience. They were given a private showing of the famous portrait bust of the Egyptian Queen *Nefertiti.* Despite my orders as director of the Collecting Point that none of the Berlin museum crates should ever be opened without my authorization, Joe Kelleher had ordered the well sealed box to be opened. Frau Hobirk, of the German staff, was called in to lift her out; if she fell an American would not be at fault. Kelleher intended to remove this more than three thousand years old masterpiece of sculpture for the pleasure of a few other MFA & A officers including Tom Howe and Edith Standen. Howe had brought with him Colonel Kluss, Chief of the Restitution Control Branch who had never seen the Collecting Point. The visitors also had a tour of the Treasure Room and were shown the Hungarian Crown and coronation regalia as well.

In 1997 Renate Hobirk Farmer remembers lifting Queen *Nefertiti* from the box for Kelleher. The bust was returned to its box until the exhibition in Wiesbaden in February 1946.

When I confronted Kelleher with my knowledge that the box had been opened he swore that he had been ordered by two generals to open it for their inspection. Sgt. Lindsay later recalls that Kelleher told him a similar story and said that inquiries were being made about the sculpture by the Egyptian government.[1]

Although I was shocked and confused by Kelleher's disobedience he was a fellow officer and I felt compelled to trust him. Other military brass had pulled rank to try and see famous works stored at the Collecting Point. Once a colonel had demanded admittance to the Treasure Room after learning that we were safeguarding the Hungarian Coronation Regalia. I agreed to show him the Crown of St. Stephen and the other relics. Suddenly he grabbed the Crown and put it on his own head! I was shocked speechless by this appalling lack of respect for a work

[1] This issue is documented in Appendix III b, page 209–214.

that is, as I had told him earlier, considered as the holy of holies by the Hungarian people (see photo page 231–232).

Nothing more was ever heard from the Egyptian government during my remaining months in Wiesbaden. Later, after the publication of Tom Howe's book, *Salt Mines and Castles*, containing his version of the incident, I realized that Kelleher had probably staged the party so as to advance his own position at our Military Government headquarters. But I now find it more important to refute a recently published account of the "discovery" of the bust of Nefertiti at the Collecting Point which has appeared in the eminent *Jahrbuch Preussischer Kulturbesitz* by Rolf Krauss. The following is a free translation:

> Alone among all the art works brought there, the Nefertiti bust created stories. It is told that the leading art officers, Kelleher and Rorimer, removed the Nefertiti bust from its box on Christmas 1945 and "they raised a glass together to the famous head of Nefertiti, which was in their charge and which they uncrated to console themselves."[2]

I object to this account. The true story will never be known.

Perhaps by usurping my authority Captain Kelleher had meant to further his plot to remove me as director of the Collecting Point. Soon afterwards I learned that in my absence on leave he had been promoting himself for this position, but Captain James Rorimer, still attached to the 7th Army, had blocked his stratagems and reinforced my command. Kelleher retreated to his post with the Military Government of Greater Hesse where he eventually succeeded to the top MFA & A position before returning to his work at Princeton in the spring of 1946.

Nefertiti was indeed a Queen and while she was our guest should have been shown every regal courtesy. In her lifetime she was the wife of Akhnaton, the enlightened Pharaoh of Egypt in the fourteenth century BC when the arts enjoyed an important renaissance. Her name proclaims her unique for *Nefertiti* means 'The beautiful one is here.' Numbered among the last works executed in the style of the Amarna workshop which was noted for its naturalism her portrait canonized feminine beauty in her era and established a standard that the world will forever acknowledge.

---

[2] Krauss, Rolf. "1913–1988, 75 Jahre Büste der Nofret Ete/Nefret-iti in Berlin, Zweiter Teil," *Jahrbuch Preussischer Kulturbesitz,* Band XXVIII, 1991 (1992), 123–157. The translation is that of my daughter Margaret Farmer Planton. The quote within the quote on page 135 is footnoted as follows: Anonymus: Patrick J. Kelleher 1918–1985, in: Record of the Art Museum, Princeton University, Vol. 44, No. 2, 1985, p. 36f. This citation leads to the unpleasant suspicion that the quote is due to Kelleher himself and represents the way he told the story around the Princeton University campus.

The bust of *Nefertiti* was excavated in the winter of 1912 by Dr. Ludwig Borchardt, a famous German Egyptologist working on the site of Akhnaton's capital at Tel-el-Amarna. In compliance with regulations Borchardt had submitted a list of his finds at Tel el Amarna to the authorities at the Cairo Museum, but they had failed to note that this bust was among them and he returned with it to Berlin. Now with the collapse of the German Reich the Egyptian government would certainly try to get her back.

Fortunately, the sculpture had been well-packed by the curators of the Berlin Egyptian Museum and Queen *Nefertiti* retained her great beauty unmarred by further damage during the months she had spent in transit and storage. But once uncrated her supervision became an additional responsibility within our Collecting Point. Word of her unveiling had spread and others came asking to see her.

With so much international attention having been focused upon the Wiesbaden Collecting Point and the vast quantities of German-owned treasures it contained, the idea occurred to me that we might stage an exhibition of our own. The shipment of the 202 had by no means depleted our storehouse of great paintings and by displaying the magnificent Queen *Nefertiti* we might be able to reassure the German people of our good will and best intentions. Gathering my staff around me we began to plan for this event which we thought we could arrange to open on 10 February 1946. Earlier exhibitions at the Collecting Points in Marburg and Munich had been resounding successes and more than mere propaganda events. With the participation of scholars like Dr. Ernst Holzinger from the *Städelsches Kunstinstitut* in Frankfurt, who spent several days each week with us as a consultant, I felt sure we could make an appropriate selection from our holdings.

Christmas time was approaching and I was determined to lift the morale of my staff by trying to create an appropriate holiday celebration. We had all been working too hard and the shipment of the 202 had been a disruptive occurence, so I wanted to do something that would solidify the fraternal atmosphere that had been developing. And as it had been a long time since I had enjoyed a family Christmas I was determined to create one. I was able to gather candy and other items from our PX that would make appropriate gifts for the children of the workmen and I had received packages of treats from my sister and others which would offer a festive if meager spread. Everyone joined in my mood and we had a wonderful celebration during which we toasted our fellowship and sang traditional carols in English and in German.

During the month of December we received two important visitors, Lt. Hans Jaffe from Holland and Captain Rose Valland. Jaffe and Valland were representatives of their countries authorized to examine the contents of the Collecting Points and identify paintings which had been looted from their public and private collections. These visits were arranged as a result of a policy, decreed by

President Truman at the time of the Potsdam Conference. There would be unilateral restitution from the United States Zone to those nations whose representatives could provide proofs of ownership to authorities at the Collecting Points. This responsibility fell especially hard upon the staff under Craig H. Smyth at the Munich Collecting Point which had received most of the looted art the Nazis had hidden in Bavaria and Austria.

Because of her work in defense of French art during the German occupation of France Rose Valland was a heroine in her own country and to the members of our MFA & A branch. Now she had been given the rank of Captain in the French First Army and was travelling through Germany tracing works of art that had passed through the *Jeu de Paume* on their way to the Nazis' repositories in eastern Germany and Bavaria. We had little to show her at our Collecting Point relating to her mission, but it was a privilege to meet someone who had so courageously and tenaciously maintained her position as conservator during the Occupation of Paris. At the time of the Liberation of Paris she was virtually a prisoner within her museum when German troops attempted to incorporate the *Jeu de Paume* within the defenses of the German military headquarters in the hotels off the rue de Rivoli. When these forces retreated a jubilant mob attempted to storm the museum looking for German fugitives and held at gun point she had to lead a search party through the basement where the museum's collections were stored. In her book *Le Front de l'art* she wrote, "I was sincerely delighted that no German soldier was found hiding there."[3] For her efforts during her lifetime she was made an officer in the Legion of Honor, a Commander of Arts and Letters and given the Resistance Medal as well as the US Medal of Freedom.[4]

The new year found us immersed in preparations for our exhibition. I had managed to locate white paint to refurbish a series of ten rooms in the old fine arts department, the *Gemäldegalerie,* that were not needed for storage and that would make an acceptable suite for the display of the exhibition I had in mind. Before the war the *Landesmuseum* had been decorated in a dark and depressing color scheme. With my newly found appreciation for contemporary styles I wanted the stark white look of a modern gallery and found bolts of white linen with which to make draw curtains for the windows. The daylight streaming in from the skylights overhead sometimes was too bright so it was necessary to cover them with transparent paper which adjusted the illumination for proper exposure. Every detail was thoughtfully considered for we knew our exhibition would draw an excited, but also critical, audience.

---

3 Valland, Rose. *Le Front de l'Art.* Paris: Plon, 1961, 207.

4 Gibson, Michael. "How a Timid Curator with a Deadpan Expression Outwitted the Nazis," *ARTNews,* Summer, 1981, 105–111.

What an accumulation of treasures I had to chose from! The *Kaiser Friedrich Museum* collection was rich in old master paintings and bronze sculptures from the Italian Renaissance and I decided to concentrate the display on these fields. There were 17th century Dutch and Flemish artists to include alongside of German masters of the 15th and 16th centuries. The Early Netherland school was represented by its leaders, Jan van Eyck, Rogier van der Weyden, Hugo van der Goes and Hieronymus Bosch. From the late middle ages we gathered an international group of small painted altarpieces and highlighted it with magnificent objects from the Guelph Treasure of the *Schloss Museum* in Berlin. And there was the collection of the Egyptian Museum from which we drew two stone sculptures from the 25th–26th dynasties to accompany the painted limestone bust of Queen *Nefertiti.*

This was the work I had waited all my life to do. I was thirty-five and an architect by training, but in spirit I was a collector and a student of beautiful objects. To have this assortment of riches at hand and the opportunity available to arrange them with care and sensitivity was the experience of a lifetime.

Our planning for the exhibition also included the preparation by Renate Hobirk of a catalogue that gave a check-list of the exhibition and a few illustrations. Its publication also offered us an opportunity to set forth the brief history of the Central Collecting Point at Wiesbaden and to recognize the contributions of our German specialists and advisors chief of whom was Dr. Ernst Holzinger. We also used a page to publish a statement of the general program of the Monuments, Fine Arts and Archives Section, of the Office of Military Government for Greater Hesse. Since until that time little had appeared that announced the vital purposes of MFA & A we used the opportunity to state our objectives:

> Restoration of civil agencies for administration of fine arts activities, and protection and preservation of the cultural heritage indigenous to Land Greater Hesse.
>
> Custody, care and protection of displaced, German-owned works of art and cultural material now stored in repositories and central collecting points in Land Greater Hesse.
>
> Location, identification and restitution of works of art and other cultural material acquired in Allied countries during German occupation.
>
> Emergency measures to prevent further deterioration of war-damaged cultural monuments.

The exhibition opened on the 10th of February. To inaugurate the festivities that evening speeches were given by the Director of Military Government for Greater Hesse and the German Minister President of Greater Hesse. The opening was exceptionally well attended by both Americans and Germans with many of our high ranking Generals present.

The exhibition turned out to be the signal for an awakened interest in art and culture. The attendance astonished us. Within the first eighteen days over 9,000 people visited the exhibition during its scheduled hours and at other times we admitted school groups and clubs. I felt a glow of pleasure in knowing that many Wiesbaden students and especially those studying art history were seeing important pictures for the first time. Older people were traveling long distances under great hardship to visit the exhibition.

We even received accolades from the German press. The semi-weekly *Die Neue Zeitung,* Munich,18 February, carried this article:

> Out of the immense treasures of art, which are kept in the Collecting Point Wiesbaden (Landesmuseum), a choice of selected works has been made, accessible to the public. In contrast to the exhibition in the House of Art in Munich, the art historical spread of the show in Wiesbaden is infinitely larger. It reaches from the primitive religious painting and church treasures of the high middle ages, includes the early Italian pictures, the masters of Germany through Renaissance, the Netherlandish and Flemish pictures of the 17th century. The enchanted visitor goes through a compendium of European masters from Cimabue until Rembrandt. Nearly all the important works of the Berlin Kaiser Friedrich Museum are to be seen, as Botticelli's "Portrait of a young man" and Mantegna's "Mary with child." Dürer's "Jacob Muffel" and the "St. Christopherus" by Konrad Witz, Rogier van der Weyden and the Master von Flemalle.
>
> In vitrines one sees the Guelph treasure coming from the Berlin Schloss museum, Sculptures by Donatello and Riemenschneider are placed in the carefully repaired rooms of the Museum, and in a special room, the beautiful head of queen Nofretete (Egyptian Museum, Berlin). The onlooker anticipates, enjoying the pictures some of the extensive protecting, preserving work, which has been done to keep the works of art from further damage. One also notices with satisfaction, when one takes the excellent catalog in hand, the firm will of the Military Government to preserve these works of art for the German people. The work of restoring, lies in hands of German specialists under the direction of Dr. Ernst Holzinger of the Städel-Institut, Frankfurt. The present show was arranged by Ministry of Education and Culture of Greater Hesse in conjunction with the detachment of MFA & A, Military Government.
>
> A continuation of shows can be expected.[5]

Among the crowds that visited our exhibition were many distinguished military visitors and other MFA & A colleagues. Joe Kelleher was beside himself with excitement over the visit of Lt. Col. Ernest T. DeWald who had left a teaching post at Princeton to serve as a Monuments Specialist in Italy. And our German staff were equally thrilled by the arrival of the Prince and Princess of Hesse who came to see our show. They had also come to the Collecting Point to retrieve the family's Holbein known as the *Darmstadt Madonna.* From all over Europe people who were hungry for a glimpse of great art came to see the Berlin pictures and sculptures that had for so long been in hiding.

---

5 *Die Neue Zeitung,* Munich, 18 February, 1946, *feuilleton.* A number of copies of this and other press reports will be found with the WIF papers, NGA, Washington, D.C. It was translated–like other German texts–by my daughter MFP.

For one of our visitors the opportunity to see again the *Kaiser Friedrich Museum* (KFM) paintings had a deeply emotional meaning. Dr. Irene Kühnel-Kunze was a staff-member of that museum and the paintings had been packed for storage under her supervision. For many months we had been communicating with her at her office in Berlin attempting to secure copies of accession books and inventories so that we could check the contents of the crates when they were opened for conservation inspections. Those lists would have been particularly useful when it came time to extract the 200 works that went to the United States under operation *Westward Ho,* but we had thus far been unable to obtain them. Moreover, we were anxious to fulfill our military directive which was to separate from the KFM collections any works of art that could be considered as loot and to inventory them before endeavoring to return them to the representatives of nations from which they had come. Any works of art that had entered any German museum collections after 1933 were under suspicion since from that time onward many museums had acquired works that had been looted or removed by punitive measures after the Nazis' introduced their cultural policies.

Dr. Kühnel-Kunze was visibly anxious to examine the paintings that had once been her responsibility and would become so again, but who knew when. Dr. Holzinger and our conservators worked with her to identify condition problems and together we made the decision that racks would be constructed to hold the paintings in open storage. Prolonged crating had already caused the varnish on the paintings to darken so removing them from their cases would be an important preventive measure.

There was a lot of tension associated with Dr. Kühnel-Kunze's visit for she certainly felt resentment over the absence of the paintings that had been sent to Washington two months earlier. Unfortunately, she was not the easiest person to work with and we had to conceal our amusement at her constantly voiced intention to "control" her paintings. Although she could not have known it while she was in Wiesbaden, she would see them again when she was invited to Washington in May of 1948 to examine the works before they were to be sent on tour.

Prior to her visit we had received a copy of a report she had written 9 January 1946 on the "Evacuation to the Saltmines of Kaiseroda and Ransbach."[6] In it Dr. Kühnel-Kunze related the history of the evacuation from her point of view:

> From the 11th to the 31st of March 1945 a great number of works of art, stored in the flak-towers near the Zoo and the Friedrichshain in Berlin, were transferred to salt-mines in Central Germany. Though transportation then was rather difficult because of the many and grave air-raids, they reached the repositories without serious damage.

---

6 A copy of this report is with the WIF papers, NGA, Washington, D.C.

> The objects meant for evacuation were only partly ready for conveyance. They also could not be packed anew, as the transport took place very precipitatedly. The cases generally were fit only for transportation within Berlin, the manner of packing being quite insufficient for a longer journey. Packing material was already hard to get during the first year of the war, as the museums had not been declared as of "primary importance" for the war. This fact may explain the different manner and quality of packing.
>
> The question whether the objects that were insufficiently packed or not packed at all should be moved away or not, caused a lively discussion and was answered differently by the responsible directors of the museum departments. It thus becomes comprehensible that objects of second rank have been transferred to the repositories together with the most precious works of art from the Berlin museums. So when the Painting Gallery evacuated its contents, the trailers that seemed not [to] be quite safe, were only loaded with so-called "depot" paintings. The paintings from the "National Gallery" had to be transported unpacked as they had not yet been prepared for conveyance. The Director of the "Painting Gallery," however, could not decide to have the paintings transported without packing. Besides some very large cases were not transferred to the new repository in the salt-mine as they could not be moved with the cage. Such were for instance the painting by Signorelli, called "Pan," the large format paintings by Rubens and Tintoretto's Annunciation. They remained in the Flakturm[7] [Flaktower].
>
> The incomplete identifying letters of the cases – many cases are only marked with the identifying letters of the section without adding "Berlin" – also can be explained by the precipitancy of the evacuation measures.
>
> The repositories for the State Museums Berlin, occupied by the American Army are: Salt-mine Kaiserroda near Merkers (Thuringia)
>
> Salt-mine Ransbach near Hattorf (Thuringia)
>
> Castle Plassenburg near Kulmbach.
>
> One transport directed from Oegeln (Mark Brandenburg) to the castle of Tannenberg (Thuringia) was surprised by war-action. It was stopped not far from Melsungen (halfway between Cassel and Bebra). American troops found it damaged by shots.
>
> The greater part of the works of art have been transferred to the salt-mine of Kaiserroda. Only one truck-load of paintings (45 cases) has been sent to the salt-mine of Ransbach, containing, it is true, cases with most valuable works of art. Ransbach was regarded as climatically unfit for a repository. It was planned to have the cases that were stored here provisionally, as soon as possible transferred to Kaiserroda. This became unfeasible by the quick progress of war-action.

Dr. Kühnel-Kunze's report continued with a list of the sections of the State Museums Berlin which I have already mentioned. She added that a case from the *Staatliches Institut für Musikforschung,* containing valuable old musical instruments, was also transferred from Berlin to Kaiseroda. She then described how Dr. Paul Ortwin Rave, director of the *Nationalgalerie* in Berlin, had moved to Merkers as responsible commissioner of the *Staatliche Museen zu Berlin:*

---

7 Flaktower Friedrichhain, a military stronghold for Anti Aircraft Artillery that was also used as a large repository of the Berlin State museums. There the remaining parts of the museum collections are said to have been destroyed in May 1945 after the capture of Berlin.

> He conducted the conferences, when Ransbach and Kaiseroda were occupied by American troops on the 4th of April 1945. According to a report by Dr. Rave, all works of art were transferred from the salt-mines Kaiseroda and Ransbach to Frankfurt/Main on April 17th by American Art Protection officers. Inadvertently no copy of the lists then composed has been forwarded to Berlin.[8]

Having outlined the history of the evacuation of the collections Dr. Kühnel-Kunze went on to discuss the condition of the objects. In her opinion the condition of the works before they were evacuated was in general perfect and even the most susceptible paintings had been well preserved as the climate of the flaktower was suitable. Regular inspections were conducted to look for minor damages of mold-growth, which could be removed. However the reports of these inspections had been lost when the flaktower burned. She then stated that as for the State Museum collections: "The short stay of about five weeks in the unsuitable climate of the salt-mine had done no damage to the objects." On the other hand:

> On some of the unpacked paintings from the National Gallery, however, that had been taken out of the mine to be transferred to Frankfurt and that were placed into the open air without being wiped immediately, the salt-(s)ediments turned into a crust. (This seems to be a chemical combination [Magnesium sulphate] that is easily soluable with cold water). In the meantime it will be known whether the influence of the salt caused serious damage or whether the salt-dust fell off all by itself. In the Ransbach mine, that had been for some time without control after the fighting, several cases with paintings have been found broken open. Dr. Rave himself packed them anew with the excelsor that had fallen out of them and nailed them provisionally. Dr. Rave is of the opinon, that nothing has been looted from the cases ...[9]

Dr. Kühnel-Kunze's report, rendered in the dry and technical language of a professional museum curator, nevertheless conveys the strenuous attempts she and her Berlin colleagues would make to justify their stewardship of their collections during the extraordinary conditions that the war had presented. For some time after her visit the postwar environment of Berlin would not permit the return of the immensely valuable works of art. The museums they had come from were now in the Russian Sector. There were no other places to store or display the collections and rebuilding plans would have to await the recovery of the German economy. Moreover, as Henning Bock observes in his 1986 history of the Berlin *Gemäldegalerie,* "On 25 February 1947, the Allied Control Commission formally abolished the State of Prussia. The Berlin Museums became collections without a country."[10]

---

[8] See also note 6.

[9] See also note 6.

[10] *Masterworks of the Gemäldegalerie, Berlin.* New York: Abrams, 1986. Translated from the German by John Gabriel, 28.

In 1984 Dr. Kühnel-Kunze published her recollections of the period.[11] The decade following the end of the war had been a difficult one for the German population and even those in the traditionally sheltered environment that a museum offers were not excluded from hardship. Most frustrating to these professionals was the absence of their collections which remained under American government control and within the jurisdiction of the regional governments, the *Länder* like that of Hesse, where the Wiesbaden Collecting Point remained operational. With the partitioning of Germany into East and West and the division of Berlin itself into two cities in 1948 it seemed risky indeed to transfer such valuable collections to an increasingly political dangerous zone. Nonetheless, an agreement for the transfer of the collections from their West German deposits to West-Berlin was eventually concluded 7 July 1955. The collections began to return in January 1956 and these transfers continued until August 1958.[12]

Once it had been seen that the Americans did indeed know how to protect Berlin art collections we were asked to store the smaller but equally prestigious collections of the *Städelsches Kunstinstitut* of Frankfurt at the Wiesbaden Central Collecting Point. The bombardment of Frankfurt had been no less intense than that of Berlin and the museum building that housed the Städel Institut and its collections was greatly damaged. There were no other suitable buildings in which to store and monitor the paintings collection since the Frankfurt *Historisches Museum* had also been totally destroyed.

The Städel collections had been put into storage with the same motives of caution and preservation that had led the Berlin curators and directors to seek secure repositories for their collections. When the director, Georg Swarzenski, had fled from the Nazis to take refuge in the United States he had encouraged the directors of the *Städelsches Kunstinstitut,* a private foundation, to name Ernst Holzinger as his successor.[13] Holzinger had been the curator of the Städel's print and drawing collection and had deeply admired the courageous collecting

---

11 Kühnel-Kunze, Irene. "Bergung – Evakuierung – Rückführung: Die Berliner Museen in den Jahren 1939–1959," *Jahrbuch Preussischer Kulturbesitz,* Sonderband 2, Berlin: Gebr. Mann Verlag, 1984.

12 Herbst, Arnulf. "Zur Geschichte des Wiesbadener Collecting Point" *Kunst in Hessen und am Mittelrhein,* 1985, is a valuable account of the period 1945–1958 because Herbst has tried to understand the motivations of the MFA & A and to credit and praise our services, something Dr. Kühnel-Kunze was never willing to do. However, he perpetuates her assessment of the building's condition at the time we took it over calling the building "only slightly damaged during the war" a gross understatement which I have tried to clarify in my descriptions in Chapter three.

13 RKM interview with Doris Schmidt, Munich, 30 April 1994. Dr. Schmidt worked for Ernst Holzinger as his secretary while continuing her studies in art history that had been interrupted by the war.

program of Swarzenski which had enriched the Städel collection with great works of twentieth century German art. With the arrival of the Nazis many of the great paintings by the German Expressionists such as Max Beckmann, Schmidt-Rotluff, Kirchner, *et.al.*, had to be removed from the collection and were sold. After the war and for the remaining years of his tenure Holzinger tried to buy back these paintings in order to restore the black hole that had opened up in the Städel's otherwise chronological display of German and international modern art.

The old master paintings and other collections that had been removed for preservation from the Städel had been placed in different castles as well as a mine in central Germany. These collections had been under the supervision of Dr. Holzinger who with his family had lived in one of the country houses that secretly served as a repository. As I have said, Holzinger had served as our curatorial consultant in Wiesbaden beginning in September 1945. Given the fact that he had witnessed at first hand the subtraction of the 202 from our depots to be "safeguarded" in the United States, his decision to place his collection with us represented a true act of faith. I treasure a letter I received in Cincinnati from Dr. Holzinger, dated 22 June 1946.

Bringing the Städel collection out of its hiding places began on 6 February 1946 when approximately 440 paintings were evacuated from their repository at Amorbach. Next to come were the works from Bad Wildungen and Rossbach which arrived on 27 and 28 February. Shipments continued in March after my departure and under the administration of my successor Captain Edith Standen. In the second shipment of 109 paintings were included some of the finest pictures of this institution: paintings by Dürer, the Master of Flémalle, Gerard David, Rogier van der Weyden, Vermeer and Botticelli.

February 1946 was crowded with events including as I have mentioned the opening of our exhibition and the visits of the dignitaries I have described. To add to our excitement there was one more delivery of works of art that sent everyone out to the courtyards for an impromptu ceremony of welcome. In the latter part of the month we received two truckloads of Jewish religious objects among which were 700 Torah scrolls. Suddenly I began to be more preoccupied with the "archives" portion of our service branch when the question arose of how to store them. The simplest solution, it seemed to me, was to build yet another set of racks and to rest these fragile illuminated scrolls horizontally upon them. Immediately workmen began constructing these racks while the shipment was carefully unloaded and carried into the Collecting Point.

Several days later I learned that through my lack of knowledge of Judaism I had handled these sacred Torahs improperly; they should have been stored vertically. We received a visit from Major Seymour J. Pomrenze who informed me in no uncertain terms of my ignorance and laid his claim to these valued treasures.

Pomrenze had been selected for the task of establishing and operating the Offenbach Archival Depot. The scrolls and a great deal more were shortly going to become his responsibility.

The story of the Offenbach Archival Depot has never received the attention given to restoration of monuments such as the Tiepolo ceilings at Würzburg or the restitution of fine arts looted by the Nazis. Those stories make gripping reading while the saga of the salvage and restitution of books, archives, manuscripts and even the Torah scrolls might seem less thrilling. Nevertheless an account of MFA & A activities in the Frankfurt area would be incomplete without a description of the rescue of the literary and scriptural treasures that the Nazis had looted with the same nefarious purposes they applied to art collections. I had been introduced to the subject by Jim Rorimer in the fall of 1945 when he took me with him to inspect an abandoned warehouse within the I.G. Farben plant at Offenbach. This building was under consideration to become the repository primarily for Jewish libraries, archives and the Torahs.

Looting of libraries became as integral to the Nazis plan for cultural domination as the looting of art collections. At first the Nazis were content to seize the writings of authors whose philosophies they wanted to discredit and obliterate and to burn them in public ceremonies. But as their own philosophies of cultural and racial imperialism took shape it was decided to institute a program of search and seizure among the libraries and archives of the nations that they sought to conquer. To accomplish all their looting and destruction the Nazis set up special organizations. The Ribbentrop Battalion[14] was the first such unit with instructions to confiscate valuable cultural materials. This Battalion had three to four hundred men and worked all over Europe. Von Ribbentrop's orders were that all scientific institutions, libraries and palaces in Russia were to be thoroughly "combed out" and everything of definitive value was to be carried off. A company commander reported:

> We reaped a rich harvest in the library of the Ukrainian Academy of Science, treasuring the rarest manuscripts of Persian, Abyssinian and Chinese literature, Russian and Ukrainian chronicles, the first edition books printed by the first Russian printer Ivan Fjodorov, and rare editions of the works of Schevtchenko, Michiewicz, and Ivan Franko.
>
> In Kharkov several thousands of valuable books in deluxe editions were seized from the Korolenko library and sent to Berlin. The remaining books were destroyed.[15]

---

14 This is identical to *Bataillon der Waffen-SS z.b.V.* or *Kommando Künsberg.*

15 Poste, Leslie I., *The Development of U.S. Protection of Libraries and Archives in Europe during World War II,* US Army Civil Affairs School, Fort Gordon, GA, (rev. ed.), August, 1964, 245.

These activities established a pattern which resulted in the eventual accumulation in Germany of storehouses full of other nation's libraries. Just as the American Army had found itself in charge of the greatest art collection ever assembled in the world, so too did it find itself to be responsible for the safekeeping of millions of books.

When the time came to deal with the restitution of libraries the Army searched among the ranks of the MFA & A for a qualified officer. Fortunately, they found Lt. Leslie I. Poste, a graduate librarian, who had been charged with the responsibility of safeguarding libraries and archives in Württemberg-Baden and was quartered in Stuttgart. It was Poste who had recognized Major Pomrenze's abilities, tapped him to organize the Offenbach depot,[16] and brought him to Wiesbaden to examine the scrolls. The only other time I had met Lt. Poste was when he had come to Wiesbaden for our meeting on 7 November 1945 to write the Manifesto but our common love of books has forged a lasting friendship.

Like so many MFA & A officers Leslie Poste's military career began with his induction as a private soldier because vision problems nixed his application to Officers Candidate School.[17] By 1943 he had just earned his Masters in Library Science and was serving as the acting librarian at Columbia College when the Army called him. With their usual placements skills they put Poste into a General Service Engineers Regiment just like mine. His regiment landed in Bristol, England, and built the same sort of temporary encampments our regiment had constructed. During a cold and miserable winter, Poste was nearly buried alive when a ditch his unit was digging collapsed upon them. The accident sent him to a hospital near Oxford for thirty days during which time he started a war-time library of paperback books. At the end of his stay the hospital wanted to keep him because he could type and spell medical terms. Still in need of physical therapy for a crushed knee he wanted to stay, but the army sent him back to his regiment. They needed typists too, but could not hold him for long. His librarian's training had finally been spotted and he became the first enlisted man to join the Library Branch of Special Services in London.

From then on Poste rose through the Army's Staff School programs which needed libraries for their instruction. After two and a half years in the Army he finally won his commission as a first lieutenant in June 1945. Poste remained in England until he was sent to Heidelberg 15 October 1945 to become an MFA & A officer with the Seventh Army. On arriving he was interviewed by my boss,

---

[16] Pomrenze was also the choice of Judge Simon H. Rifkind, on leave from the federal bench and the Adviser on Jewish Affairs to General Eisenhower, and of Koppel Pinson, a representative of the American Joint Distribution Committee serving in Germany at the time.

[17] RKM interview with Leslie Poste, Rochester, NY, August 1993.

Captain James Rorimer. Jim never failed to be impressive on first meeting and Poste was awed by his stories of MFA & A's preservation missions on behalf of looted art. On the other hand, virtually nothing had been done about the looted libraries: "it's up to you," Rorimer said and then inquired if Poste could drive a car. He could not. That same afternoon he received a half hour's instruction. Thus prepared, Lt. Leslie Poste set out to rescue some of the finest libraries of Europe.

For their looting of libraries the Nazis had employed the same tactics, rationale and personnel that had carried forward their looting of art. The Ribbentrop Battalion receded to the background with the growth of the *Einsatzstab Reichsleiter Rosenberg,* the group that was responsible for the bulk of the looting done by Germans in the areas they occupied throughout Europe. In a 1948 article Poste summarized their tactics:

> The new watchdog of Nazi culture, the Einsatzstab Reichsleiter Rosenberg [ERR], placed in the Wehrmacht by Hitler was charged with collecting cultural materials under the guise of utilizing them "for scholarly purposes." With headquarters in Berlin, its regional branches in Amsterdam, Brussels, Paris, Belgrade, Riga, Minsk, Kiev and Ratibor, looted systematically. Each Hauptarbeitsgruppe [regional branch] had subregional offices [Arbeitsgruppen] and local centers [Sonderkommandos]. In eastern Europe, for example, there were eleven subregional offices and seven local centers.
>
> Through these collecting points the Berlin administration of the ERR directed German army quartermaster general troops to seize book collections and other cultural materials. Books poured into the Berlin office from field units. In their efforts to eradicate Judaism, Freemasonry, democracy, republicanism, and other anti-Nazi movements, the ERR collecting teams and the Wehrmacht visited 375 archival institutions, 402 museums, 531 institutes, and 957 libraries in eastern Europe alone.
>
> The looted materials were divided among various German institutions for "research purposes" under the direction of the Institut der NSDAP zur Erforschung der Judenfrage [Institute (of the Nazi party) for Research on the Jewish Question] located in Frankfurt. Actually the sheer bulk of the cultural resources displaced by the ERR was a blessing in disguise; the difficulties of handling the millions of pieces gathered within a short time unquestionably saved priceless volumes from the bonfire ...
>
> Allied bombings of Frankfurt caused the hurried removal of the Institut der NSDAP zur Erforschung der Judenfrage to the small village of Hungen. Here hundreds of thousands of volumes were literally flung into six repositories, scant attention being given to protecting the materials from the elements or theft. Thousands of books, for instance, were found heaped in one small brickyard. The evacuation and sorting of the repositories revealed portions of the Bibliotheca Rosenthaliana, the Spinoza, Rothschild, Collegio Rabbinico Italiano, YIVO (Yiddish Scientific Institute) and other famous collections.[18]

---

[18] Poste, Leslie L. "Books Go Home From the Wars," *Library Journal,* December 1, 1948, 1699.

As a preliminary measure in July 1945 our MFA & A headquarters had arranged to transport some 130,000 looted books from the sub-cellars of the building that had housed the *Institut zur Erforschung der Judenfrage/Weltdienst* to the Rothschild Library in Frankfurt. There were 1,200,000 items in six different repositories in Hungen awaiting similar relocation.

This was the situation prior to Poste's appointment. Now he was asked to make a needs survey since the Rothschild library was clearly inadequate to house the books that were then being discovered in repositories throughout Germany. Among his recommendations Poste suggested that detailed cataloguing be dropped to expedite early restitution and that the operations be moved across the Main River to the property of the I.G. Farben plant at Offenbach. The new site was a five story reinforced concrete loft building. In these commodious quarters the tempo of sorting operations was increased from about 300 books a day to the point where millions of items were handled expeditiously.

Poste also knew that he was not the right man for the proposed job of director of the Collecting Point. For this position one would have to know German, Hebrew and Yiddish. Miraculously, the right man was already in Germany serving with Poste in Württemberg/Baden. Major Seymour Pomrenze, an archivist at the National Archives, Washington, had served with the OSS in the Far East during 1945, before his posting to Stuttgart. Not only did he have the language skills but also he had had sufficient higher level military experience to be able to slash through administrative red tape and secure 200 workers for his operational plan.

On 2 March 1946 a basic directive was issued by the Office of Military Government for Greater Hesse that declared the Offenbach Archival Depot to be a "first priority" Monuments, Fine Arts and Archives "restitution project." The director was empowered to establish and maintain liaison with all Allied and other officially designated restitution officers assigned or attached to the United States Forces European Theater and to assist them in making books and other materials clearly identifiable as to country of origin available for restitution. Authorization was also given to the director of the Offenbach Archival Depot to make recommendations as to the disposition of such books as were not identifiable as to country of origin.[19] Within one month the first restitution was made: a barge was dispatched to the Netherlands with over 500 cases of materials belonging to that nation's institutions and individuals.[20]

Subsequently promoted to the rank of Colonel, Pomrenze continues to serve as a military archivist and as a consultant to the Jewish Institute in New York City

---

19 Poste, see note 15, 263.

20 Poste, see note 18, 1701.

where he was interviewed for this book. During the war Pomrenze had served in the China, Burma, India theater. He had been happy to have avoided serving in Germany and had only gone to Stuttgart in late 1945 at the request of the Archivist of the United States who asked him to help with the reconstruction of German archives. Suddenly finding himself in command of the archival Collecting Point at Offenbach he faced many of the same challenges that I had faced months earlier in Wiesbaden. The I.G. Farben building needed repairs and protection against the winters and he also had to attempt to enforce security controls. As he recalls, "... although I used to pull security inspections and had men and women searched by men and women, going in and out, ... we had some very valuable little books and manuscripts and items and they were very ingenious in hiding them in the most unmentionable places. So this was a real problem."[21]

Pomrenze was given his command of the Offenbach archives at the beginning of March 1946 and remained at that post until June. During that time Offenbach was declared the zonal Collecting Point and truckloads of books began arriving from all over Germany to be added to the initial shipments from Frankfurt. As the shipments increased so did the complexity of the work. Pomrenze recalls:

> I was very concerned about the fate of these materials. Stationed with me in Offenbach as a military officer was a unique individual, a very decorated officer whose name was Isaac Bencowitz. Isaac Bencowitz, for personal reasons was anxious to become the Director of the Depot and I was very anxious that he should become my successor. So, we went through the usual military channels, which were irregular, because you can't win in the regular channels and the people in Wiesbaden, who were the headquarters of Hesse, they were very happy to cooperate since this was a peculiar assignment. Bencowitz brought to the depot many qualifications that I did not have. Number one, he was familiar with eastern European languages, which I know nothing about. Particularly Russian, he spoke Russian very fluently. Also, he was a hero of some stature, I think he had five or seven Purple Hearts, he was wounded in World War I and World War II. Also he was a PhD chemist and this had a bearing on the mission because he knew how to handle documents that were wet and frayed and so on. Also he brought to bear some very intelligent solutions to problems, which I guess I didn't think about. He set up a way of identifying the materials through the ex libris which were in many of the materials.[22]

Bencowitz' system of identification was based upon a photographic record established to reproduce the *ex libris* which were the stamps and other marks of ownership found for the institutions and private collections of all the countries. These marks were eventually published in two volumes and bear silent testimony to the systematic looting conducted by the Nazis. There are 4,015 library marks

---

[21] Unpublished text of an oral history audio document: Colonel S. J. Pomrenze, Interview August 14, 1989, Concerning the Jewish Cultural Reconstruction Project, Restitution of Materials Looted by the Nazis. Transcribed by the Hebrew Union College Museum, Los Angeles, and placed on deposit at the Jewish Institute New York City.

[22] See note 21.

of which 2,277 were from Eastern Europe. These books were in 35 different languages and 75% of the unidentified books were of purely Jewish significance.

To facilitate his identification process Bencowitz had a conveyer belt built. Each worker was responsible for three or four *ex libris.* The opened books passed along on the conveyer belt and the worker pulled out the ones for which he was responsible. In this very elementary way libraries were sorted and reassembled to await retrieval by their owners or when possible restitution through the channels set up by the US Military Government.

After the war when Leslie Poste chose to write his doctoral dissertation on the MFA & A and its archival responsibilities, Captain Bencowitz shared with an entry from his diary written during this period.

> I would walk into the loose document room to take a look at the things there and find it impossible to tear myself away from the fascinating pile of letters, folders and little personal bundles. Not that what you held in your hand was so engrossing, but rather what the next intriguing item might be. Or, in the sorting room I would come to a box of books which the sorters had brought together into one fold ... books from a library which once had been in some distant town in Poland, or an extinct Yeshiva. There was something sad and mournful about these volumes ... as if they were whispering a tale of yearning and hope long since obliterated.
>
> I would pick up a badly worn Talmud with hundreds of names of many generations of students and scholars. Where were they now? Or, rather where were their ashes? In what incinerator were they destroyed? I would find myself straightening out these books and arranging them in the boxes with a personal sense of tenderness as if they had belonged to someone dear to me, someone recently deceased.
>
> There were thousands of loose family photographs without any identification. How dear all these tokens of love and gentle care must have been to someone and now they were so useless, destined to be burned, buried, or thrown away. All these things made my blood boil ... How difficult it is to look at the contents of the depot with the detachment of someone evaluating property or with the impersonal viewpoint of scholarly evaluation.[23]

Under Bencowitz' management the staff of the Offenbach Collecting Point swelled to a maximum of 176 employees in April 1946 and then diminished in stages until fewer than twenty were working there in April 1949. During this time more than two million books were returned. Bencowitz left Offenbach on terminal leave in October 1946. For a time he was succeeded by Theodore Heinrich who was also the director of the Wiesbaden Collecting Point. A fulltime director and civilian employee, Joseph A. Horne, took over in January 1947 staying only a year and relinquishing the position to James Kimball, the last director of the Offenbach Archival Depot which closed in 1949.

---

[23] Poste, see note 18, 1703.

During the earliest months of its operation the Offenbach archive was visited by a number of scholars and national representatives who had come searching for the remnants of looted libraries and other materials. Among them was Koppel S. Pinson who spent the period from October 1945 and September 1946 in Germany as Educational Director for Displaced Jews in Germany and Austria for the American Joint Distribution Committee (JDC). Pinson worked in the Depot from March to October 1946 withdrawing unidentified books classified as "non-valuable" which could be sent to the Jewish DPs in refugee camps.[24] Pinson was eager to restore the benefits of libraries to these survivors who had lost everything in the conflagration of their society that we have come to know as the Holocaust.

In November 1945 Pinson had visited the Rothschild library before the establishment of the Offenbach archive and began his effort to gain release of these books through appeals to General Lucius Clay. He proposed specific guidelines for the selections and Clay authorized the loan of 25,000 volumes to the JDC in January 1946. At the time of his departure in October that year he had removed 20,000 volumes.

More than a year later, in February 1947, the historian and Holocaust authority Lucy S. Dawidowicz arrived in Offenbach on a similar mission. She had learned that 5,000 volumes of the official quota had never been removed and from her work with the Joint Distribution Committee she knew that the need for books in the camps was still acute. Dawidowicz also had a personal mission. She was seeking the remnants of the YIVO (Yiddish Scientific Institute) library of Vilna, Lithuania, where she had studied and matured as a scholar.

From that Place and Time is Dawidowicz's memoir of the decade of the Holocaust. It covers the years, 1938 to 1947, which she spent first as an American student studying Jewish history in Vilna and then in the United States from where she watched in horror as the Jews of Europe were nearly obliterated. Burdened with guilt over having abandoned her people, she returned to Europe after the war as a worker for relief organizations. Her experience at Offenbach is a bitter tale, but one that led to the restitution of the YIVO library to the new headquarters of the Institute in New York. For two months she labored among the boxes of unidentified books sorting out those which had belonged to YIVO and to other libraries.

In March 1947, the US Military Government Restitution Branch yielded to requests from the Joint Distribution Committee and agreed that the libraries could be shipped to the United States and announced that Seymour Pomrenze,

---

24 Pinson, Koppel S. "Jewish Life in Liberated Germany. A study of the Jewish DPs," *Jewish Social Studies* 9, 1947, 101–126.

now an archivist at the Library of Congress, would return to Offenbach to escort the shipment to its new home. Pomrenze arrived on 16 June and the next day the shipment was on its way. Lucy Dawidowicz had completed her mission. Of her time at Offenbach she wrote:

> When I worked, holding the orphaned books in my hands I often thought that it was easier to be with amkho, the living people, than with these inanimate remnants of the world the Germans had destroyed. The human survivors had a will to live and even, at times, a will to forget, but the books had been dumb witnesses to mass murder. They were the relics of six million murdered Jews.[25]

The last years of the Wiesbaden Collecting Point were under the directorship of Captain Theodore Heinrich who was also *Land* Chief. In April of 1949 the control of the Collecting Point was turned over to the trusteeship of the Hesse Arts Administration under Director Prof. Ernst Holzinger who had been involved since 1945. From 1950 to 31 October 1958 there were 17 shows which involved much borrowing throughout Germany. Restitution shipments continued to be made from Wiesbaden to the end of August, 1952; the records of the Collecting Point were then shipped to the State Department in Washington, D.C. On 7 July 1955 the Prussian Cultural District was formed; the last collections were returned by October 1958 when sufficient museum spaces had been recreated. The story of the Wiesbaden Collecting Point was in the hands of time.

---

[25] Dawidowicz, Lucy S., *From that Place and Time,* New York: Norton, 1989, 322.

Chapter six: The Search for Missing Treasures

More than fifty years later the interest in the story of the shipments to the Wiesbaden Collecting Point continues. Even though the Roberts Commission went out of business in 1946 and the Collecting Points were emptied and closed in 1951 interest in gold, the salt mines, missing trains, and stories of art looted by the Nazis, Russians, and the Allies have persistently occupied a place in the international press. As time passed European museum administrations assumed their normal routines, the search for missing works commenced and rumors began to circulate concerning the most notorious discrepancies between inventory documents and visible evidence.

For example, it was known that in May 1945 a fire in one of the Berlin flaktowers established at the park of *Friedrichshain,* should have destroyed works of art that were too large to make it on the trucks headed for the West in March and April 1945 (Merkers and eventually to Wiesbaden) or were left behind because there was a lack of transport capacity during the last days of the war.[1] But who set the fire and did anyone have time to retrieve anything from it before? Many authors have speculated on this event during the last five decades.

With the sudden and nearly miraculous disappearance of the Berlin Wall and the retreat from East Germany of the Soviet government, the reunification of Germany became a reality, I had thought never to see. Thinking of the Berlin art collections one could now begin to imagine a time when the divided collections could be reassembled and when objects both known and rumored to have been removed to Russian museums might be restituted. Perhaps some of the paintings from the flaktower might reappear.

Well before the excitement of November 1989 when the Berlin Wall was crumbling I was engaged in the search for the works of art which were said to have been evacuated from the Berlin museums, but had never arrived at the Wiesbaden Collecting Point. In 1987 I had begun a correspondence with a German archaeologist, Dr. Klaus Goldmann, who is a curator at the *Museum für Vor- und Frühgeschichte* (Pre- and Early History Museum) situated in the museum complex at the Charlottenburg Palace in West Berlin. Goldmann had been engaged by a German documentary film company which wished to produce a feature for

---

[1] Kühnel-Kunze, Irene. "Bergung – Evakuierung – Rückführung. Die Berliner Museen in den Jahren 1939–1959," *Jahrbuch Preussischer Kulturbesitz,* Sonderband 2, Berlin: Gebr. Mann Verlag, 1984, and Wermusch, Günter, *Tatumstände (un)bekannt. Kunstraub unter den Augen der Alliierten,* Braunschweig: Westermann, 1991.

German television on the efforts of the Allies to bring about the restitution of German art treasures after the war. The film company invited me to come to Washington where they would be videotaping Goldmann's activities as a researcher. It was proposed that an interview between Goldmann and me would be videotaped for use in their production. A date was set for our meeting on 16 July 1987. Although the wording of the letter of invitation I received was decidedly vague, I looked forward to the opportunity to discuss my work at the Collecting Point and to meet Dr. Goldmann.

Then in his fifties, Goldmann was only a small boy when the war ended in Germany. He had come upon the story of the Collecting Points established by the US Army as a result of his research undertaken for his museum. He had learned that, like those of the *Kaiser Friedrich Museum,* crates from his museum's collections had once been stored at Wiesbaden following their removal from the Frankfurt *Reichsbank.* Following his initial research in German archives he arrived in Washington in the summer of 1987. He hoped to find among the MFA & A archives more records which might lead him to the whereabouts of treasures formerly belonging to the Pre- and Early History Museum that he had been unable to locate. He was planning to interview other surviving MFA & A officers whose experiences might have bearing on his quest. With this series of interviews Goldmann opened many new doors in his search for treasures and rekindled my interest in the work I'd been a part of so many years ago.

In 1971 Goldmann was newly employed at the Pre- and Early History Museum where he and his colleagues were assigned to preparation of a permanent installation for their Bronze Age collection. Before the war the collections of that museum had been located in the *Martin Gropius Bau* near the old Anhalter Railway Station and Potsdamer Platz. This area had been heavily damaged by bombing during the war and afterwards was carved through by the Berlin Wall. The Department of Pre- and Early History traditionally had been part of the greater administrative structure of the *Staatliche Museen zu Berlin* whose larger parts of the collections had been shown on the so called Museum Island. This department was affiliated and neighbored with the Ethnographic Museum. Even before the war the ethnographic collections, but not the prehistoric, were scheduled to be moved to the new museum facility in the West-Berlin suburb of Dahlem. (In the 1950s space in this Dahlem museum complex had been given to the paintings collection of the former *Kaiser Friedrich Museum*). The *Martin Gropius Bau* was ruined, so the Prehistoric Museum reopened after war's end in the former building of the Ethnographic Museum which could be repaired. But ultimately, in 1960, the Pre-and Early History Museum found its home within the Charlottenburg Palace complex where it has its own building, the *Langhansbau.* There it presents an excellent chronological display of rare materials dating from the beginning of mankind during the Old Stone Age through the Bronze- and Iron Age up to the Middle Ages.

While planning for the new Bronze Age display Goldmann consulted the old catalogues of his department in order to see what had been done with the collections by his pre-World War II predecessors. He was seeking to know what objects had been shown previously and what had been the state of research on the collections before that work had been interrupted by the war. When he began to study the catalogues and inventories he realized that many of the most important objects of the pre-war collection were not listed in the current inventories kept by his department in Charlottenburg.

At the time when he was doing this work Goldmann was aware that the pre-war collection was presently divided between museum departments in the West and East sectors of Berlin. As a first step of his research for the whereabouts of the missing parts, he had to reconstruct the different periods of packing and sheltering the objects during the war in Berlin. He reasoned that when the contents of the collections had been prioritized for evacuation the best finds, what he calls "the highlights," had been selected for swift removal to safekeeping in the West (this was an order by the responsible ministry to all departments for the handling of the evacuation in March 1945) and that other less significant or less portable objects had remained behind awaiting further transportation. Those objects which had found their way to the Wiesbaden Collecting Point were now in his custody. But the others could be in East Germany if they had not been either destroyed or looted. The curators of the two departments who were separated by the Berlin Wall, nevertheless had clandestine contacts with one another and inquiries could be made concerning objects that were listed in the former catalogues but now appeared to be missing at both locations.

Most conspicuous was the absence of the so-called *Treasure of Priam.* This was the hoard of gold objects from Troy collected by the famous German archaeologist Heinrich Schliemann and given to the Berlin museum in 1881. Missing too were the famous *Eberswalde gold finds,* as well as hundreds of significant jewelry and weapon finds. There were at that moment no records of these objects which could be located in either museum. After much searching through files one list appeared, a packing list of some thirty crates containing all the materials that were placed in storage at the Prussian State Bank strong room in 1941, before it was transferred to the Flaktower at the Zoological Gardens *(Flakturm Zoo).*

This was a great discovery for it disclosed what had been packed by the curators at the beginning of the war and the list itemized the very treasures for which Goldmann was looking. The survival of the list was remarkable because it appeared to Goldmann that after the war most of the museum files had been combed through and many critical lists had been removed or lost. But the crate list for the Prussian Bank strong room, made to satisfy their inventory requirements, had escaped destruction because it had been filed separately with papers having nothing to do with the collections. From this point Goldmann could begin his own archaeological studies of the Berlin museums' wartime procedures and the events of collection management which took place during the American and Soviet occupations of Berlin.

Minus the highlights, Goldmann's installation at the Pre- and Early History Museum was completed, but his search for the missing objects continued. With the publication of Irene Kühnel-Kunze's book in 1984[2] he hoped to learn from an eyewitness and integral participant what might have happened to the crates that had been removed from the Prussian State Bank strong rooms to the tower at the Zoo wherefrom at least the 6 crates in the Wiesbaden Collecting Point had been sent westward at the end of the war. But to his dismay, her accounts contained no additional information that would aid him and indeed provoked an even more intense curiosity because of omissions and conflicts with the data he had already discovered.

Until Goldmann began his recent research rumors of the whereabouts of the Trojan gold had been based on the story of the former director of Goldmann's department Wilhelm Unverzagt. He, who held the position from 1926 to 1945, had said that he had turned over three cases containing the most precious objects of his museum to a high ranking Russian commission; one of the commissioners, he said, was the former director of the Moscow Tretyakov Gallery. Today Goldmann says it is known that this man was not a member of the Russian Trophy's Commission, a group that followed their army into Berlin and began to scour its museum storerooms and other hiding places looking for loot, the Germans had taken in the USSR during the war and shipped to Berlin.

But, in 1987 at the time of our meeting, Goldmann discounted the truth of Unverzagt's story. If the Russians really had the *Treasure of Priam* why had it never been displayed? At that time – and even till the early nineties – most of the East German museum directors were convinced that the Soviets had returned in 1958/59 to the GDR all the trophies, they had taken in their occupation zone 1945 to 1948. What was missing, surely was destroyed and lost during and after the war, they believed. The war booty from Berlin museum collections had been prominently shown in different exhibitions in the USSR in 1958. Most conspicuously, they had carted away to Moscow the Pergamon Altar sculptures and then returned them in 1958 to their former home on the Museum Island. The building was renovated, its collections were reinstalled and it became a centerpiece of the GDR's efforts that its capital should become a tourist destination. Display of the *Treasure of Priam,* if it had been returned to the GDR in 1958 too, would have complemented the ensemble of museum marvels which one could see there since the mid-1960s.

---

[2] See note 1.

Wilhelm Unverzagt also reported after the end of World War II that a number of crates from his museum collection had been sent to the Grasleben salt mine near Helmstedt. This was one of the hiding places west of Berlin for collection storage since 1944. Later, in March 1945, the Berlin museums were in favor of even more distant storage places such as the Merkers mine. Only in early April of 1945 Grasleben was used again as a shelter, when Merkers had been captured by the U.S. Army. Doubting the Unverzagt story that the *Treasure of Priam* had gone east, Goldmann trained his attention upon the recorded chronology of activities of the museum personnel who were responsible for the safekeeping and subsequent westward movement of the art collections. Crating of the most valuable works had begun in 1939 when the war broke out for it was feared then that the British had the means to bomb Berlin. Works of art were initially sent to bank strong rooms until the presumably more secure new built flaktowers were ready to receive them in 1941. There were several flaktower-systems. The largest was the *Flakturm Zoo* and the second the *Leitturm* (radartower) Friedrichshain.

It is beyond doubt that inventory lists for the contents of all the crates with works of art were made before they went to the strong rooms and then to the flaktowers. Following standard custodial procedures, copies of these lists would have gone with the collections when they were evacuated. According to Kühnel-Kunze, evacuation to the mines was relatively orderly even given the fact that it was done with insufficient transport and under fire. While the collections were stored in the mines they were under the supervision of curators who continued to control them by systematizing the arrangement of the crates and, in the case of the paintings and prints, making periodic inspections to check for mold or moisture. Inventories of the crate contents would have been essential to this work. But, as Goldmann discovered, such lists as still do survive in German archives are lists of crates scheduled for transport and their contents are not itemized for reasons of security. For example Goldmann located a numerical list of thirteen crates from his museum containing archival material and found eleven of them, but the first two crates which were thought to contain the complete inventories of the evacuated collection were missing.

From a search for golden treasure Goldmann's attention turned to a quest for missing documents. If the inventories he sought were not in German archives perhaps they had been gathered up in the mines by the US Army when they occupied the country in April, 1945. If so they might be in Washington and it was with the goal of searching in the National Archives that Goldmann came to the US in 1987 hoping also to interview surviving members of MFA & A who had evacuated the mines and would have been as conscious as he of the importance of lists and inventories.

Reviewing his research Goldmann began to theorize about the political events of the spring of 1945 which would have bearing on the fate of art collections. To begin with it was necessary to establish at what point Hitler had finally been persuaded to order the evacuation of the flaktowers and bank strong rooms so as to begin to move the assets of the Third Reich to the west. Works of art were considered as a part of the flow of foreign currency including gold and other monetary assets which were to be moved in the direction of the Western Allies with the hope that somehow a peace accord could be reached through which these assets would be retained for the next German state.

Speculation on this flow of treasure inevitably led Goldmann toward the network of conspiracy theories which have been described by historians and journalists since the end of World War II. What would Hitler and his Nazi leaders have done to spare their country from total defeat and how far would the representatives of the western governments have been willing to go to obtain a cease-fire and an end to the war in 1944 or early 1945? Goldmann was influenced by his reading of *The Secret Surrender* by Allen Dulles, former chief of the Office of Strategic Services (OSS), the later Central Intelligence Agency (CIA) and the man who guided the top secret *Operation Sunrise* which brought about the Nazi surrender in Italy.[3] The movement of the assets of the Reich seems fully documented, but when exactly did it get underway and who was masterminding its execution? These are matters not disclosed in the files of the National Archives pertaining to the MFA & A. Instead, Goldmann believes, answers to his questions will one day be found in the intelligence files of the US Treasury department.

With regard to the activities of the MFA & A, Goldmann theorized that there could have been a superior echelon of military officers which were working with or themselves were members of the OSS working for Dulles who was stationed in neutral Switzerland. According to his theory these officers could have had advance knowledge of the contents of the mines and access to the inventories so that they were able to enter them to remove the most valuable objects for safe-keeping. He knew that nearly all underground stores with objects of art were found by so-called Target Forces of the Intelligence Services and that most of the inventories that were with the evacuated goods, disappeared.

The rationale for this belief is deeply rooted in present day understanding of the diplomatic discussions of reparations and restitution in kind which are noted in the Appendix I to this book (see "The Roberts Commission"). From an altruistic viewpoint the United States would have wanted to safeguard as much as possible of the German patrimony from confiscation by the Russians or for use as barter

---

3 Allen Dulles, *The Secret Surrender*, New York: Harper & Row, 1966, is a tale of thrilling events and turbulent negotiations which could lead one to many imaginings. But because its focus is on the situation in Italy it contains no mention of works of art in Germany.

in the negotiations of the allies. A less charitable reading of the theory would mark the United States as no worse and no better than the others when the time came for repatriation of "safeguarded" goods. After all, in Goldmann's view, the United States government had been unwilling to return the Hungarian Crown and royal regalia until the Carter Administration. Perhaps, Goldmann thought, the *Treasure of Priam* was still in Fort Knox.

It was with those questions in mind that Goldmann approached me for an interview. What could I tell him of my experiences in the MFA & A and what would I know that might support his conspiracy theories. There was little I could offer him beyond my recollections of our staff discussions at the time of the shipment of the 202. So profound had been my belief in the integrity of the Roberts Commission and the MFA & A that I was shocked to learn that removal of the entire *Kaiser Friedrich Museum* collection had been under active discussion and that my colleagues in Frankfurt and Höchst had been trying valiantly to stall the execution of a directive ordering its movement to the United States. As I said before, I had been kept completely in the dark and learned with total surprise just what the other MFA & A officers had had no trouble in believing. They thought that the *Kaiser Friedrich Museum* collection had been targeted because it contained the right works of art to fill holes in the collections of major American museums. My outrage had expressed itself in my call for a protest action. Now I can look back with some amazement to see just how significant that protest was.

Sitting face to face in a Washington hotel room, I recounted to Goldmann the shock and disappointment I felt when I received the telegram ordering the shipment to the United States of two hundred paintings from the *Kaiser Friedrich Museum* collections that were stored under my supervision at the Wiesbaden Collecting Point. I relived for him the events of the 6th and 7th of November 1945 when my fellow officers and I gathered to write the Wiesbaden Manifesto. At that moment he appeared as if struck by lightning and he called a halt to the taping while he struggled to understand the significance of my recollections.

With great excitement Goldmann said to me: "That's it! The protest was the turning point. It was the most important moment in the history of the MFA & A because it meant that nothing further could be moved."

Goldmann's research into what he calls the "archaeology of World War II," revived a lot of speculations and gave encouragement to others who would like to explore the mysterious losses and rumors of thefts which have surrounded the events of the post war period. Although the documentary feature that was made from the videotapes done in Washington had little exposure (it was shown only in Northern Germany) the experience marked a turning point for me as I began to take notice of the many writers who had entered the field of research into looted art. On 12 November 1987 the German magazine *Der Stern* published an inflammatory article about the American Army's involvement in the rescue and salvage of German works of art. The title "Die Spur führt nach Amerika," ("The Path Leads to America") certainly caught my attention. My interview with Klaus Goldmann was a part of this article. I began to sort my archives, search for any new articles, and write about Wiesbaden with my daughter. I certainly wanted the truth about the MFA & A to be known.

In the spring of 1988 I received a letter from Cay Friemuth enclosed with a complimentary copy of the German documentary. Friemuth explained that the film which was largely concerned with Goldmann's fruitless search for the *Treasure of Priam* had not measured up to the producer's expectations and that Goldmann and one of the producers intended to continue working on the subject. "This time," Friemuth wrote, "not under the auspices of mysterious losses of works of art, but in order to commemorate the achievement of American MFA & A, looked upon with gratitude by the following generations." Friemuth introduced himself by saying that he was a young art historian who had been studying British MFA & A and had been asked by Goldmann to help with the scientific part of the video project. He said in part:

> I was honoured with a look at the video-recordings and at your letters to Dr. Goldmann and I share his feeling of deep respect in the face of your personal integrity, openness and idealistic endeavor to contribute to the clearing up of the top-secret traffic of works of art in occupied Germany. Your own courageous initiative of November, 1945 is the best proof for the non-involvement of American MFA & A. You were, and you still are the central figure and we largely depend on your (and your daughter's) collaboration if our project is to be successful.[4]

Friemuth's assurances regarding the purposes of a further collaboration were indeed welcome because in December of 1987, after my first meeting with Klaus Goldmann a most disturbing article had appeared in the New York magazine *Art and Antiques.* The essay by Sol Chaneles, former chairman of the Department of Criminal Justice at Rutgers University was titled "The Great Betrayal; Where are the 16 million works of art stolen by the Nazis during World War II? An exclusive report on the most tragic case of plundering and counter-plundering in history."[5] My MFA & A friends and I had never been contacted by him, but misinformation about us and our activities was presented.

Chaneles jumped through many issues with the clear attitude that the MFA & A mission was a failure. He took the entire list of 123 names published in the 1946 Report of the American Commission and proceeded to mixup their roles and duties. Cay Friemuth wrote that Chaneles "was mixing up responsibilities between the institutions which were working absolutely independently from (and

---

4 Cay Friemuth to Walter Farmer, Hamburg, March 22, 1988. WIF papers.

5 Chaneles, Sol. "The Great Betrayal," *Art and Antiques,* (December, 1987), 93.

partially against) each other."[6] It appears that he did read some memoirs of my colleagues, but distorted the information. For example he claimed: "Many (MFA & A officers) lived in luxurious villas, hotels and castles."[7] While there is an element of truth in this, those situations were anything but "luxurious," with many of us sharing small rooms, eating at canteens (when we took time to eat) and really bathing only once a week when fresh clothing was issued.

Towards the end of his essay Chaneles quoted Edith Standen whom he says told him, "of MFA/A staffers 'borrowing' works of art for their quarters or to decorate the palatial temporary homes of general staff officers," and that she went on to say: "There were many shady characters in the unit."[8] These out of context and distorted quotations brought a rebuttal from Edith which was published in the March issue of *Art and Antiques*. As hers was the only letter written by an MFA & A officer to be published I will quote one paragraph.

> I do not know of any work of art that was appropriated by an MFA/A officer; of the men and women I knew personally, not one could have been capable of such an action. We were officers in the Army of the United States, we obeyed army regulations, submitted the appropriate reports, and lived in the same way as other Military Government officials. The officials who served during the war with the invading armies, such as James Rorimer, lived like other soldiers and, by their conservation work, have earned the eternal gratitude of all lovers of art.[9]

Goldmann's theories on loot gained further exposure through an article published 25 January 1988 in *Insight*. The author, Derk Kinnane Roelofsma, had skillfully woven together the accusations of the German journalists in *Stern* magazine with those of Sol Chaneles as published in *Art and Antiques* along with new claims Chaneles had made in interviews given since its publication. Once again my comments to Klaus Goldmann on the selection procedures for the 202 were referenced along with many of his other charges.[10] Certainly the rediscovery of the Quedlinburg treasure in America added validity to these theories.

A new contact made in the late 1980's was Michael J. Kurtz of Annapolis, Maryland. His 1985 dissertation entitled *Nazi Contraband: American Policy on*

---

6 Cay Friemuth to Walter Farmer, Hamburg, March 22, 1988.

7 Chaneles, see note 5, 101. It is true that both Rorimer's *Survival* and Tom Howe's *Salt Mines and Castles* describe the variety of MFA & A living quarters, but always with airs of amusement and touches of irony that should have been unmistakable.

8 Chaneles, see note 5, 103.

9 "Letters," *Art and Antiques*, March, 1988, 22. Copies of these unpublished letters are to be found with the WIF papers.

10 Roelofsma, Derk Kinnane. "Europe's Search for its Missing Art," *Insight*, 4, January 25, 1988, 50.

the Return of European Cultural Treasures, 1945–1955[11] brought new information. For his dissertation Kurtz had made use of great quantities of unpublished sources principally from the Departments of State and the Army as well as those of the National Gallery of Art and his text was meticulously documented. Kurtz strongly defended the actions of the MFA & A:

> MFA/A staff members did recover some 15 million cultural items from 1,400 repositories located in the American Zone of Occupation. Fully 75 percent of these items were eventually judged as legitimately German and returned to their owners. 3,750,000 items, not the 200,000 Mr. Chaneles alleges, were returned to the countries from which the Nazis looted them. Also, Mr. Chaneles does not seem to be aware that international agreements of the period required return of the looted cultural items to the country of origin. The American government did make several exceptions. Items were returned to individuals who fled Communist Eastern Europe rather than to the countries involved and heirless Jewish property (approximately 300,000 items) was turned over by OMGUS in 1949 to a Jewish successor organization. Jewish Cultural Reconstruction, Inc.[12]

Another new contact in the late 1980's was Lynn Nicholas who was deeply involved in the research for her own publication, *The Rape of Europa: The Fate of Europe's Treasures in the Third Reich and the Second World War* (1994). On 12 April 1988 she presented a paper on her work at IFAR (Institute for Art Research) in New York and defended the MFA & A.[13]

My correspondence with Cay Friemuth resulted in his coming to Cincinnati in December 1988. In advance of his visit I worked with Kay Rorimer to make it possible for Friemuth to meet other living MFA & A officers and to have appointments with Lynn Nicholas and Michael Kurtz, both of whom gave him valuable assistance. While working with Cay Friemuth, I continued an active correspondence with Klaus Goldmann. Our contact and friendship was further strengthened by Margaret's visit with Goldmann in the fall of 1988.

The result of Friemuth's visit and other research was his book *Die geraubte Kunst,* published in 1989. In his Chapter Four, "Westward Ho – auf nach Amerika!" Friemuth published the telegram I received ordering the shipment of the 202 and the full text of the Wiesbaden Manifesto along with quotations from my letters to Josselyn. I believe that his intention was to place the righteous action of the protesters in bold contrast to the other stories he told concerning the actions of Roberts Commission members including Francis Henry Taylor and of Army General Lucius Clay. As a young German historian he had the inclination to share with Klaus Goldmann the belief that there were many instances of looting

---

[11] Published in the Modern American History series of Garland Publishing, Inc. 1985.

[12] "Letters", *Art and Antiques,* March, 1988, 22.

[13] Text of her talk is in WIF archives.

by American troops and certain plans to plunder the art of Germany on the part of Americans involved in the controversy over reparations. Even so, after he recited a familiar list of accusations, Friemuth offered this assessment.

> War reparations are not theft. No possessions in the world can compensate a people like the Americans, whose country remained undamaged in the Second World War, for the lives of the young men who died freeing Europe. Just in light of the idealism of the American arts officers does the seizing of cultural treasures by the American Army take on a bad smell. It is no wonder that these officers, foremost Walter Farmer, want to see that the treasures will again be displayed and that the people who are holding items back for the future will be exposed.[14]

The collapse of the Berlin Wall in November, 1989 forever altered Klaus Goldmann's life, as it did so many others who had grown up in a divided Germany. Goldmann had been involved in assisting Cay Friemuth with his manuscript while quietly continuing his own pursuit of leads to the *Treasure of Priam*. Now with reunification an immediate reality, Goldmann's work load increased. He wrote to Margaret on 10 June 1990:

> You will understand that the new situation in Berlin and Germany has brought many new problems for us – but all problems can and will become solved, I am absolutely sure! So we are preparing the reunification of our Berlin-Museums and from both sides we started to make an inventory of all the losses, burnt or stolen during the war. All this was very difficult before the fall of the wall. Now it is possible to make studies in the state archives in the USSR. So I have been during the second half of May in Moscow and Leningrad together with my friend and colleague Dr. Kernd'l, who speaks Russian fluently. We got some very interesting papers from German sources, the Russians had confiscated in 1945, even lists of our Berlin Antiken-Museum, where the Russians had written their numbers of objects, they had taken as "reparations." Now we can control, what really came back to Germany. It seems they will open their hidden store-rooms. Nevertheless – there are many other highlights of European art in similar hidden places in your country, as you have seen with the example of the "Quedlinburg" – treasure.[15]

Goldmann's publication efforts continued to be fruitful. An article in the 11 October 1990 *Frankfurter Allgemeine* reviewed his conspiracy theories centered upon his discoveries concerning a rumored U.S. "Operation Gold Cup" and repeated his assertions that the *Priam treasure* must be in the United States. He sustained this position in his fall 1992 book *Vernichtet, Verschollen, Vermarktet. Kunstschätze im Visier von Politik und Geschäft. (Destroyed, Missing, Marketed: Art Treasures in the Cross-Hairs of Policy and Trade)*, a collection of stories drawn from his research and earlier publications and written with Günter Wermusch.[16]

---

[14] Friemuth, Cay. *Die geraubte Kunst,* Braunschweig: Westermann, 1989, 116.

[15] Klaus Goldmann to Margaret Farmer Planton, Berlin, June 10, 1990.

[16] Published by MUT-Verlag, Asendorf.

The cracks in the door between East and West opened the way for conversations, visits and access to sources for publications from the East. In 1990 and 1992 the German and Russian governments were discussing their legal foundations for negotiations about "missing art." "Both sides agree that art treasures which disappeared or were unlawfully misappropriated, which are not in their territory, will be returned to their owners or successors."[17] Goldmann quickly turned his attention to Russia as the daring articles by Konstantin Akinsha and Grigorii Koslov, two Moscow art historians, revealed that missing works of art and the Trojan Gold were in hiding in the "Soviet Union."[18] On 29 December 1992 he wrote in a letter to my daughter: "after some more years of research I only can repeat, what I said long ago: Walter's "Wiesbaden Manifesto" is the highlight of personal engagement and courage in the field of art during World War II."[19]

In 1992 I was contacted by a German reporter for the Associated Press who wrote a story that was eventually published 17 January 1993, in *The Salt Lake Tribune.* The occasion was a meeting to be held in Dresden between German and Russian governmental officials and art experts that would inaugurate a bilateral restitution commission which had been called for in a 1991 treaty between those countries. Along with Goldmann's theories the story introduced those of a new player, Kenneth Alford, a Richmond, Virginia, banker who for twelve years had been digging into US military archives for clues to German art allegedly plundered by US soldiers. I was pleased to state, as I had so many times, that soldiers would be soldiers and there had been looting on all sides, but the MFA & A had not been a part of it. "We all wanted to save the German owned works of art from being stolen by us or anybody else."

This article also revealed that Klaus Goldmann now knew where Priam's treasure was! He was quoted as having said that: "Along with artifacts from a Bronze Age gold find north of Berlin and other highlights of (his) museum, the gold of Troy was packed in 26 crates that records show were taken to the Soviet Union." In the summer of 1993 the Russians made the official announcement to the world that they were in possession om the *Treasure of Priam.* The excitement was still clear in Goldmann's voice when he called Ohio in October of 1994 to tell

---

[17] "Russia's Hidden Treasures in the cellars of the Pushkin," *Economist,* December 24th 1994–January 6th 1995, p. 62.

[18] A series of articles began with Konstantin Akinsha and Grigorii Kozlov, "Spoils of War: The Soviet Union's Hidden Art Treasures." *ARTnews* 90, April 1991, 130–141. Konstantin Akinsha and Grigorii Kozlov with Sylvia Hochfield, *Stolen Treasure – the Hunt for the World's Lost Masterpieces,* London, Weidenfeld & Nicholson, 1994 and *Beautiful Loot – The Soviet Plunder of Europe's Art Treasures,* New York, Random House, 1995.

[19] Letter from Klaus Goldmann to Margaret Farmer Planton, dated Berlin 29. 12. 92. WIF papers NGA, Washington, D.C.

us he had visited the Trojan Gold in Moscow. He thanked me for all the help and support I'd given, all the while proclaiming that the MFA & A had not touched the gold. Only time will tell if the treasures will ever return to Berlin; at least now they can be seen and studied again. In 1994–95 news story upon story revealed that Russian basements contained paintings and collections which were thought to have been destroyed.

The culmination of the revelations of the early 1990's was the January 1995 symposium, "The Spoils of War, World War II & Its Aftermath: the Loss, Reappearance, & Recovery of Cultural Property." The symposium was organized by The Bard Graduate Center for Studies in the Decorative Arts under Director Susan Weber Soros. The open public forum brought together all the international players, brought the issue of restitution up to date and was to "help foster a cooperative atmosphere in which the resolution of these problems can be achieved." The publication of Lynn Nicholas's award winning *The Rape of Europa* in 1994 had also helped set the stage for this open dialogue.

The symposium lasted for three exhilarating days and hosted 48 speakers. This remarkable setting afforded me the opportunity to explain to the world what we had done in Wiesbaden and how the Manifesto had been written. Each on the panel moderated by MFA & A Edith Standen and including MFA & A officers Craig Hugh Smyth and S. Lane Faison, Art Intelligence Officer Bernard Taper, and Art Looting Investigation Unit Director James S. Plaut described their personal experiences. After our panel presentation a Russian expressed how sorry he was that they had not acted like the Americans. Sparks flew through the air as government and museum officials stated their cases. Both Ambassador Hagen Graf Lambsdorff and Minister Counselor Dr. Armin Hiller spoke representing the German government. Several Russian participants revealed that more missing artworks are in their country, many in private hands. The Russian plans, previously unknown to many, for a huge cultural museum similar to Hitler's Linz Museum were shown. The symposium was ended by Ambassador Lambsdorff coming forward and reading aloud in English the entire Manifesto; it was a deeply emotional moment for me.

The New York Times, which my daughter and I picked up at the airport on January 23, 1995, presented the complicated controversy to the public. "Revelations and Agonizing on Soviet Seizure of Artwork" quoted Irina Antonowa, Director of the Pushkin State Museum: "The war is not ended so long as we have not settled these questions."[20] On Sunday, February 12 a second article brought

[20] Ralph Blumenthal, "Revelations and Agonizing on Soviet Seizure of Artwork," *The New York Times*, January 25, 1995, C 11; and "Without Portfolio: Wartime Art Daredevils," February 12, 1995, 32.

"Wartime Art Daredevils" up to date. The exhibition "Twice Saved" at the Pushkin State Museum of Fine Art in Moscow and "Hidden Treasures Revealed" at the State Hermitage Museum in St. Petersburg in 1995 continued the controversy in the world press and heightened political tension. In preparing *The Spoils of War* for publication in 1997, editor Elizabeth Simpson notes "The optimism that prevailed in the first half of this decade has yet to be realized in the second."[21]

It was the respect shown for the Manifesto during the symposium, I believe, which brought the German government to the decision to award me a medal. Dr. Ruth Meyer, in beginning the writing of these memoirs had made inquiries about my receiving some recognition. The significance of the Manifesto was now clear. As Goldmann had stated, further shipments of major German art treasures to the United States were slated. "The 202 were only the tip of an iceberg. If the plotters had had their way more shipments might have followed, all under the guise of safekeeping."[22] The political climate could have favored more art shipments under pretense of "safekeeping," but by January 1946 the story of the protest and the text of the Wiesbaden Manifesto had been so publicly circulated that Operation "Westward Ho, Watteau" could not continue.

On September 27, 1995 German President Roman Herzog signed the award for me to receive *Das Grosse Verdienstkreuz der Bundesrepublik Deutschland.* I wish to express my deep gratitude to Dr. Ruth Meyer, Ute Papke, President Cincinnati – Munich Sister City, Ambassador Hagen Graf Lambsdorff, Dr. Armin Hiller, Prof. Dr. Henning Bock, and Dr. Klaus Goldmann for helping to obtain this award for me. On February 9, 1996, German Vice-Chancellor and Minister for Foreign Affairs Dr. Klaus Kinkel presented me with the award and hosted a luncheon at Petersberg near Bonn. He stated: "Ladies and gentlemen, Walter Farmer's enduring achievement as an officer in charge of art protection is in his firm belief that cultural heritage is at the disposal of no-one, not even the victors in war. The standards of international law, reaffirmed in the 'Wiesbaden Manifesto,' are still highly relevant to today's global debate on the return of art treasures transferred as a result of war."[23] I was proud to accept the award in the name of all of the MFA & A officers.

The award trip also included a week in Berlin. For the first time I saw many of the magnificent treasures I had cared for in crates. My daughter, friend Ted Gantz and I were warmly received by the Directors of the museums. A totally

---

[21] Simpson, Elizabeth (ed.). *The Spoils of War, World War II and its Aftermath: The Loss, Reappearance, and Recovery of Cultural Property*, New York: Harry N. Abrams, 1997, 15.

[22] RKM interview with Klaus Goldmann, Berlin, May 3–4, 1994.

[23] Full text in WIF-papers, NGA, Washington D.C.

new experience for me was the group of reporters who were following the story. The German interpreters and my daughter were right there for me and they made sure I rested my 85 year-old bones. This was a very personal and rewarding trip.

Soon after returning home, Margaret and I began working on the article about the Manifesto Prof. Dr. Werner Knopp had asked us to write for the 1996 *Jahrbuch Preussischer Kulturbesitz.*[24] I welcomed this opportunity to clearly explain the actions and intentions of the MFA & A for a German publication and to stay in touch with Klaus Goldmann and any further developments. What other discoveries might there be?

The press about my award had also caught the attention of the *Grand Lodge of Ancient Free and Accepted Masons of Germany.* They invited me to come to Germany to receive the Humanitarian Prize of German Freemasons, a sincere honor since I am not a Mason. In July 1996 their magazine titled *Eleusis* published a lengthy article about the Manifesto and an editorial by Ulrich Wolfgang, "No Offense hurts so deeply as the theft of Cultural Heritage."[25]

On 10 May 1997 in Fürth, Germany, I accepted the honor with humility "in memory of a great humanitarian, a man who was given tremendous authority and had the power to lead. General Dwight Eisenhower actually took the time to proclaim his belief in saving the culture of Europe by writing, "an order to protect cultural heritage before the invasion of Italy on the 29th of December 1943." Dr. Goldmann was on stage to give remarks about the Manifesto. A personal letter from Hungarian Prime Minister Gyula Horn, an earlier recipient of this award, is a treasured keepsake.

The Fiftieth Anniversary of D-Day is over, the anniversary of the 20 August 1945 arrival of the art shipments at the refurbished Collecting Point and the November 1945 declaration of the Wiesbaden Manifesto have passed. That protest saved my country from humiliation an embarrassment. I will always be proudest of the moment when I found the courage to stand up and shout *we must stop this!* without thinking of the personal consequences. It is my eternal wish that all the missing art treasures will be recovered and that they will be available for the whole world to see.

---

24 Walter I. Farmer und Margaret Farmer Planton: The Wiesbaden Manifesto of 7. November 1945 in: *Jahrbuch Preussischer Kulturbesitz* 33, Berlin 1997, 91–119.

25 *Eleusis* Beiträge zur Kultur aus freimaurerischer Geisteshaltung. Frankfurt/M. No. 51, July 1996, 4.

Walter Ings Farmer, Time Line

1911	born on July 7 in Alliance, Ohio to Fred Elihu and Alice Matilda (Putland) Farmer
1935	Bachelor of Arts and Bachelor in Architecture from Miami University, Oxford, Ohio
1935–42	designer with A. B. Closson, Jr. Company in Cincinnati, Ohio
1936–70	lecturer at the Cincinnati Art Museum
1942	married Josselyn Liszniewska on February 19 in Cincinnati, Ohio, divorce 1946
1942	entered service of the U.S. Army in March
1945–46	member of the Monuments, Fine Arts and Archives Commission for the Protection and Salvage of Artistic and Historic Monuments in War Areas of the U.S. State Department; Director of the Wiesbaden Collecting Point. The Wiesbaden Manifesto was written on 7 November 1945.
1946–49	designer with Foley's and founder of the Contemporary Art Museum in Houston, Texas
1947	married Renate Wichelmann Hobirk on 15 June in Houston, Texas; divorce 1966
1949	daughter Margaret Cornelia Farmer born on February 13
1949–97	designer and owner of Greenwich House Interiors in Cincinnati, Ohio; recipient S. M. Hexter award in 1963, Factory's Top Plants of the Year award in 1967, and Designer's Choice award F. Schumacher and Co. in 1972
1950–67	lecturer University of Cincinnati, Ohio
1973	received Doctor of Humane Letters from Miami University, Oxford, Ohio
1978	founder of the Miami University Art Museum, Oxford, Ohio
1987	published *In America Since 1607* with Margaret Farmer Planton, editor
1987	met Dr. Klaus Goldmann in Washington D. C.
1995	spoke at the Symposium: "The Spoils of War, World War II & Its Aftermath: the Loss, Reappearance, & Recovery of Cultural Property."
1996	awarded Das Grosse Verdienstkreuz and published "The Wiesbaden Manifests of 7 November 1945" in Jahrbuch Preussischer Kulturbesitz
1997	awarded the Humanitarian Price of the Year by the Grand Lodge of Ancient Free and Accepted Masons of Germany in May
1997	passed away on 9 August in Cincinnati, Ohio

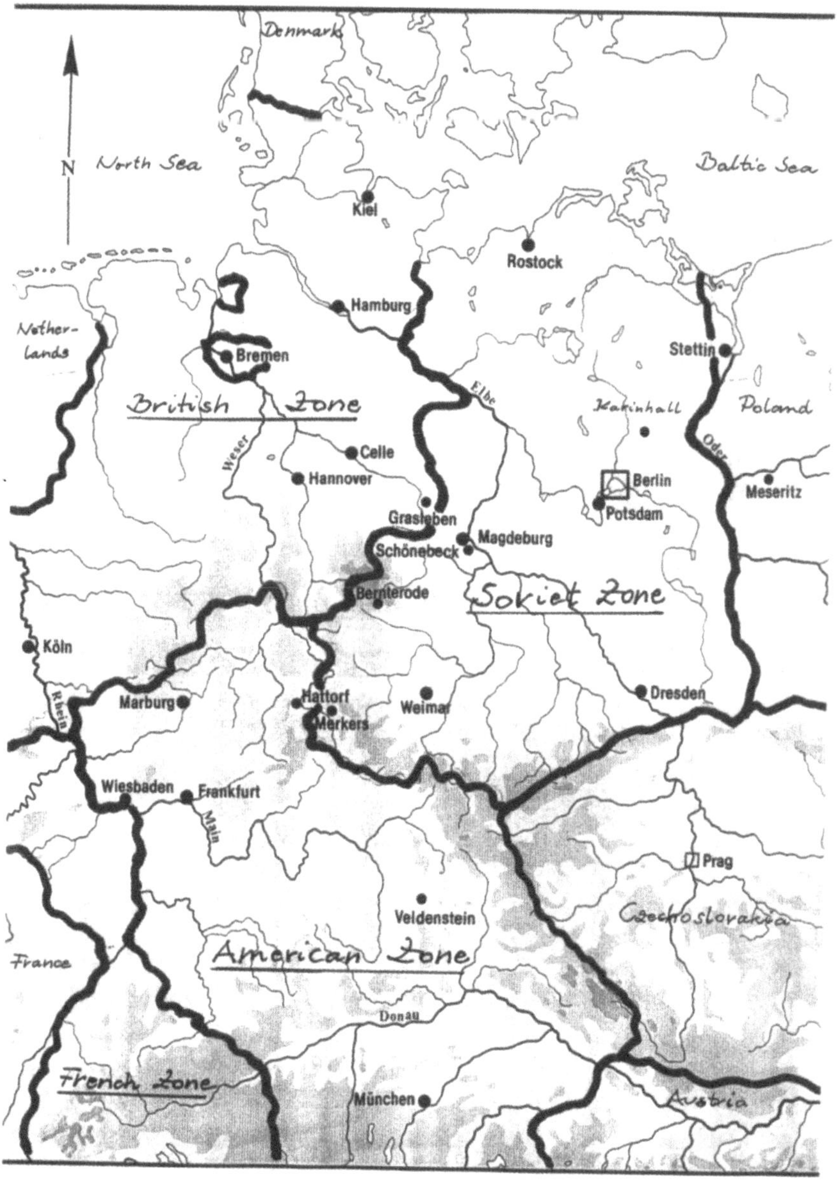

Germany 1945. Allied Occupation Zones

Appendix I

Dr. Ruth K. Meyer, former director of the Taft Museum in Cincinnati (see page 2), wrote this text **The Roberts Commission** when preparing the first draft of this publication. It gives the political background of the establishment of the MFA & A during World War II.

The Roberts Commission

Ruth K. Meyer

On 29 December 1943 General Eisenhower issued the following letter concerning the preservation of historic monuments which clarified and gave the highest official sanction to the Monuments, Fine Arts and Archives policy. This statement, issued during military operations in Italy, was made public by President Roosevelt at a White House Press Conference on 15 February 1944.

> Today we are fighting in a country which has contributed a great deal to our cultural inheritance, a country rich in monuments which by their creation helped and now in their old age illustrate the growth of the civilization which is ours. We are bound to respect those monuments so far as war allows.
>
> If we have to choose between destroying a famous building and sacrificing our own men, then our men's lives count infinitely more and the buildings must go. But the choice is not always so clear-cut as that. In many cases monuments can be spared without any detriment to operational needs. Nothing can stand against the argument of military necessity. That is an accepted principle. But the phrase "military necessity" is sometimes used where it would be more truthful to speak of military convenience or even of personal convenience. I do now want it to cloak slackness or indifference.
>
> It is a responsibility of higher commanders to determine through AMG Officers the locations of historic monuments whether they be immediately ahead of our front lines or in areas occupied by us. This information passed to lower echelons through normal channels places the responsibility on all Commanders of complying with the spirit of this letter.[1]

On 26 May 1944 General Eisenhower issued the following letter concerning the preservation of historical monuments, which was an enlargement over the policy of his directive for Italy:

> Shortly we will be fighting our way across the Continent of Europe in battles designed to preserve our civilization. Inevitably, in the path of our advance will be found historical monuments and cultural centers which symbolize to the world all that we are fighting to preserve.
>
> It is the responsibility of every commander to protect and respect these symbols whenever possible.
>
> In some circumstances the success of the military operation may be prejudiced in our reluctance to destroy these revered objects. Then, as at Cassino, where the enemy relied on our emotional attachments to shield his defense, the lives of our men are paramount. So, where military necessity dictates, commanders may order the required action even though it involves destruction to some honored site.
>
> But there are many circumstances in which damage and destruction are not necessary and cannot be justified. In such cases, through the exercise of restraint and

---

1 Report of the American Commission for the Protection and Salvage of Artistic and Historic Monuments in War Areas, Washington, D.C., 1946, 48–49.

> discipline, commanders will preserve centers and objects of historical and cultural significance. Civil Affairs Staffs at higher echelons will advise commanders of the locations of historical monuments of this type, both in advance of the front lines and in occupied areas. This information, together with the necessary instruction, will be passed down through command channels to all echelons.[2]

General Eisenhower's statement represented a milestone along a policy route that had been laid down over the course of seventy years. In 1874, after the Franco-Prussian War, European leaders decided to act together to bring to an end the historic practice of looting which had always expressed the victors' revenge upon the vanquished.[3] Recorded history shows that from the beginning of time looting had been virtually enshrined as a right and privilege of the conquerors. Only slowly had sentiments against the practice developed. The early Nineteenth century witnessed the first attempts on the part of European nations to assert the concept of a national cultural heritage having both an artistic integrity and unity. Gradually it was agreed that this national cultural heritage should be protected during time of war from flagrant pillage and needless destruction. As a result some of the loot that had been gathered by Revolutionary and Napoleonic armies of France was returned to countries such as Italy which had lost the four horses from the facade of the cathedral of St. Mark in Venice to the French invaders.

The combatants in the Franco-Prussian War had demonstrated alarming new developments in the technology of warfare. Participants in a series of subsequent international conferences now recognized the urgent need to attempt to influence military behavior. With both greater firepower and swifter mobility armies could extend their battles more widely across the countryside and cause greater destruction of civic properties. At the 1874 Brussels Conference a consensus was achieved that cultural and educational property even where state-owned should be treated as private property and thus be exempt from seizure. The intention was to prohibit armies from fortifying buildings with historical significance which might be destroyed in the process of their use and defense.

Two more conferences at The Hague in 1899 and 1907 were intended to regularize the rules of warfare and curtail its wanton destructiveness. Convention No. 4, "Laws and Customs of War on Land,"[4] approved at the second conference, contained articles in its attached regulations that became essential statements in international law on the protection of property. Article 47 forbade pillaging

---

2 See note 1, 102.

3 Kurtz, Michael J. *Nazi Contraband: American Policy on the Return of European Cultural Treasures, 1945–1955.* New York: Garland, 1985. The "Introduction" provides a review of the events leading up to the Brussels conference.

4 Parry (ed.), *Consolidated Treaty Series* vol. 205, p. 345 See also: Simpson, Elizabeth (ed.): *The Spoils of War, World War II and its Aftermath: The Loss, Reappearance, and Recovery of Cultural Property*, New York: Harry N. Abrams, Inc., 1997, 278f.

while Article 56 specifically stated that the seizure or destruction of cultural institutions, historical monuments and works of art and science was properly the subject of legal proceedings. European and non-European powers including the United States, Germany, Russia, France and Great Britain signed this agreement.

The work of these international conferences did little to alter the conduct of the combatants in World War I. The Germans had burned a part of the University of Louvain and bombarded Reims cathedral. Soldiers had used church towers in Belgium and France for their artillery spotters and had pillaged private homes indiscriminately gathering up works of art as booty. These actions were viewed as desecration and looting by the Allies and their resentment found its expression in the treaty that concluded peace at the end of the war.

Through the Treaty of Versailles drafted and signed in 1919 attempts were made to force the Germans to make reparations for works of art that were lost by compelling the total restitution of treasures like the Ghent Altarpiece.[5] In the year 1821 portions of this multipaneled work had been legally acquired as parts of the renowned English Collection of Edward Solly by the Prussian King. Now under the terms of Article 247[6] they would be forced to make the work whole again by giving up both the panels they had purchased as well as the panels they had recently looted from Ghent. Article 247 of the Versailles Treaty required the repair of damage done to the University of Louvain. These treaty provisions embodied language that established the principle of using works of art as reparations, that is to say as compensation for other destroyed works of art. The restoration of public buildings was also mandated. After World War II the principles of reparations and restitution would have even greater significance in the context of the work done under the auspices of the Roberts Commission and the MFA & A and are central to this story.

These artistic and cultural issues were not the only Versailles Treaty articles that would provoke negative feelings on the part of the Germans towards the Allies and extend verbal hostilities into the post war period. Indeed they were probably minor when seen in comparison with the articles that forced the Germans to acknowledge guilt for starting the war, to give up their claim to the industrial heartland of the Ruhr valley, to ship all of the coal produced in their mines to Belgium and France where mines had been destroyed and to reduce their army down to a standing force of 100,000 men.

The founding of the League of Nations created a new international body that was intended to preserve the European peace by providing among other things a

---

5 See note 3, 6.

6 Israel (ed.), *Major Peace Treaties in Modern History 1648–1967*, vol. 3 (1967) p. 1535. See also note 4, 281.

forum for discussion of controversies resulting from the implementation of the Treaty of Versailles. Its International Museums Office was urged to draft new conventions in an attempt to focus on the protection of the fine arts during wartime.[7]

The growing burden of complying with the Versailles Treaty provided Adolf Hitler with the substance for his speeches before the newly formed National Socialist Party gatherings in Munich during the 1920s.[8] As their propaganda officer Hitler preyed upon the resentment of the German people for the treatment they had received as losers in the conflict. Their nation had been forced to pay large sums of money as reparations for the economic losses of the winners, the French and the English. The near total collapse of the German economy at the end of that decade and widespread unemployment fueled an appetite for revenge. When the rising aggression of the Nazi party coupled with the ingrained German desire to be a dominant world power led to the outbreak of war in September 1939, it was too late for international diplomacy to insure the protection of artistic monuments and personal property. Belated efforts by the Secretary General of the League of Nations to draft a declaration covering basic principles of preservation found only a few adherents: Belgium, Greece, the Netherlands, Spain and the United States.

The framers of the Hague Conventions who wrote these rules were seeking to prevent not only the physical destruction of buildings dedicated to public worship, art, science or charitable purposes, historic monuments and hospitals that were found to be in the way of troop maneuvers, but also to protect their contents from looters. With their words the Hague delegates had wanted to put an end to the historic practice of gathering trophies of war. Of course this was a wholly idealistic goal, born in an age that had just seen the results of what modern warfare could accomplish. But where would you draw the line and how would you deal with the lingering grievances of one country against another? To reverse the effects of the practice of looting would have entailed the rearrangement of the world's great public art collections built up over centuries and for the most part containing loot from one civilization as prized and captured by another. For every great displaced monument that can be named there are those who would justify their actions in removing it from its context or from its original owners as being an act of safekeeping and cultural stewardship.

---

[7] Report, "The Director's Committee of the International Museums Office to the International Committee on Intellectual Cooperation for the Year 1937/38, Together with a Preliminary Draft International Convention on the Protection of Historic Buildings and Works of Art in Time of War." File "League of Nations – Draft of International Agreement to Protect Arts and Monuments in Time of War," Correspondence RG 239, National Archives.

[8] Flood, Charles Bracelen. *Hitler: The Path to Power.* Boston: Houghton Mifflin, 1989.

After reviewing fifty years of eye-witness accounts, journalists' studies and academic scholarship one has to conclude that an arts policy based upon the looting and destruction of other nations' cultural wealth was a fundamental aspect of Nazi governance. Although the sales of looted art were supposed to be part of Göring's economic plans, one can also say that the motivation for Nazi cultural looting was principally emotional, rooted in their ignorance and hatreds and fundamentally had little to do with their economic policies. Some of the artistic property stolen from others was sold at auction or bartered through dealers and funds were allocated to different military units. But the money raised was also used to obtain works more pleasing to the tastes of Hitler and his malevolent band of art connoisseurs. A great deal more looted art was simply warehoused, placed in storage for purposes that events never allowed to be revealed.

Their reign of terror began in the spring of 1933 with the Reichstag fire and street violence during parliamentary elections. Afterwards, Hitler and his cabinet dominated by Nazi party members were granted dictatorial powers by a German electorate that had lost all faith in their traditional leaders. Failure of the Weimar government, which had been democratically elected and leftward leaning opened the way for a Nazi government that would be hard on the communists and scornful of the democratic center. Their real target of course was the Jewish people. Their program of aggression against the Jews became clear with the passing of the Nuremberg laws of 1935 which stripped the Jews of their citizenship, imposed restrictions on their ability to earn a living and exposed them to venomous personal violence. A key element of the Nazi effort was the destruction of the economic and financial position of their foes. All Jewish assets were seized and a key element in this onslaught was the seizure of artistic, literary and cultural property ranging from the sentimental to the priceless.

Despite its seeming impracticality the Hague Convention existed as the statement of enlightened international opinion in the 1930s when the Nazis began their systematic campaigns of aggression against the Jews. From a half century's perspective it is now evident that Hitler and the leaders of the Nazi party who surrounded him had a cultural policy that was based on their irrational and vicious anti-Semitism. Their contempt for the rights of personal property was as total as their contempt for the concept of national self-determination which was displayed in 1938 with the annexation of Austria.

The conquest of Austria by means of annexation represented a personal conquest for Hitler who had been born in an Austrian community in 1889. After his tyrannical father's death his mother, whom he adored, moved her family to Linz where she had been born. Hitler left school at the age of sixteen and wanted to launch a career as an artist. He had a flair for drawing and a romantic temperament fueled by dreams of the messianic glory which he hoped to achieve through a union of art and social activism. He went off to Vienna at the age of eighteen to try for a place in the Academy of Fine Arts. When he was refused he turned to the Architectural School, but could not be considered there because he had not attended the *Oberrealschule*. Just at this time came the news of the death of his mother breaking his last tie to home.

Hitler stayed on in Vienna for five more years pretending to be an art student and cherishing the ideal of becoming a self-trained architect. When money from home ran out he lived in charitable institutions. He had devised a program of readings in art, history, and philosophy and attended performances of Wagner's operas when he could afford them. Hitler painted watercolors for the souvenir market and oils to fit inside of frames which improved their sales in frame maker's shops. This meager existence ended when he moved to Munich in 1913 to escape conscription into the Austro-Hungarian Empire's army.

Twenty-five years later Hitler took his revenge on Vienna and its residents who had failed to see his genius. Now he wanted to lower Vienna to the status of a third class city. He was determined to establish Linz, his mother's birthplace, as the cultural and economic capital of the Thousand Year Reich and to build a museum with the richest collection in Europe. During the late 1930s as his plans were taking shape, Hitler had a number of art advisors beginning with an old friend, Heinrich Hoffmann. Hoffmann was a photographer who got rich from his monopoly of photographs of Nazi proceedings.[9] Seeing that the job of building Hitler's collection was going to be beyond his powers, Hoffmann recruited others such as the dealers Maria Almas-Dietrich in Munich and Karl Haberstock in Berlin.[10] They began to consult with Hitler to gain an estimation of his tastes and then set out to assemble his personal collection while enriching themselves with finders fees along the way.

To give the project greater stature it was proposed that the Linz Commission be established for the purpose of making the acquisitions for Hitler's museum. Haberstock suggested that Dr. Hans Posse, formerly director of the *Dresden Gemäldegalerie* be appointed as director for Linz. After Hitler's army invaded Austria, Posse and Haberstock followed the troops to begin their acquisitions. Among the first collection to be visited was that of the Austrian branch of the Rothschild family.

Hitler particularly wanted to regain the crown jewels and coronation regalia of the defunct Holy Roman Empire which were stored in Vienna. Since 1424 the crown jewels had been the prized treasure of the German city of Nuremberg until 1796 when, at the approach of French troops, Emperor Franz II had moved them to Vienna. The treasure was returned to Nuremberg in 1938.

---

9 Nicholas, Lynn H.: *The Rape of Europa*. New York: Alfred A. Knopf 1994, p. 31.

10 See note 9, p. 32–34, for a thorough discussion of the formation of the Linz Commission.

Systematic looting of Jewish property increased after *Reichskristallnacht* (Crystal Night, 9 November 1938), and Munich was one of the main centers of activity. Panicked Jews were now fleeing Germany and others were being forced into concentration camps. The Nazis seized everything except their family portraits. No compensation was given and money obtained when items were sold on the international art market was put into a special bank account for the police.

Once the European conflict began more powerful figures were involved. Hermann Göring, Chief of the *Luftwaffe* and Hitler's confidant, was an avid collector and fancied that his taste in art far was superior. By the end of the war Göring had six residences crammed with art. The most lavishly decorated was *Carinhall*, his estate forty miles north of Berlin, named for his first wife.

One of Göring's sources of acquisitions was the *Einsatzstab Reichsleiter Rosenberg* (*ERR, Einsatzstab für die besetzten Gebiete*), the *Reichsleiter Rosenberg* Task Force for the Occupied Territories. Hitler established the ERR in 1939 and empowered its leader, the vehemently anti-Semitic party theoretician Alfred Rosenberg, to collect cultural materials "for scholarly purposes." In January 1940, Hitler gave Rosenberg the task of seizing all Jewish and Masonic archives, libraries and places of worship. The aim was to establish a post-war academy for the study of the "degenerate" Jewish race. The ERR had headquarters in Berlin, and branch offices in Amsterdam, Brussels, Paris, Belgrade, Riga, Minsk and Kiev. ERR collecting teams worked independently or with the German military to make their raids on the homes of the Jews and the public and private institutions.

Göring overpowered the weaker Rosenberg and used the ERR as his personal agency for collecting art especially in France. Specially installed exhibitions were arranged for him at the *Jeu de Paume* Museum which the ERR had taken over as its warehouse and gallery facility. More than 20,000 objects had been confiscated from 203 Jewish owned collections. Eventually, 138 freight car loads of loot were removed.[11]

What Göring and company did not know was that all the while there was a spy in their midst. At the ERR headquarters in the *Jeu de Paume* works of art to be sent from France were first inventoried and evaluated by a system Göring had decreed. The permanent collection of that museum had been put in storage and remained under the control of art conservator Rose Valland, a Louvre staff member. Initially, the Germans had agreed that Valland could remain at her post to supervise her collection and to monitor the inventory processes of the ERR so

---

[11] National Archives, RG 239/85, OSS/ALIU CIR 1, Plaut. "Activity of the ERR in France," August 15, 1945. Lt. Comdr. James S. Plaut, (USNR) was an MFA & A officer and a fellow Cincinnatian.

that the French museum administration would know what was being removed to Germany. This courtesy was quickly dispensed with once Goering arrived on the scene, but Valland tenaciously stayed on the job employing one excuse after another. The ERR needed her as a housekeeper to maintain the building during its occupation. She seized this opportunity to note down the contents and destination of the shipments that began to depart from France. Valland made notes that the ERR was sending the loot to the German castles of Neuschwanstein, Chiemsee, Kogl, Weisenegg, Nikolsburg and the Monastery of Buxheim. Memorizing daily events, at home each night she updated her journal. After the Nazi defeat Rose Valland guided MFA & A officers to recovery of these collections.[12]

In Belgium the Nazis focused on national treasures. Their most provocative action was the "recapture" of the Van Eyck *Altarpiece of the Mystic Lamb* which had been restored to the church of St. Bavon in Ghent after World War I in accordance with the terms of the Treaty of Versailles. In 1940, fearing once again for its safety the Belgians decided to send the altarpiece to the Vatican for safekeeping. However, when Italy entered the war this plan was changed and the altarpiece was placed in the custody of the French government at the *Chateau de Pau*. It remained in France until July 1942, when Hitler ordered the Vichy government to relinquish the masterpiece. Next *The Mystic Lamb* was brought to Germany where it would be stored at Schloss Neuschwanstein until the fall of 1944, when that castle was deemed unsafe and the altarpiece was taken to the salt mine at Altaussee in Austria.[13] Its eventual liberation and restitution to the Belgians is one of the most frequently told success stories symbolic of the mission of the MFA & A.

Another Belgian altarpiece which had been dismembered was a target of Nazi looters. Dirk Bouts, *The Last Supper,* from the Church of St. Pierre in Louvain had previously lost its wings through legitimate sales to German museums before World War I. The Versailles Treaty had restored them to the Belgians through its articles covering reparations. In 1942, the Germans returned to capture their prize again.

A final attack on Belgian cultural patrimony occurred in September 1944. German officers arrived in Bruges to seize the sculpture of the Madonna and Child by Michelangelo which had been a civic treasure since the 16th century. Now the

---

12 Valland, Rose. *Le Front de l'art*. Paris: Librairie Plon, 1961. It is her first personal account of the years 1939–1945. Her book formed the basis for Simon, Matila. *The Battle of the Louvre: The Struggle to Save French Art in World War II.* New York: Hawthorn, 1971.

13 Rorimer, James J., and Gilbert Rabin. *Survival.* New York: Abelard Press, 1950, and Howe, Thomas Carr. *Salt Mines and Castles.* Indianapolis, New York: Bobbs-Merrill, 1946 give accounts of these rescues. See also Nicholas, Lynn H. *The Rape of Europa.* New York: Knopf, 1994, 407–444.

pretext for its removal was the advance of the American army who would surely desecrate it. It was man-handled into a truck lined with mattresses by a group of sailors and carted away for "safekeeping." Along with the van Eyck altarpiece it also went to Altaussee.

In Eastern Europe the story was worse. The Nazis thought the Poles were a sub-human species and viewed the other Slavs of Eastern Europe with total contempt. The great Veit Stoss altarpiece (1477–87) commissioned by the King of Poland and placed in a church in Cracow was seized because Stoss was from Nuremberg, thus a German and to the Nazis there was no such thing as Polish art or culture. The work was returned by MFA & A officers in 1946.

The situation in Russia after the June 1941 invasion was still more barbaric. Destruction was wrought on a large scale as the Nazis had absolute contempt for the Russians. In Novgorod they blew up the Church of St. Sophia, built in 1050 and filled with irreplaceable frescoes and icons. Before they were expelled from Russia, the Germans destroyed 427 museums in Leningrad, Smolensk, Stalingrad, Novgorod, and Poltava. From a variety of sources an MFA & A officer estimated that 375 archival institutions, 402 museums, 531 institutes and 957 libraries in Eastern Europe were looted or destroyed.[14]

In Italy, because of the alliance between Hitler and Mussolini, an art acquisition team from the German government was received in Rome in 1937. At first they wanted to obtain the sculpture of the Discobolus of Myron, but since it was the registered property of a prince, they were unsuccessful. Eventually; despite opposition from Italian art authorities 34 unopened crates were sent to Germany.[15]

Nazi art policy also aimed to suppress the activities of living German artists who were Jewish or of Jewish ancestry. They were particularly harsh towards works of modernist tendency which Hitler despised and labeled as degenerate art. Many German artists even if they were not Jewish saw their works burned and destroyed, collectors of modern art were harassed and the great school of art and design, the *Bauhaus*, founded in Essen and later established at Weimar, simply went out of existence.

The creation of the American Commission for the Protection and Salvage of Artistic and Historic Monuments in War Areas must be seen against this back-

---

14 Poste, Leslie I. *The Development of U.S. Protection of Libraries and Archives in Europe during World War II,* US Army Civil Affairs School, Fort Gordon, GA, [rev.ed.], August, 1964, 74–78.

15 Siviero, Rodolfo. *Second National Exhibition of the Works of Art Recovered in Germany,* Florence: Sansoni, 1950, 13.

ground of events in Germany.[16] From the mid-1930s onward reports of Nazi activities were brought back to this country by tourists and refugees, journalists and intelligence agents, students and scholars. After the outbreak of war leaders of exiled governments and the finance ministers of the European allies meeting separately recognized their growing obligation to establish policies that would enable the recovery of the national and personal property that the Nazis were carrying away. Although the British nation was not experiencing the problem of looting its leaders sympathized with their allies' concerns and wanted to be supportive in the matters of cultural restitution and reparations.

The British also understood the value of protecting the reputation of their Army which was would be fighting on the continent. The Italians had already charged the British with destruction of ancient Roman ruins in North Africa and this had led eventually to the appointment of Sir Leonard Woolley as Archaeological Advisor to the Director of Civil Affairs in the War Office. While Sir Leonard came to view the whole cultural preservation effort as a public relations campaign to ensure that the good name of the British Army would also be preserved, collaboration between the Americans and British on this mission proved to be essential.

While it would be wrong to think that the reports of the Nazis' looting were only met with apathy in the United States, nothing much had happened before President Roosevelt established the National Resources Planning Board which was charged to begin organizing for possible war.[17] Among its many units was the Committee on Conservation of Cultural Resources (CCCR) directed by the American Council of Learned Societies and made up of the Librarian of Congress, the Archivist of the United States, the Directors of the National Gallery of Art and the National Museum of American Art with representatives from the American Association of Museums and the American Institute of Architects. Other representatives came from the War Department and from Civil Defense.

Responding to rumors about European museums preparing their collections for storage the CCCR debated the need for a similar effort in the United States. Lacking confidence in the speed and effectiveness of committee procedures by late 1941 museum leaders in New York, Boston, Philadelphia and Washington were working independently to move their collections into hiding. Many were following advice contained in a pamphlet on packing and evacuation of collec-

---

[16] See note 1. It is the official publication on the work of the Roberts Commission prepared shortly after its conclusion.

[17] Nicholas, *The Rape of Europa,* Chapter 8, provides an excellent account of the formation of the Roberts Commission and the diplomatic, political and military policies which its activities encompassed. Before its publication Michael Kurtz's *Nazi Contraband,* (see note 3) was the most reliable source of information.

tions in wartime written by George Stout, chief of conservation at the Fogg Museum, Harvard University. Apolitical and generally suspicious of museum directors as a breed, Stout's dedication to the fundamental principles of art conservation and preservation marks him as one of the principal contributors to the establishment of the MFA & A and among its most dedicated officers.[18]

In the fall of 1942 certain leaders in the academic and museum communities met to discuss their fears of the coming destruction and to plan possible action. Participants included William B. Dinsmoor, President of the Archaeological Institute of America; Francis Henry Taylor, Director of the Metropolitan Museum of Art, New York; Paul J. Sachs, Associate Director of the Fogg Museum of Art, Harvard University; and David Finley, Director of the National Gallery of Art, Washington. Later they were joined by Archibald MacLeish, the Librarian of Congress.

This self-appointed group met to debate various methods of insuring that the US government would have policies in place regarding cultural preservation and restitution of looted art after the end of the conflict. Deciding that to meet those goals they would need the mandate of the President, they next approached Chief Justice Harlan F. Stone because of his independent status as the head of the nation's judiciary and because of his position as chairman of the Board of Directors of the National Gallery of Art. They wanted Stone to serve as a figure of authority who would sign a letter they intended to write to President Roosevelt.

Dated 8 December 1942 a letter Stone sent to Roosevelt asked the President for a Statement of Policy supporting the protection of fine arts and monuments. It also asked for the creation of a presidential committee "for the protection and conservation of works of art and of artistic or historic monuments and records in Europe."[19] Showing the group's cognizance of British policies, Stone's letter also noted the proposed commission's potential usefulness in combating enemy propaganda and in assisting with the eventual restitution of stolen objects.

In a second letter to the President Stone, now writing for himself, presented some additional requests.[20] He strongly suggested that the US Government urge the British and the Russians to create similar committees so that these committees would then pool their resources to provide qualified personnel and information necessary to protect art works. Stone envisioned the creation of a subcommittee under the three national commissions assigned to collect data on looted property

---

[18] The George Stout papers, Archives of American Art, provide an intimate and unpublished look into the formation of the Roberts Commission and the activities of the MFA & A.

[19] US Department of State, *Foreign Relations of the United States: Diplomatic Papers, 1943*, vol. 1, *General*, Washington, D.C.: US Government Printing Office, 1963, 469.

[20] See Nicholas: *The Rape of Europa*, 212.

and receive restitution claims. The expanded proposal suggested an international system of information gathering and cooperation not unlike that which the MFA & A eventually achieved although without anticipated governmental sponsorship.

Roosevelt routed Stone's letter to Secretary of State Cordell Hull because it touched on so many diplomatic and political issues. On 24 December 1942 Hull replied to the President that the idea had a great deal of merit, but would need the approval of the Joint Chiefs of Staff who could then authorize military protection of fine arts and monuments during combat operations.[21] Hull made special mention of the advantage in proclaiming concern for protecting the symbols of civilization and giving the Allied cause a moral boost. Given the positive nature of Hull's reply Roosevelt wrote to Stone four days later that he had referred the proposal to the appropriate agencies for comment, and he expected unanimous agreement with the objectives involved.

Months passed and it was revealed that the Secretary of State, Cordell Hull, never received Roosevelt's letter authorizing him to contact the military.[22] Belatedly the matter was referred to the Joint Chiefs of Staff who replied that they saw no military advantage to the idea of a national commission for the protection of cultural items. The President decided to intervene directly and on 24 April Roosevelt let Justice Stone know that the military would cooperate so long as cooperation would not hinder military actions.

Cordell Hull now drafted the concept for the American Commission for the Protection and Salvage of Artistic and Historic Monuments in Europe. On 23 June 1943 Roosevelt approved Hull's outline and the process of gathering acceptances from proposed commission members got underway. Chief Justice Stone had declined to head the commission so the honor passed to Justice Owen J. Roberts who agreed to serve in Stone's place and gave his name to the group. The Roberts Commission united members from concerned private institutions such those named previously: William B. Dinsmoor of the Archaeological Institute of America, Francis Henry Taylor of the New York Metropolitan Museum of Art, and Dr. Paul J. Sachs of the Fogg Museum at Harvard. Former Governor of New York, Alfred E. Smith, was a newcomer to the group. Government representatives included David Finley and Huntington Cairns of Washington's National Gallery of Art; Herbert Lehman, Chief of the Foreign Relief and Rehabilitation Corporation; and Archibald MacLeish, the Librarian of Congress.

---

[21] Cordell Hull to Franklin D. Roosevelt, 24 December 1942, in: 1940–1944 Decimal File (840–403), Record Group 59, National Archives.

[22] Kurtz. *Nazi Contraband,* 66.

Paul Sachs played a crucial role in the Roberts Commission. He was a founding member of the American Defense-Harvard Group (ADHG) which had organized shortly after the United States entered the war in order to provide intelligence assistance through liaisons with the Office of Strategic Services (OSS). Through the art history courses he had taught at Harvard Sachs had trained many men and women who had become curators and museum directors. Now he would have an opportunity to share in the training of officers who would be doing civil affairs work in future liberated or occupied countries. The Office of the Provost Marshal General of the Army, which organized and operated the newly created School of Military Government in Charlottesville, Virginia, wanted to provide its candidates with information on preservation issues. Sachs helped organize a sub committee of the ADHG which prepared lists of institutions and monuments needing protection. The same group oversaw the writing of manuals on conservation for implementation in the field. Through his position on the Roberts Commission Sachs was able to effect a collaboration between this group and another formed by the American Council of Learned Societies which was aided by refuge scholars from Europe who were preparing lists, maps and catalogs of monuments and movable cultural objects.

The more immediate challenge was to get men of the caliber of Paul Sachs' students into military service and have them assigned to the units that would be moving into territories where works of art would be threatened. In the fall of 1943 the War Department's Civil Affairs Division (CAD) yielded to the pressure of the Roberts Commission and the Monuments, Fine Arts and Archives Branch was born.[23] Without the determination of key Roberts Commission members this could have been nothing but a paper victory because the War Department had inflexible personnel policies. The Department would not directly commission civilian experts nor would it intervene to influence assignments made by theater commanders. Despite its status within the War Department the CAD was a staff office in Washington and was nearly powerless to affect the conduct of officers in the field who failed to see preservation as a military priority. Time and again the purpose of the Roberts Commission was compromised by their inability to get personnel assigned to staff the elaborate organization they envisioned. This pointed up the weakness of the link between the civilian commission and the military establishment and led to the difficulties the MFA & A officers encountered in carrying out their missions.

With the coming of spring 1944, the academic groups had completed most of the handbooks, lists, atlases and guides which were to be distributed to military personnel in advance of the invasion of the Continent. The more difficult task

---

[23] Kurtz. *Nazi Contraband,* 72.

of establishing policies for the eventual restitution of works of art was underway, but proceeded with glacial slowness. Through their scholar contacts members of the Roberts Commission were learning of the magnitude of the job that lay before them. The ERR's plunder of the art collections in occupied countries and the activities of the Linz Commission had been verified by intelligence reports. Once the Allies had landed in Italy and France these reports increased alarmingly, but by mid-summer 1944 there was still no agreement as to how the mechanics of restitution and claims for reparations would be handled by the Great Powers. The members of the Roberts Commission felt they were operating in a vacuum since they did not have representation at the conference tables in Washington and in London where these issues were being debated.

Over the course of the next year until the summer of 1945 when the war had ended the Allies wrangled over many issues regarding the future of Europe and the governance of a defeated Germany. Not the least was the problem of how to restore those elements of each national culture which had been damaged, destroyed or relocated because of the Nazis refusal to honor the international conventions on artistic preservation and their widespread activities as looters. Debate at the conference tables centered on two words and their definitions: *restitutions* and *reparations*. At its simplest restitution means the act of restoring, the return of an object to its previous owner. Its secondary meaning brought complexity to the discussion: "the act of making good, or of giving an equivalent for any loss, damage, or injury."[24] By insisting upon the parity of both meanings the French and the Belgians, still grieving over losses from World War I, hoped to receive works of art legally owned by Germany as replacements and in compensation for lost objects now that the Germans would once again be forced to submit to the terms of a peace treaty. The French promoted the concept of a committee that would consider their claims and make suitable rewards to them from the German art repositories that would come under Allied occupation government command.

The theory of cultural reparations was also intimately linked to restitution and likewise depended upon multiple definitions of that word. At the Allied conferences reparations meant more than "1. a repairing or being repaired; restoration to good condition." This definition applied to the issue of monetary "reparations," *i.e.* currency to be used to rebuild a damaged monument. It was the second and third meanings of reparations that energized the French: "3. a making of amends; a making up for a wrong or injury" and "4. anything paid or done to make up for something else; compensation; specifically (usually pl.),

---

[24] Webster's New Twentieth Century Dictionary, Second Edition. New York, Simon & Schuster 1979, p. 1544.

compensation by a defeated nation for damage done to civilians and their property in a war, payable in money, labor, goods, etc."[25]

Months passed while this terminology and its potential applications were debated. The Allies could not agree on how to legislate restitution and reparations by means of treaties. Which of the many commissions studying the problem should write the policies? Who should vote on their implementation? Who should supervise Germany's compliance with their regulation? Should it be the European Advisory Commission established in October 1943, a forum where the Big Three considered political questions arising from the impending defeat of Germany, or should it be the United Nations, fledgling successor to the old League? Another contender was the Council of Allied Ministers of Education which represented more countries than the Big Three and which had commissions actively studying the matter of the destruction and looting of libraries and archives.

From the tangle of debate it emerged that the American and the British leaders were reluctant to participate in authorizing any final plans for cultural restitution and repatriation in the post war period. Nevertheless, from a sense of fair play and out of respect for those Allies who had lost so much, governmental representatives did continue to participate vigorously in all of the study groups and planning commissions. All the while, the Russians displayed only token participation, offering no plans of their own and giving the impression that they would not have endorsed a mutual international effort.

Nevertheless, the need for postwar cultural policies urged by the Roberts Commission seemed to have achieved some success. August 1944 saw the creation of British and American planning groups for the eventual occupation of Germany.[26] The American group, formally designated United States Group, Control Council (Germany), had a Monuments, Fine Arts and Archives branch. Three months later in November a new structure for the USGCC was drawn that created a division for Reparations, Deliveries and Restitution (RDR). The MFA & A Branch was attached to this division and retained its place in the subsequent organization of the Allied Control Council, the planned governing body for occupied Germany.

At this stage Allied conferees focused on means to prevent the movement of works of art in German territory. It was feared that the Nazis might try to move their incredible hoard of loot out of the country and by sale of these treasures gain the assets required to stage a return to power. The specter of a resurgent German army awakened the military to the arguments of the Roberts Commis-

---

25 See note 24, p. 1532.

26 Kurtz. *Nazi Contraband,* 85.

sion and authorities at Supreme Headquarters, Allied Expeditionary Forces (SHAEF), issued Military Government Law No. 52 on 26 September 1944 in which any transaction involving a work of art or cultural material of value or importance, regardless of ownership or control, was forbidden.[27]

During the same month efforts proceeded to draft a military directive on arts protection policies for American armed forces. It was adopted by the Army in December 1944. Capt. Mason Hammond, was appointed as the first Monuments Specialist officer and was now stationed in London with Francis Henry Taylor, who had taken a leave from duties as director of the Metropolitan Museum to consult with the European Advisory Commission and to work with military advisors preparing the *Handbook for Military Government in Germany Prior to Defeat or Surrender.* Part 3, Chapter 16, paragraph 1186 states, "it is the policy of the Supreme Commander to make measures to facilitate the eventual restitution of works of art and objects of scientific or historical importance which may have been looted from United Nations Governments or nationals."[28] This was an early victory for the MFA & A branch.

But publication of this directive represented only a small gain for the Roberts Commission and the MFA & A since they were still unable to make a substantial impact on the State Department planners or their colleagues in the War Department in Washington. Conflicting points of view with regard to the post war future of Germany created a tangle of political and diplomatic intrigue so dense that the issues of cultural restitution were all but invisible except to its partisans. In the end the State Department never took any formal actions to endorse any of the draft policies and guidelines over which the Commission and its advisors had labored for two years.

The chance to establish an international policy for cultural restitutions and reparations was lost; in fact it was overtaken by events. As the Allied armies moved into Germany from both the east and the west there was no longer time to bring about agreement between the Western allies and the Russians who were bent on extracting retribution for the destruction of their monuments and the looting of art in their country during the Nazi attacks early in the war. Allied forces began to come upon the hundreds of storage places the Germans had chosen as repositories for their own art and that which had been looted. Roberts Commission members and the few MFA & A officers were now arriving on the continent from London and hoped to prevent even greater destruction and dispersal than that which had already occurred. The military handbook and Eisenhower's statements only proclaimed American adherence to general principles of restitution

---

[27] Kurtz. *Nazi Contraband,* 88.

[28] See note 27, 88–89.

and conservation of Germany's cultural heritage. There were no specific directions given on how to achieve these goals.

The experience of MFA & A officer Walker Hancock may serve to illuminate the situations that were encountered even before the German surrender. When the US entered the war Hancock had been a professor of sculpture at the Pennsylvania Academy of Fine Arts. During his student years he had won a prize to study art in Rome for three years, 1925–28, and had made several return visits to Italy during the 1930s.[29] He was fluent in Italian and at the beginning of the war had tried to enlist in the Air Force intelligence service, but been rejected for medical reasons. He tried the Navy, but they were slow in responding with his commission, so he had been drafted into the Army as a medic. He was rescued from that service when his entry was chosen in a sculpture competition to design an air medal and he was ordered to Washington and stationed at the Army War College. There Hancock's Italian training and language skills were appreciated and he was sent to work at the Pentagon. In this assignment he learned of the formation of the MFA & A and applied for a transfer to the newly formed unit. From Washington he was sent to London to the office of British Colonel Geoffrey Webb where the binational policies of MFA & A were being drafted. Hancock worked on the directive that was issued as a statement by General Eisenhower before the Normandy invasions.

During 1943 and 1944 Hancock worked with the first MFA & A officers on the preparation of guide books for the Army officers which were meant to prepare them for their anticipated roles as preservationists. They were given maps and texts describing the location of major monuments and histories of the places in France they would soon be defending and liberating. He became a good friend of George Stout, the former Fogg Museum conservator, who had first sounded the alarm to American museum colleagues and had pursued the establishment of the Roberts Commission two years earlier. When preparations for the Normandy invasion were completed the MFA & A London group began planning for the subsequent invasion of Germany.

When Walker Hancock entered northwest Europe with the First Army he took up his duty as a Monuments Specialist Officer to see that Eisenhower's directive to the Allied troops was enforced. Only ten MFA & A officers were sent into the field with the British and American armies north of the Alps. Hancock later recorded his experiences in an article published in the *College Art Journal* of May 1946 in which he said:

> In the American armies such essential items as transportation, clerical assistance, labor or authority to bring about necessary action were for the most part obtained

---

[29] RKM interview with Walker Hancock, August, 1993.

> by means of any entreaties, cajolings or other tricks at the command of the individual officer. Empty-handed before a task of such magnitude, he could sustain himself only with the thought that whatever he accomplished was just so much better than nothing.[30]

The war was not over when Hancock followed the troops into Aachen that March of 1945. In Charlemagne's former capital he wanted to make sure that the city's museums and the cathedral were going to be kept safe once the remaining citizens were evacuated and American troops moved in. His work next took him farther into the Rhineland where moving within range of enemy guns he tracked down reports of repositories. One of the greatest of these was the Siegen mine where George Stout had learned the Aachen cathedral treasures had been hidden.

Escorted by the vicar of the cathedral and accompanied by Stout, Hancock and other Army personnel entered the mine outside the town of Siegen. The area had been under Allied bombardment for three months and the mine had become a refuge for the townspeople who had been staying there for weeks fearing the arrival of the Americans. Passing through this crowd, Hancock and Stout were led down a tunnel to a locked door. The man who opened it was startled to see the vicar in such company, but led the way down a passage to a room containing more than 400 paintings of the finest quality. There were also stacks of cases from the museums of Bonn, Cologne, Wuppertal, Essen and Münster. Other cases contained church treasures from Essen, Cologne, Siegburg and Metz as well as Aachen plus the contents of the Beethoven house in Bonn.

Despite environmental conditions that would be hazardous to the precious contents of the Siegen mine everything had to remain there under guard while the US Military Government was being established. Months would pass before Hancock would return to rescue these treasures of German art which remained in limbo until the authority of the United States army to transport them was established.

Creation of an effective Military Government for Germany was hindered by a complex structure that had two different, and often competing fronts of authority. Overall command was in the hands of General Eisenhower, who had two hats. He was the military Governor of the United States Zone and Commander-in-Chief of SHAEF and its American successor, as of 28 June 1945, United States Forces European Theater (USFET). Eisenhower's Deputy Military Governor, Lucius Clay, appointed 31 March, headed the relatively small policy-making body, the United States Group Control Council (Germany). Implementation was in the hands of USFET.

---

30 Hancock, Walker: "Experiences of a Monuments Officer in Germany," *College Art Journal*, May, 1946, 271.

This duality was cumbersome. During the first four months of the occupation, the MFA & A branch in the RDR Division of USGCC (Germany) developed policies relating to conservation of Germany's heritage and the restitution of looted cultural items. Operational responsibility for inspecting repositories, protecting cultural objects, and implementing restitution procedures resided with MFA & A officers stationed with local Military Government detachments (E Teams) scattered throughout the zone. But, these teams were under direct control of USFET and not USGCC or its RDR division.

Eisenhower continued the further split in Military Government structure by retaining operational responsibilities in the Military Government section of USFET, though he renamed it the Office of Military Government US Zone (OMGUS). Military Government offices were created for the new *Länder* of Bavaria, Württemberg-Baden, Greater Hesse, and the enclaves of Bremen and Berlin. Each of these regional Military Governments had MFA & A offices. But throughout the occupation there was never a unified MFA & A structure despite the common missions that the officers performed. The MFA & A was never fully commissioned.

To cope with the need to secure the repositories and make arrangements for the storage of works of art OMGUS authorized the creation of a number of regional Collecting Points. These would be administered by the Military Governments set up in each *Land* and included Munich for Bavaria, Wiesbaden and Marburg for Greater Hesse, Stuttgart for Württemberg-Baden along with others which were only briefly active. The *Land* military were charged with implementing restitution and also had the final say in allocating personnel for the MFA & A function. In OMGUS, at General Clay's insistence, only about six people were assigned to the MFA & A section. In the *Land* Military Governments, a high point of fifteen officers was reached in August 1945. Thereafter, there were usually no more than two or three individuals assigned in each *Land* to MFA & A work.

In late May and June of 1945, Clay and his top staff were preoccupied with getting the Allied Control Commission operational. They wanted to postpone all cultural restitution activity such as the evacuation of the Siegen mine until there was an Allied agreement, which given the impasse on the EAC, was highly unlikely. Clay did not want to divert limited American resources to what he regarded as a non-essential area, and he wanted to avoid diplomatic problems that unilateral action might cause. The Cultural Advisor in the USGCC, John Nicholas Brown, was alarmed at the potential for harm to valuable items and consequently to America's reputation. While on a tour of the occupied zone in May 1945 Brown urged Clay to make exceptions including return of internationally recognized masterpieces such as the *Altarpiece of the Mystic Lamb* to Ghent and Michelangelo's *Madonna and Child* to Brugge.

Prior to the Potsdam Conference held in July and early August Clay's staff came up with new tactics on restitution: works of art would be divided into three categories. Category A, easily identified looted works of art; Category B, looted art for which the Germans alleged proper payment had been made; and Category C, German art stored in the American Zone for safekeeping. USGCC staff proposed immediate return of Category A items and mechanisms to permit the restitution of Category B objects, with a proviso that reserved for future Allied agreement whether or not these items were accountable as reparations payments. And, in a surprising new maneuver they also counseled *transfer of Category C items to the United States.* Clay explained this reasoning to Sumner McKnight Crosby, a professor of medieval art at Yale University on leave of absence to advise the Roberts Commission and a true believer in the creed of restitutions and cultural preservation. Since the United States did not intend to claim industrial reparations, Clay said, it might want at some point intangibles such as art.[31]

Reluctantly parented and begrudged offspring of a political union, the Allied Control Council, the branch was tardily whelped in the late summer of 1944 and the recruitment of specialists was a word of mouth affair. MFA & A never was officially commissioned as a "unit," a "branch," or a "corps," although it certainly had its own "esprit." The Roberts Commission, advised by the chair of its personnel committee, Paul Sachs, and his colleague, W. G. Constable of the Boston Museum of Fine Art, had been making staffing recommendations to the War Department since the spring of 1943. Many of those who were tapped had already joined one of the service branches. The pattern of their appointments had been set in May 1943 when the first, Captain Mason Hammond of Air Force Intelligence, was ordered to Africa as Adviser on Fine Arts and Monuments to the US Army. US Forces were then preparing to land in Sicily and it was hoped that Hammond, who was a Professor of Classics at Harvard, would have the expertise and authority to be effective in steering Army commanders away from the archaeological sites of Southern Italy.

MFA & A officers for Germany were recruited in 1945. Lieutenants Thomas Carr Howe, Jr. and Craig H. Smyth came from the Navy as did Charles Parkhurst. Howe had previously served as the director of the Palace of the Legion of Honor in San Francisco. Smyth and Parkhurst had been working at the National Gallery of Art in Washington. Army Lt. James Rorimer (later Captain) had been the curator of medieval art at the Cloisters of the Metropolitan Museum of Art. Lt. Charles Kuhn, had been at Harvard before entering the Navy and would return there again to direct its collections of German art housed in the Busch Reisinger Museum.

---

31 Kurtz. *Nazi Contraband,* 125.

The MFA & A officers shared a fundamental commitment to the cause of preservation. Above any other concerns they would first ask what does the work of art need in order that its condition be preserved and secondly they would ask how to determine its ownership. After the rampage of the Nazi "culture vultures" they believed in cultural repatriation because as Francis Henry Taylor had written the art of a country was "part of the spirit and heritage of these subject peoples."[32] Craig Smyth summed up this attitude when he wrote, "It was a deep satisfaction for military personnel in the MFA & A Service to be part of an operation which they saw to be pure in heart."[33]

Each of these officers brought to his duties the curator's special knowledge: how to identify a masterpiece, how to inspect its condition for damage, and how to pack it for storage or transport. These were the skills which would be needed at the repositories where the displaced and looted art was stored and at the Collecting Points to which it would be taken. In the case of the architectural monuments, the MFA & A officers who were assigned to mobile Army units, as Rorimer had been, could do little more than report damage they had observed and post signs placing the church or chateau off-limits. As it had turned out the rapid advance of the Americans into Germany and the unexpected surrender of the Germans left little opportunity for the MFA & A to repair or restore a monument. One striking example was the preservation of the Tiepolo ceiling paintings at the Residenz in Würzburg carried out by John Skilton in June 1945,[34] he found materials to cover the destroyed roof.

---

[32] Smyth, Craig Hugh. *Repatriation of Art from the Collecting Point in Munich after World War II*, The Hague: Schwartz/Maarssen/SDU Publishers, 1988, quoted from a letter from Francis Henry Taylor to Paul Sachs dated 4 December 1942, National Archives, RG 239, Box 53.

[33] See note 32, 20.

[34] Skilton, John D. Jr., *Defense de l'art europeen*, Paris: Les Editions Internationales, 1948.

Appendix II

This report prepared by Capt. Edith Standen and Renate Hobirk gives a complete list of the contents of the Wiesbaden Collecting Point as they recorded them. This list records the broad spectrum of the holdings of the WCCP and the dates of arrival and departure. No original packing lists of the Berlin State Museums or of the property from any other institution which came to Wiesbaden were ever made available to the staff. This list can not necessarily be used as detailed evidence of the numbers on crates, of the number of objects (many crates were never opened), or possibly of the correct names of the crates' owners. It is a most important document representing all their work done in less than one year after the opening of the Wiesbaden CCP.

COPY*

U.S. FORCES, EUROPEAN THEATER
GERMANY

7 November 1945

1. We, the undersigned, Monuments, Fine Arts and Archives Specialist Officers of the Armed Forces of the United States, wish to make known our convictions regarding the transportation to the United States of works of art, the property of German institutions or nationals, for puposes of protective custody.

2. a. We are unanimously agreed that the transportation of these works of art, undertaken by the United States Army, upon direction from the highest national authority, establishes a precedent which is neither morally tenable nor trustworthy.

b. Since the beginning of United States participation in the war, it has been the declared policy of the Allied Forces, so far as military necessity would permit, to protect and preserve from deterioration consequent upon the processes of war, all monuments, documents or other objects of historic, artistic, cultural or archaeological value. The war is at an end, and no doctrine of "military necessity" can now be invoked for the further protection of the objects to be moved, for the reason that depots and personnel, both fully competent for their protection, have been inaugurated and are functioning.

c. The Allied Nations are at present preparing to prosecute individuals for the crime of sequestering, under the pretext of "protective custody", the cultural treasures of German-occupied countries. A major part of the indictment follows upon the reasoning that even though these individuals were acting under military orders, the dictates of a higher ethical law

* Copy of the mimeographed paper in WIF Papers. Retyped from this in its original shape.

made encumbent upon them to refuse to take part in, or countenance, the fulfillment of these orders. We, the undersigned, feel it is our duty to point out that, though as members of the Armed Forces we will carry out the orders we receive, we are thus put before any candid eyes as no less culpable than those whose prosecution we affect to sanction.

3. We wish to state that from our own knowledge, no historical grievance will rankle so long, or be the cause of so much justified bitterness, as the removal, for any reason, of a part of the heritage of any nation, even if that heritage may be interpreted as a prize of war. And though this removal may be done with every intention of altruism, we are none the less convinced that it is our duty, individually and collectively, to protest against it, and that though our obligations are to the nation to which we owe allegiance, there are yet further obligation to common justice, decency, and the establishment of the power of right, not of expediency or might, among civilized nations.

/s/Stephen Kovalyak
/t/STEPHEN KOVALYAK
1st Lt. Inf., 0314411
(U.S. Zone)

/s/Patrick J. Kelleher
/t/PATRICK J. KELLEHER
Capt., TC, 01944717
Office of Military
Government for Land
Great Hesse

/s/Lamont Moore
/t/LAMONT MOORE
2nd Lt., AUS,02011967
Office of Military
Government (U.S. Zone)

/s/Samuel Ratensky
/t/SAMUEL RATENSKY
1st Lt., AUS, 02025813
Office of Military
Government for Land
Great Hesse

/s/Charles P. Parkhurst, Jr.
/t/CHARLES P. PARKHURST, Jr.
Lt., (jg), USNR, 298080

/s/Sheldon W. Keck
/t/SHELDON W. KECK
2nd Lt., AUS, 020255818

Office of Military
Government (U.S. Zone)

Office of Military
Government for Stadt-
kreis and Landkreis
Marburg

/s/Edith A. Standen
/t/EDITH A. STANDEN
Capt. WAC, L 117136
Office of Military
Government
(U.S. Zone)

/s/Walter I. Farmer
/t/WALTER I. FARMER
Capt., CE. 01108653
Office of Military
Government for Stadt-
kreis Wiesbaden

/s/Walker K. Hancock
/t/WALKER K. HANCOCK
Capt., Inf., 0515315
Office of Military
Government for
Stadtkreis and Land-
kreis Marburg

/s/Julius H. Buchman
/t/JULIUS H. BUCHMAN
Capt., FA, 01171068
Office of Military
Government for Stadt-
kreis Frankfurt

/s/Frederick C. Shrady
/t/FREDERICK C. SHRADY
2nd Lt., AUS, 02025315
Office of Military
Government for Land
Great Hesse

/s/Richard H. Kuhlke
/t/RICHARD H. KUHLKE
1st Lt., Ord., 01556305
Office of Military
Government for Stadt-
kreis Frankfurt

/s/Everett P. Lesley, Jr.
/t/EVERETT P. LESLEY, JR.
Capt., QMC, 01581907
The General Board,U.S.
Forces, European
Theater

/s/Theodore A. Heinrich
/t/THEODORE A. HEINRICH
2nd Lt., AUS, 02015985
Office of Military
Government for Regie-
rungsbezirk Kassel

/s/Clyde M. Harris
/t/CLYDE M. HARRIS
1st Lt., CE, 01116157
Office of Military
Government for Regie-
rungsbezirk Hessen

/s/Doda Conrad
/t/DODA CONRAD
1st Lt., AUS, 01691535
Office of Military
Government (U.S.)

/s/Edwin C. Rae
/t/EDWIN C. RAE
Capt., AC, 81643246
Office of Military
Government for Bavaria

/s/William A. Lovegrove
/t/WILLIAM A. LOVEGROVE
1st Lt., C?P, 01797674
Office of Military
Government (U.S. Zone)

/s/Edward J. Putrux
/t/EDWARD J. PUTRUX
Capt., QMC, 01575023
Office of Military
Government for Regie-
rungsbezirk Niederbayern
and Oberpfalz

/s/Walter W. Horn
/t/WALTER W. HORN
1st Lt. Inf., 01326328
Office of Military
Government (U.S. Zone)

/s/J. T. Morey
/t/J. T. MOREY
1st Lt., CE, 01113367
Office of Military
Government for Regie-
rungsbezirk Oberbayern

/s/Robert A. Koch
/t/ROBERT A. KOCH
1st Lt., AUS, 02011971
Office of Military
Government for Wurt-
tenberg - Baden

/s/Dale V. Ford
/t/DALE V. FORD
2nd Lt., CE, 01112695
Office of Militar Government
for Landkreis Heilbronn

/s/Thomas C. Howe, Jr.
/t/THOMAS C. HOWE, Jr.
Lt. Comdr., USNR, 237833
Office of Military
Government (U.S. Zone)

The following officers have expressed agreement with the sentiments of this paper but do not feel at liberty to sign any statement:-

JAMES J. RORIMER
Capt., AUS, O-537225
Office of Military Government
(Western District)

LESLIE J. POSTE
2nd Lt., AUS, 02025871
Office of Military Government
(Western District)

W.B. VAN NORTWICK
Capt., Inf. (Armd), O-1108653
Office of Military Government
for Stadtkreis Wiesbaden.

The following officers have expressed similar sentiments by means of separate letters to Major L.B. La Farge:-

JOHN H. COULTER
Lt. Cmdr., USNR, 13699
Office of Military Government
for Bavaria.(U.S.)

CRAIG H. SMYTH
Lt., USNR, 173178
Director, Munich Collecting Point

EDWARD E. ADAMS
CAPT., QMC, O-444547
Office of Military Government
(U.S. Zone)

HARRY D. R. GRIER
Capt., Inf., O-1305768
Office of Military Government
for Germany (U.S.)

KURT F. HAUSCHILDT
2nd Lt., AC., O-1540391
U.S. Headquarters Berlin District

The names listed above include 32 of the 35 MFA&A Specialist Officers now in Europe assigned to headquarters in Germany. No contact has been possible with the remaining three officers owing to the shortage of time and the distances involved.

It may also be noted that, while no attempt has been made to ascertain the opinion of the enlisted men and civilians in the Monuments, Fine Arts and Archives organization, nor of the personnel of American Monuments, Fine Arts and Archives organizations outside of Germany, all the individuals in these categories who have read this paper have expressed complete agreement with its sentiments.

German State Museum owned

Source or Owner	No. of cases or Items	Type of Material	WIE No.'s	Shipment	Status
Collections of Berlin State Museums					
I Antiken Abt.	89 cases	Classical Antiquities	between 1-1663	I 20-31 Aug 45	Spot checked.
II Ägyptische Abteilung	163 cases	Egyptian Antiquities	" 1-1663	I " "	Spot checked.
III Islamische Abteilung	49 cases	Ceramics, Sculpture, Carpets	" "	I " "	Checked by Frau Dr. Kühnel.
IV Gemälde Galerie	988 200	Paintings Paintings	" "	I " " I	Checked by Frau Dr. Kühnel. Out-Shipm. No. I 20 Nov 45
V Skulpturen-Abteilung	350 cases	Sculptures	" "	I " "	In process of checking.
IV Frühchristlich-byzantinische Sammlung	7 cases	Painting, Sculpture Ceramics, Jewelry	" "	I " "	Spot checked
VII Kupferstichkabinett	2300 portfolios	Prints, Drawings	1500	I " "	Spot checked. Accession lists screened. No easily identifiable loot.

German State Museum owned

Source or Owner	No. of cases or Items	Type of Material	WIE No.'s	Shipment	Status
VIII National-Galerie	391	Paintings	between 1-1663	I 20-31 Aug 45	Checked by Frau Dr. Kühnel.
"	2	Paintings	" " "	I "	Out-Shipment No 1 20 Nov 45
	288 cases	Decorative Arts	" " "	I "	Spot checked
IXa Schloss-Museum	30 cases	Tapestries	2045 B	XIII 13 Oct 45	Not processed.
	3 cases	Prussian Regalia	1839-1841	IX 17 Sept 45	Not processed.
b Kunst-gewerbe Museum	41 cases	Porcelaine	between 4413-4415	LIX 10 May 46	Not processed
	45 cases	Decorative Arts	between 1-1663	I 20-31 Aug 45	Spot checked
X Zeughaus	39 cases	Arms, Uniforms	between 1-1663	I???? 1 ????	Spot-checked,
	31 c???	???	" " "		Uniforms fumigated
"	51 cases	Flags etc	between 4413-4415	LIV 10 May 46	Not processed.
XI Museum für Deutsche Volkskunde	30 cases	Folk Art	" " "	I 20-31 Aug 45	" "
XII Völkerkunde-museum	92 cases	Ethnological Col-lection	" " "	I "	Spot checked
XIII Ostasiati-sche Kunst-abteilung	4 cases	Ceramics, Sculpt.	" " "	I "	Spot checked

German State Museum owned

Source or Owner	No. of cases or Items	Type of Material	WIE No.'s	Shipment	Status
XIV Museum für Vor- und Früh-geschichte	6 cases	Prehistorical Art	between 1-1663	I 20-31 Aug 45	Not processed
XV Staatl. Kunstbiblio-thek	14 cases 742 portfo-lios	Books and Plates	" "	I "	Spot checked
Collection of Verwaltung Schlösser u. Gärten, Pots-dam	6	Tapestries	4025 B	XIII 13 Oct 45	Not processed. Addi-tional 11 tapestries not identified.
	54 cases	Books, Engravings	4413-4415	LIV 10 May 46	Not processed.
	270	Paintings	4425	LIX 29 May 46	Photographed and Property Cards made at Marburg MAR 138-407
	3 cases	Books	4425 (MAR 319, 360, 361)	LIX 29 May 46	Not processed. Be-lieved to be part of Library of Fred. the Great.
	17	Furniture	4425 (MAR 3439-3458)	LIX 29 May 46	Not processed.
	3 cases	Porcelain, Glass Bronces	4425 (MAR 3457-3610, 2585-2699)	LIX "	Not processed.
Garnisonkirche	1 case	Textiles	4425 (MAR 410)	LIX "	Not processed

German Museum owned, Land Greater Hesse

Source	No. of objects	Type of Material	WIE No.'s	Shipment	Status.
Kassel Landesmuseum	55 cases	31 cases Prints and Drawings 12 cases Sculptures 12 cases objects d'art	between 1927-2009 " " " "	XXII - 5 Dec 45 " " " "	Not processed. Spot checked, no objects identifiable as removed from occupied countries discovered. Will be returned to Kassel.
Archeol. Museum Wiesbaden	20 cases 7	Sculptures, Ceramics Tapestries	between 3296-3322 " "	XXXIII 5 Mar 46	Not opened
Staatsarchiv Wiesbaden	1 case	Meussbach-Dillenburg Archives	1908	XIV 25 Oct 45	Stated by Netherlands Archival Representative to be not subject to restitution. Will be returned to Staatsarchiv, Wiesbaden
Städel and other Frankfurt Museums and private owners	approx. 20.000	Paintings Scuoöture, Drawings, Prints etc.	between 2051-2452 2453-2540 2541-2826 2827-3164 3166-3295 3323-3380 3385-3561 3624-3690 4059-4190	 XXVII 8 Feb 46 XXVIII 14 Feb 46 XXIX 14 Feb 46 XXX 21 Feb 46 XXXII 28 Feb 46 XXXIV 9 Mar 46 XXXVII 16 Mar 46 XL 21 Mar 46 XLV 10 Apr 46	In process of screening. Objects identifieable as having been removed from occupied countries restituted, internal loot of unknown ownership segregated, internal loot of known ownership listed.

German-Museum owned, Land Greater Hesse

Source	No. of objects	Type of Material	WIE No.'s	Shipment	Status.
Städel and other Frankfurt Museums and private owners. (cont.)	approx. 20.000	Paintings Sculpture Drawings Prints etc.	between 4191-4393 4197-4272 4298-4364 4365-4411	XLVI 16 Apr 46 XLIX 25 Apr 46 LI 29 Apr 46 LII 8 May 46	In process of screening. Objects identifiable as having been removed from occupied countries restituted, internal loot of inknown ownership segregated, internal loot of known ownership listed.

German-Museum Owned, Other Länder - US Zone

Institution	No. of objects or cases	Type of Material	WIE No.'s	Shipment	Status
Mannheim (Escheberg re-pos. through Marburg CCP)	34	Textiles	2014-2045	XIII 13 Oct 46	Not processed. Lists available.
Karlsruhe Museum	193	Paintings and Prints	between 1860-1888	XII 13 Oct 46	Screened for foreign purchases.
Staatsgalerie Stuttgart	1	Painting	3910	XLII 22 Apr 46	Returned to Stuttgart authorities Out-Shipment No 9 26 June 46

Loot from Poland

Source or Owner	No.'s of objects	Type of material	WIE No.'s	Shipment	Status
Lüneburg (Grasleben)	13 cases	Archeological material	between 1-1769	I 20-31 Aug 45	Out-Shipment No 4 17 April 46
Lüneburg (Grasleben)	773	Church Treasures	between 1-1769	I 20-31 Aug 45	Out-Shipment No 4 17 April 46

Hungarian State owned

Source or owner	No.'s of Objects	Type of material	WIE No.'s	Shipment	Status
Hungarian State	1 chest	Coronation Regalia	1842	IX 17 Sept 45	Sent to Munich Out-Shipment No 4 17 Apr 46

Objects readily identifiable as having been removed from France

German Holder	No. of objects	Tape of material	WIE No.'s	Shipment	Status
Frankfurt Museums (cont)	15	Sculptures	4198/1, 4250 4298, 4299 4373, 4375, 4378/1 4378/2, 4380, 4381, 4388/1, 4411	XLIX 25 Apr 46 LI 25 Feb 46 LI 8 May 46	Out-Shipment No 3 24 May 46 " " " " " "
	10	Drawings	4305/1, 4305/3-9 4305/11, 4305/12	XLI 21 Mar 46 " "	Out-Shipment No 3 24 May 46 " " "
	1	Print	4305/2	XLI 21 Mar 46	" " "
ELHAG Tauberbischofs-heim	33 4 13 22 4 9	Furniture Ceramics Paintings and Engravings Metalwork Sculpture Textile	3562-3616 " " " " " " " " " "	XXXVIII 16 Mar 46 " " " " " " " " " "	Out-Shipment No 3 24 May 46 " " " " " " " " " " " " " " "
Private Owners Frankfurt	1 5	Sculpture Sculptures	4412 4417-4421	LIII 9 May 46 LVI 18 May	Out-Shipment No 3 24 May 46 " " "

Objects readily identifiable as having been removed from France

German Holder	No. of objects	Type of material	WIE No.'s	Shipment	Status
Dr. Eckermann Wiesbaden	1	Chandelier	1664	IV 23 Aug 45	Out-Shipment No. 3 24 May 46
Haberstock, Karl	4	Paintings	1816, 1821, 1818, 1824	VI 23 Aug 45	Out-Shipment No. 3 24 May 46
Philipp Frank Heidelberg	1	Drawing	252	XIX 21 Nov	Out-Shipment No. 3 24 May 46
" "	16	Paintings Drawings Sculptures	1843-1858	X 21 Sept 45	Out-Shipment No. 3 24 May 46
Bertha Deutsch Wiesbaden	10	Paintings	1911-1920	XVII 14 Nov 45	Out-Shipment No. 3 24 May 46
Stadt Heidel-berg	1	Armor	262	XIX 21 Nov 45	Out-Shipment No. 3 24 May 46
Kunsthalle Karlsruhe	33 14 11 5 2 3 1 1	Paintings Drawings Metalwork Ceramics Prints Sculptures Woodwork Enamel	1860-1888/12	XII 12 Oct 45 " " " " " " " " " " " " " "	Out-Shipment No. 3 24 May 46 " " " " " " " " " " " " " "

Objects readily identifiable as having been removed
from France

German Holder	No. of objects	Type of material	WIE No.'s	Shipment	Status
Haus Solms Karlsruhe	24	Paintings	3623/9-34	XXXIX 20 Mar 46	Out-Shipment No. 3 24 May 46
	1	Drawing	3623/24	" "	" "
	1	Ceramics	3622	" "	" "
	527	Paintings, Prints etc	3623/36	" "	" "
	1 case	Household furnishings	3617	" "	" "
Adam Kramer Fulda (Marburg)	3	Woodreliefs	2011-2013	XXIV 13 Dec 45	Out-Shipment No. 3 24 May 46
Frankfurt Museums	24	Paintings	2212, 2223, 2399	XXVII 8 Feb 46	Out-Shipment No. 3 24 May 46
			2431		" "
			2870	XXVIII 14 Feb 46	" "
			2870, 3017	XXX 21 Feb 46	" "
			3325/1, 3325/2	XXXIV 9 Mar 46	" "
			3635, 3662, 3717	XL 21 Mar 46	" "
			3756, 3766		
			4061/1, 4061/2	XLV 10 Apr 46	" "
			4061/33, 4062/1		
			4063/1, 4064/1		
			4065/1, 4065/2		
			4066/1		
			4325	LI 29 Apr 46	" "
	15	Sculptures	2854	XXX 14 Feb 46	" "
			4108/1, 4108/2	XLV 10 Apr 46	Out-Shipment No. 3 24 May 46

Material from French Zone

Institution	No. of objects or unopened cases.	Type of material	WIE No.'s	Shipment	Status
Stiftung Heylshof, Worms	10	Paintings	1828-1830 1832-1838	VII 9 Sept 45	Processed
Städtische Gemäldegalerie und Altertumsmuseum, Mainz	33 50 124	Paintings Manuscripts Antiquities (Jewels etc)	1890-1907 " " " "	XX 27 Nov 45 " " " "	Not processed " " " "
Ludwigshafen	1	Painting	4034	XLIII 22 Mar 46	Not processed

Objects readily identifiable as having been removed from Holland.

German Holder	No. of objects	Type of material	WIE No.'s	Shipment	Status
Haberstock, Karl	1	Tapestry	4058	XLIV 24 Mar 46	Out-Shipment No. 5 1 May 46
Staatsarchiv Wiesbaden	62	Archives of Family Meuselbach Dillenburg	1890	XIV 25 Oct 45	Restitution stated by Netherlands Representative to be not necessary. Will be returned to Staatsarchiv Wiesbaden.
Kunsthalle Karlsruhe	26	Paintings	1861/3, 1861/4 1865/6, 1867/13 1867/20, 1869/4 1870/4, 1871/4 1872/1, 1872/2 1872/3, 1874/7 1879/2, 1879/4 1879/6, 1880/1 1881/1, 1882/2 1883/15, 1884/4 1884/5, 1884/8 1886/5, 1887/1 1864/2 4022	XII 12 Oct 45 XLIII 7 July 46	Out-Shipment No. 2 27 Mar 46 Out-Shipment No. 5 5 May 46 Out-Shipment No. 5 5 May 46
Haus Solms Karlsruhe	14 3 cases 446	Paintings Rugs Misc. items	3118/1-6 3123/1-8 3619-3621 3623/37	 XXXIX 20 mar 46 XXXIX 20 Mar 46	 Out-Shipment No. 2 27 Mar 46 Out-Shipment No. 5 1 May 46
Prof. Hethlage	2	Paintings	2047, 2048	XXIV 12 Oct 45	Out-Shipment No. 5 1 May 46

Objects readily identifiable as having been removed from Holland

German Holder	No. of objects	Type of material	WIE No. s	Shipment	Status
Städel-Institut Frankfurt/M	1	Sculpture	4263	XLOX 25 Apr 46	Out-Shipment No 5 1 May 46
" "	3	Painting	3408, 3649, 4300	XXXVII, 16 Mar 46 XL 21 Mar 46 LI 29 Apr 46	Out-Shipment No. 8 " "
Art dealer Frankfurt/M	2	Paintings	4427, 4428	LX 31 May 46	Out-Shipment No. 8
Art dealer Frankfurt/M	6 17 2	Paintings Drawings Maps	4429-4430	LXI 18 Jun 41	Ready for shipment.
Art dealer Frankfurt/M	3	1 Painting 1 bronze bell 1 candlestick	4431-4433	LXII 24 Jun 46	Ready for Shipment.

Material from British Zone

Institution or private Owner	No. of objects or unopened cases	Type of material	WIE No.'s	Shipment	Status
Kupferstichkabinett, Wallraf-Richartz Museum Köln	72 boxes 8 bundles	Prints	Not given	0 July 45	Out-Shipment No 7 4 June 46
Stadt Museum Düsseldorf	12 small packages and cases	Coins and Inventory	1839	VIII 12 Sept 45	Out-Shipment No 7 4 June 46
Kaiser-Wilhelm Museum und Heimathaus des Niederrhein, Krefeld	73 cases	Paintings, Sculptures etc.	between 3937-4057	XLIII 22 Apr 46	Out-Shipment No 7 4 June 46
Kunstgewerbe Museum, Köln	1 case	contens unknown	4044	XLIII 22 Apr 46	Out-Shipment No 7 4 June 46
Graf von Moltke Köln	2	Paintings	4021/1-4021/2	XLIII 22 Apr 46	Out-Shipment No 7 4 June 46
Georg Farbach (Dealer) Köln	15 cases	furniture and Procelaine	3896-4057	XLIII 22 Apr 46	Out-Shipmet No 7 4 June 46

Internal - Loot

German Holder and owner (if known)	No. of objects	Type of material	WIE No's	Shipment No.	Status
Kunsthalle Karlsruhe		Paintings	1867/19 1867/16	XII 12 Oct 45 " "	Property Cards made " "
Finanzamt Heidelberg and Mannheim	4		1865/5 1883/3	" " " "	" " " "
Polizeipräs. Heidelberg					
Institut für Erforschung der Juden-frage	90 4 18 68 1	Paintings Paintings Prints Drawings Box of Silver	3165/1-90 4422 " " 4424	XXXI 21 Feb 46 LVII 21 May 46 " " " " LVIII 24 May 46	Some owners, inclu-ding Alfred Oppenheim, identified.
University of Heidelberg, owner: Frau Leontine Gold-schmidt.	1	case said to contain cul-tural objects.	between 3896-4057	XLIII 22 Mar 46	Unopened, claim received, forwarded to Berlin.
Frankfurt Museums	34	Paintings	2020, 2445 2721, 2725 3113, 3132 3325/21	XXVII 8 Feb 46 XXIX 14 Feb 46 XXX 21 Feb 46 XXXIV 9 Mar 46	

Internal - Loot

German Holder and owner (if known)	No. of objects	Type of material	WIE No.'s	Shipment No.	Status
Frankfurt Museums (cont.)	16	Paintings	3445, 3446 3465, 6466	XXXVII 16 Mar 46	not processed
			4065/1, 4065/3 4065/26	XLV 10 Apr 46	"
			4384, 4385	LII 8 May 46	"
	15	Drawings	4305/13??? 4305/19	LI 29 Apr 46	"
			4423/1-10	LII 8 May 46	"
	2	Prints	4305/14 4305/15	LI 29 Apr 46	"
Karlsruhe	12	Paintings	3623/38/1- 3623/38/12	XXXIX 20 Mar 46	not processed

Nazi - Owned

Source	No. of objects	Type of material	WIE No.'s	Shipment	Status
Reichsbankneben-stelle, Heidelberg, through G 2 7th Army. Called „Hitler" or „Frank" Collection	16	Paintings	534, 1770, 1783, 1827	V 31 Aug 45	Processed Cards forwarded
Karl Haberstock, stated to have been bought from Non-Jewish Collections	3	Paintings	1823, 1817, 1814	VI 5 Sept 45	Processed, Cards forwarded
Karl Haberstock, stated to have been bought from Non-Jewish Collections	3 17	Paintings Paintings	1813, 1826, 1815 between 1927-2009	VI 5 Sept 45 XXII 5 Dec 46	Processed, Cards forwarded " "
Karl Haberstock, source unknown	2 2 4 3	Paintings Paintings Wood-carved Coat of Arms Sculptures	1809, 1825 4194, 4195 1786-1789 1790-1792	VI 5 Sept 45 XLVII 19 Apr 46 VI 5 Sept 45 VI 5 Sept 45	Processed, cards forwarded Not processed. Processed, cards forwarded Processed, Cards forwarded

Nazi - Owned

Source	No. of objects	Type of material	WIE No.'s	Shipment	Status
Sieger	19	Paintings	1804, 1798, 1794,	VI 5 Sept 45	Processed, Cards forwarded
			1803, 1801, 1796,	" "	" "
			1797, 1802, 1793,	" "	" "
			1822, 1810, 1811,	" "	" "
			1807, 1805, 1806,	" "	" "
			1819, 1808, 1820,	" "	" "
			1795	" "	" "
	4	Paintings	1923-1926	XXI 28 Nov 45	" "
	1	Sculpture	1812	VI 5 Sept 45	" "
	2	Books of prints	1799-1800	VI 5 Sept 45	" "
	2	Chasubles	1785	VI 5 Sept 45	" "
Goebbels house, Berlin	1	Painting	1910	XVI 30 Oct 45	Processed, cards forwarded
Gurlitt Hamburg	171	Paintings and Drawings	between 1927-2009	XXII 5 Dec 45	Processed, cards forwarded
G. Schmückle, Stuttgart	31	cases	between 1896-4057	XLIII 22 Mar 46	Not opened
Reichsstatthalterei, Stuttgart	37	cases porcelaine and glassware	between 3896-4057	XLIII 22 Mar 46	Not opened
	2	Paintings	3909, 3911	" "	"

Private Property deposited for safe keeping

Source or Owner	No. of objects	Type of material	WIE No.'s	Shipment	Status
Henkell Wiesbaden	2	Sculpture	1922, 2010	XVIII 20 Nov 45 XXIII 12 Dec 45	Property Cards made
Katzenstein Wiesbaden	3 1	Paintings sculpture	3381-3383 4303	XXXV 10 Mar 46 LI 29 Apr 46	Checked for condition. To be returned to owner on demand.
Volbach Estate Wiesbaden	1	Painting	3384	XXXVI 11 Mar 46	Checked for condition. To be returned to owner on demand.
Dr. Simon Wiesbaden	22	Furniture	4196	XLVIII 23 Apr 46	Not processed. To be returned to owner on demand.

Copy

Wiesbaden Collecting Point
Wiesbaden
Germany

19 November 1945

Receipt of Custody List of German - Owned Works of Art Designated for Shipment to the National Gallery of Art, Washington, D.C., U.S.A., for Safekeeping.

Case 1 (165)(10)

1. Giovanni Di Paolo, Legend of St. Clara 2171 (2 panels)
2. Jan van Eyck, Crucifixion 525 F
3. Master of Flémalle, Portrait of a Man 537 A
4. Altdorfer, Nativity 638 B
5. Konrad Witz, Crucifixion 1656
6. Elsheimer, St. Christopher 1707
7. Lucas van Leyden, Chess Players 574 A
8. Cranach, Lucretia 1832
9. Jan van Eyck, Giovanni Arnolfini 523 A
10. German Master (C.1400) Christ, Madonna, St. John 1837
11. Bouts, Madonna and Child 545 C
12. Elsheimer, Landscape with weeping Magdalena 1973
13. Cologne Master (C.1350) Madonna Enthroned, Crucifixion 1627
14. Altdorfer, Christ's Farewell to his Apostles 1883
15. Giovanni Di Paolo, Christ on the Cross 1112 B
16. Lorenzetti, P. Death of St. Humilitas 1077 A
17. Schongauer, Nativity 1629
18. Holbein, Portrait of a Man 586 B
19. Antonello da Messina, Portrait of a Man 18 A
20. Domenico Veneziano, Martyrdom of St. Lucy 64
21. Elsheimer, Holy Family 2039
22. Elsheimer, The Drunkeness of Noah 1843
23. Bouts, Virgin in Adoration (Fragment) 545 B
24. Petrus Christus, St. Barbara and a Carthusian Monk 523 B
25. Jan van Eyck, Knight of the Golden Fleece 525 G
26. French Master (C. 1400) ~~Triptych~~ 1620 DIPTYCH
27. Breughel, Two Monkies 2077
28. Altdorfer, Landscape with Satyr Family 638
29. Massys Magdalene 574 C
30. Jan van Eyck, Madonna in the Church 525 C
31. Petrus Christus, Portrait of a Girl 532

Acknowledge Receipt 19 Nov 1945
signed Lamont Moore
Lamont Moore 0-2011967
2nd Lt. AUS
MFA & A Spec O.

This is a certified copy:
Harry W. Adler
HARRY W. ADLER
[illegible]

Facsimile of the original case list of the "202", dated 19 Nov. 1945, assigned to Lamont Moore. WIF Papers.

Receipt of Custody List of German - Owned Works of Art Designat-
for Shipment to the National Gallery of Art, Washington, D.C.
U.S.A., for Safekeeping (Continued)

Case 2 (203) (6)

✓32. Lorenzetti St. Humilitas Raises a Nun 1077
✓33. Dürer, Madonna 557 H
✓34. Memling, Madonna and Schild 528 B
✓35. Mantegna Cardinal Mezzarota 9
✓36. Pollaiuolo, David 73 A
✓37. Cranach, Frau Reuss 1907
✓38. Jan van Eyck, Man with a Pink 525 A
✓39. Van der Weyden, Charles the Bold 545
✓40. Mostaert, Portrait of a Man 591
✓41. Van der Weyden, Portrait of a Woman 545 D
✓42. Watteau, Italian Comedians 470
✓43. Dürer, Hieronymus Holzschuher 557 E
✓44. Dürer, Young Woman 557 G
✓45. Geertgen, John the Baptist 1631

Case 3 (279) (19)

✓46. Raphael, Madonna Terranova 247 A
✓47. Domenico Veneziano, Adoration of the Kings 95 A

Case 4 (293) (81)

✓48. Gossaert, Christ on the Mountain 551 A
✓49. Botticelli, Venus 1124
✓50. Calf, Stillife 948 F

Case 5 (2) (27)

✓51. Van der Weyden, Bladelin Altar 535

Case 6 (273) (22)

✓52. Simon Marmion, Altar of St. Omer (Two Panels) 1645,1645 A

Case 7 (5) (28)

✓53. Fouquet, Etienne Chevalier & St. Stephen 1617
✓54. Dürer, Madonna with the Goldfinch 557 F

Case 8 (224) (15)

✓55. Raphael, Madonna Diotalevi 147
✓56. Giorgione, Portrait of a young man (VV) 12 A
✓57. Lippo Memmi, Madonna and Child 1067

Acknowledge Receipt 19 Nov 1945

signed Lamont Moore
Lamont Moore 0-2011967
2nd Lt AUS
MFA & A Spec.O

This is a certified
copy:

Harry A. Adler
Harry A. Adler
Captain C.E.

Receipt of Custody List of German-Owned Works of Art Designated for Shipment to the National Gallery of Art, Washington, D.C., U.S.A., for Safekeeping (Continued)

Case 9 (9) (14)

58. Bottecelli, Frame only for Giuliano de Medici 106 B
59. Signorelli, Portrait of a Man 79 C

Case 10 (310) (84)

60. Bronzino, Portrait of a Young Man 614
61. Bronzino, Portrait of a Young Man 347 I
62. Squarcione, Madonna and Child 27 A
63. Palma Vecchio, Young Woman 197 B
64. Palma Vecchio, Portrait of a Man 174

Case 11 (530) (37)

65. Hans Baldung Grien, Altar of Halle 603 A

Case 12 (295) (18)

66. Rembrandt, Rabbi 828 A
67. Rembrandt, Joseph and Potiphar's Wife 828 H
68. Rembrandt, Vision of Daniel 828 F
69. Hobbema, Landscape 1984
70. De Hoogh, The mother 820 B

Case 13 (140) (71)

71. Westphalian Master (C. 1250) Triptych 1216 B
72. Austrian Master (C. 1410) Crucifixion 1662
73. Cologne Master (C.1400) Life of Christ 1224
74. Baldung Grien, Pyramus and Thisbe 1875

Acknowledge Receipt 19 Nov 1945
signed Lamont Moore
Lamont Moore 0-201967
2nd Lt AUS
MFA & A Spec. O.

This is a certified copy:
Harry A. Adler
Harry A. Adler
Captain C.E.
Adm. Officer

Receipt of Custody list of German-Owned Works of Art Designated for Shipment to the National Gallery of Art, Washington, D.C., U.S.A., for Safekeeping, Cont.

Case 14 (196) (41)

75. Bronzino, Ugolino Martelli 338 A
76. De Hoogh, Party of Officers and Ladies 1401
77. Steen, The Christening 799 D
78. Daumier, Don Quixote, NG-10488

Case 15 (116) (46)

79. Lotto, Christ's Farewell to his Mother 325
80. Titian, Strozzi, Child 160 A
81. Del Piombo, San Dago Knight 259 A
82. Guardi, The Balcon Ascension 501 F
83. Piazzetta, in Venice (Guardi) 1836
84. Tiepolo, Rinaldo and Armida 459 D
85. Tintoretto, Old Man 298 B

Case 16 (74) (34)

86. Rubens, Perseus and Andromeda 785
87. Baldung, Lamentation for Christ 603 B

Case 17 (1887) (GV3)

88. Bosch, St.John on Patmos 1647 A
89. Sassetta, Mass of St. Francis 63 D
90 Botticelli, Somonetta Vespucci 106 A
91. Masaccio, Birth Platter 58 C
92. Rembrandt, Landscape with Bridge 1932

Case 18 (162) (123)

93. Del Piombo, Roman Matron 259 B
94. Rembrandt, John the Baptist 828 K
95. Van der Velde, The Farm 922 C
96. Filippino Lippi, Allegory of Music 78 A
97. Verocchio, Madonna and Child 108
98. Verocchio, Madonna and Child 104 A
99. Mainardi, Portrait of a Man 86
100. Tura St. Christopher 1170 C
101. Tura, St.Sebastian 1170 B

Case 19 (13) (30)

102. Patinir, Rest on the Flight 608
103. Memling, Madonna Enthroned 529
104. Burkmair, Holy Family 1732
105. Geertgen, Madonna 1853
106. Cranach, Rest on the Flight 564 A
107. Master of Flémalle, Crucifixion 538 A
108. Master of Virgin, Among Vergins Adoration of Kings 1672
109. Memling, Madonna Enthroned with Angels 529 D
110. van Cleve, Young Man 615
111. van Leyden, Madonna and Child 584 B
112. Bouts, Madonna 545 C

Duplicate No. 11

This is a certified copy:
Harry W. Adler
Harry W. Adler
Captain C.E.
Adm. Officer

Acknowledge Receipt 19 Nov 194
signed Lamont Moore
Lamont Moore 0-201196
2nd Lt. AUS
MFA & A Spec. O

- 4 -

Receipt of Custody List of German-Owned Works of Art Designated for Shipment to the National Gallery of Art, Washington, D.C., U.S.A., for Safekeeping, Cont.

Case 20 (73) (23)

✓113. Botticelli, Madonna of the Lilies 102 A

Case 21 (45) (117)

✓114. Poussin, Amaltea 467
✓115. Poussin, St.Mattheus 478 A
✓116. Lorrain, Italian Coast Landscape 448 B
✓117. Velasquez, Countess Olivares 413 E

Case 22 (564) (61)

✓118. Tizian, Venus with Organ Player 1849
✓119. Velasquez (?) or Sacchi (?), Alessandro del Borro 413 A

Case 23 (308) (38)

✓120. Castagno, Assumption of the Virgin 47 A
✓121. Bellini, The Resurrection 1177 A

Case 24 (554) (39)

✓122. Rubens, Isabella Brant 762 A
✓123. Rubens, Madonna Enthroned with Saints 780
✓124. Rembrandt, Rape of Proserpina 823
✓125. Rembrandt, Susanna and the Elders 828 E
✓126. Simone Martini, Burial of Christ 1070 A
✓127. Masaccio, Three Predellae 58 A, B, E
✓128. Masaccio, Four Saints (4panels) 58 D
✓129. French c. 1400, Coronation of the Virgin 1648

Case 25 (82) (74)

✓130. Master of Darmstdt Passion, Altar Wings (2) 1205/06

Case 26 (83) (75)

✓130 a. Master of Darmstadt Passion, Altar Wings (2) 1205/06

Case 27 (195) (118)

✓131. Caracciolo, Cosmas and Damian 1981
✓132. Tintoretto, Doge Mocenigo 2145
✓133. Pannini, Colosseum 454 A
✓134. Amigione, Lady as Diana 1659
✓135. Strozzi, Judith 1727

This is a certified copy:
Harry W. Adler
Captain C.E.
Adm. Officer

Acknowledge Receipt 19 November 1945
signed Lamont Moore
Lamont Moore 0-2011967
2nd Lt. AUS
M Fa & A, Spec.O

Receipt of Custody List of German-Owned Works of Art Designated for Shipment to the National Gallery of Art, Washington, D.C., U.S.A., for Safekeeping, Cont.

Case 28 (144) (62)

✓136. Cossa, Allegory of Autumn 115 A
✓137. Signorelli, Three Saints 79
✓138. Signorelli, Three Saints 79
✓139. Piero di Cosimo, Mars, Venus and Amor 107

Case 29 (139) (26)

✓140. Behemian c. 1350, Glatzer Madonna 1624
✓141. Giotto, Death of the Virgin 1884

Case 30 (307) (24)

✓142. Lippi, Adoration of the Child 69

Case 31 (298) (35)

✓143. Rubens, Andromeda 776 C
✓144. Bottecelli, St. Sebastian 1128

Case 32. (200) (33)

✓145. Breughel, Duch Proverbs 1720

Case 33 (320) (57)

✓146. Van der Weyden, Marienaltar 534 A
✓147. Van der Weyden, St. Johnsaltar 534 B

Case 34 (17) (21)

✓148. Amberger, Cosmograph Sebastian Münster 583
✓149. Holbein, Old Man 586 D
✓150. Raphael, Solly Madonna 141
✓151. Altdorfer, Rest on the Flight 638 B
✓152. Gossaert, Baudouin de Bourbon 586 A
✓153. Veneziano, Portrait of Young ~~XXX~~ Woman 1614
✓154. Dürer, Holzschuher Portrait 557 E
✓155. Seghers, Landscape 808 A
✓156. Sassetta, Legend of St. Francis 1945
✓157. Rembrandt, Minerva 828 C
✓158. Rembrandt, Self-Portrait 810
✓159. Ter Borch, The Concert 791 G
✓160. Botticelli, Guiliano de Medici 106 B
✓161. Baldung, Graf Löwenstein 1842
✓162. Di Credi, Young Girl 80

This is a certified copy:
Harry A. Adler
Harry W. Adler
Captain C.E.
Adm. Officer

Acknowledge Receipt 19 November 1945
signed Lamont Moore
Lamont Moore 0-2011967
2nd Lt. AUS
M Fa & A Spec.O

Receipt of Custody List of German-Pwned Works of Art Designate
for Shipment to the National Gallery of Art, Washingron, D.C.,
U.S.A., for Safekeeping. (Continued)

Case 35 (534) (29)

✓163. Ouwater, Raising of Lazarus 532 A
✓164. Holbein, George Giesze 586

Case 36 (291) (56)

✓165. Corregio, Leda and the Swan 218
✓166. Carpaccio, Entombment of Christ 23 A
✓167. Tiepolo, St. Agatha 459 B

Case 37 (1885) (228)

✓168. Chardin, The Draughtsman 2076
✓169. Hals, Hille Bobbe 801 C
✓170. Hals, Portrait of a Young Man 800
✓171. Vermeer, Man and Woman Drinking Wine 912 C

Case 38 (1875) (246)

✓172. Calf, Sitllife 948 D
✓173. Guardi, St.Mark's Plaza in Venice 501 G
✓174. Hals, Singing Boy 801 A
✓175. Ruijsdael, Haarlem View 885 C
✓176. Tiepolo, Carrying of the Cross 459 C

Case 39 (1881) (243)

✓177. Hals, Nurse and Child 801 G
✓178. Rembrandt, Tobias and the Angel 828 N
✓179. Rembrandt, Hendrickje Stoffels 828 G
✓180. Hals, Tyman OOsdorf 801 H

Case 40 (1861) (5)

✓181. Hals, Portrait of a Young Woman 801
✓182. Terborch, Fatherly Advice 79
✓183. Steen, Inn Garden 795
✓184. Chardin, Stillife 1944
✓185. Vermeer, Young Woman with a Pearl Necklace 912 B

This is a certified copy:
Harry W. Adler
Harry W. Adler
Captain C.E.
Adm. Officer

Acknowledge Receipt 19 Nov 1945
signed Lamont Moore
Lamont Moore 0-2011967
2nd Lt AUS
M FA & A Spec. O

Receipt of Custody List of German-Owned Works of Art Designated for Shipment to the National Gallery of Art, Washington, D.C., U.S.A., for Safekeeping. (Continued)

Case 41 (1864) (233)

✓186. Tizian, Lavinia 166
✓187. Tizian, Self Portrait 163
✓188. Tizian, Portrait of a Young Man 301
✓189. Mantegna, Presentation in the Temple 29

Case 42 (304) (36)

✓190. Konrad Witz, Decision of Redemption 1673
✓191. Rubens, St. Caecilia 781

Case 43 (1882) (2)

✓192. Rembrandt, Man with Gold Helmet 811 A
✓193. Rubens, Landscape (Shipwreck of Aeneas) 776 E
✓194. Rembrandt, Old Man with a Red Hat 828 J
✓195. Watteau, French Comedians 468

Case 44 (536) (40)

✓196. De la Tour, St. Sebastian 2046
✓197. Caravaggio, Amor 369
✓198. Rembrandt, Moses Breaking Law Tablets 811
✓199. Watteau, Fête Champetre 474 B
✓200. Koninck, Dutch Landscape 821 A
✓201. Manet, In the Wintergarden Nat.Gal. No. AI 550

Case 45 (8) (20)

✓202. Fra Angelic, Last Judgment (3 Panels) 60 A

Acknowledge Receipt 19 Nov 1945
signed Lamont Moore
Lamont Moore 0-2011967
2nd Lt. AUS
M FA & A Spec. O

This is a certified copy:
Harry A. Adler
Harry A. Adler
Captain C.E.
Adm. Officer

List of Paintings from the Kaiser Friedrich Museum: the "202"

Altdorfer, Albrecht
German c. 1480-1538

1. Departure of the Apostles
   Panel 16 3/4 x 12 3/4
2. The Nativity
   Panel 14 1/8 x 10
3. Landscape with a Satyr Family
   Panel 9 1/16 x 7 7/8
4. Rest on the Flight into Egypt
   Panel 22 7/16 x 15

Amberger, Christoph
German c. 1500-1561/62

5. The Cosmographer, Sebastian Munster
   Panel 21 1/4 x 16 1/2

Amigoni, Jacopo
Venetian c. 1675-1752

6. Portrait of a Lady as Diana
   Canvas 52 3/8 x 37

Angelico, Fra
Florentine 1387-1455

7. The Last Judgment
   Panel Center: 40 1/2 x 25 3/4
   Wings: 40 1/2 x 11 1/8

Antonello da Messina
Venetian c. 1430-1479

8. Portrait of a Young Man
   Panel 12 5/8 x 10 1/4

Austrian c.1410

9. The Crucified Christ Mourned by Mary and John
   Panel 33 1/2 x 31 7/8

Austrian c.1425

10. The Dead Christ Mourned by Mary and John
    Panel 9 7/8 x 13 3/8

Baldung, Hans (Grien)
German 1475/80-1545

11. Count vonLowenstein
    Panel 18 7/8 x 13 1/2
12. Pyramus and Thisbe
    Panel 36/5/8 x 26 1/4

This list was published by the National Gallery of Art for the exhibition which was held in Washington D.C., March 17 – April 18, 1948

Baldung, Hans (Grien) contd.	13. Mourning over the Body of Christ Panel 54 3/4 x 36 5/8 14. Saint George; Saint Catherine (a-b) Panel Wings each: 47 5/8 x 11 15. The Adoration of the Magi (c) Panel 47 5/8 x 27 1/2 16. Saint Mauritius; Saint Agnes (d-e) Panel Wings each: 47 5/8 x 11
Bellini, Giovanni Venetian c. 1430-1516	17. The Resurrection of Christ Panel 59 1/4 x 50 3/4
Bohemian c. 1350	18. Madonna and Child with Donor (Archbishop Ernst of Prague) Panel 73 1/4 x 37 3/8
Bosch, Hieronymus Dutch 1462-1516	19. Saint John on Mount Patmos Reverse: Passion of Christ Panel 15 3/4 x 10 3/8
Botticelli, Alessandro Forentine 1444/45-1510	20. Simonetta Vespucci Panel 18 11/16 x 13 3/4 21. Madonna and Child with Singing Angels Panel Diam. 52 1/8 22. Giuliano de' Medici Panel 22 3/8 x 15 1/4 23. Saint Sebastian Panel 76 3/4 x 29 1/2 24. Venus Canvas 62 1/4 x 27
Bouts, Dirk Dutch 1410/20-1475	25. Madonna in Adoration Panel 9 7/16 x 5 11/16
Bouts, Dirk (?)	26. Madonna and Child Panel 11 x 7 11/16
Bronzino, Angelo Florentine 1502-1572	27. Portrait of a Youth Panel 29 1/4 x 23 1/4 28. Ugolin Martelli Panel 40 1/8 x 26 3/8 29. Portrait of a Young Man Panel 33 7/8 x 26 3/8

Brueghel, Pieter, the Elder Flemish 1525(?)-1569	30. Flemish Folk Sayings Panel 46 x 64 1/8 31. Pair of Fettered Apes Panel 7 7/8 x 9
Burgkmair, Hans German 1473-1531	32. The Holy Family Panel 28 3/4 x 20 13/16
Campin, Robert (Master of Flemalle) Flemish c.1378-1444	33. The Crucifixion Panel 30 3/8 x 18 1/2 34. Portrait of a Man Panel 11 1/4 x 7
Caracciolo, Giovanni Battista Neapolitan 1570-1637	35. Two Physicians in the Role of Saint Cosmos and Saint Damian Canvas 38 3/4 x 50 1/4
Caravaggio, Michelangelo da Roman 1573-1610	36. Conquering Love Canvas 61 5/8 x 44 5/8
Carpaccio, Vittore Venetian c. 1455-1525/26	37. Burial of Christ Canvas 58 3/4 x 73 3/4
Castagno, Andrea del Florentine 1423-1457	38. The Assumption of the Virgin Panel 59 1/16 x 62 1/4
Chardin, Jean-Baptiste-Simeon French 1699-1779	39. The Draftsman Canvas 32 1/8 x 25 5/8 40. Still Life with Pheasant Canvas 28 3/4 x 23 5/8
Christus, Petrus Flemish c. 1446-1472	41. Saint Barbara Presents a Carthusian Monk to the Madonna Panel 7 1/2 x 5 1/2 42. Lady Talbot Panel 11 x 8 1/4
Cleve, Joos van, the Elder Flemish 1485-1540	43. Young Man with a Glove Panel 24 3/8 x 18 1/2
Cologne c. 1350	44. Madonna and Child Enthroned (a) 45. Crucifixion (b) Panel Each: 19 5/8 x 13 1/2

Cologne c. 1400	46. The Life of Christ Panel 32 1/4 x 43 3/4
Correggio (Antonio Allegri) Parmese 1494-1534	47. Leda and the Swan Canvas 61 1/2 x 76 3/4
Cossa, Francesco del Ferrarese 1435-1477	48. Allegory of the Harvest Panel 45 1/4 x 29 1/2
Cranach, Lucas, the Elder German 1472-1553	49. Lucretia Panel 14 x 8 1/2 50. Rest on the Flight into Egypt Panel 27 1/8 x 20 1/16 51. Frau Reuss Panel 20 7/16 x 14 1/8
Credi, Lorenzo di (?) Florentine 1459-1537	52. Portrait of a Young Lady Panel 19 x 12 3/4
Darmstadt Passion, Master of the Middle Rhenish c. 1440	53. The Madonna Enthroned (a) Panel 79 1/2 x 41 1/2 54. Adoration of the Magi (b) Panel 79 1/2 x 42 1/2 55. The Holy Trinity (c) Panel 79 1/2 x 42 1/2 56. Story of the Cross Panel 79 1/2 x 42 1/2
Domenico Veneziano Florentine	57. Martyrdom of Saint Lucy Panel 9 7/8 x 11 1/4
Domenico Veneziano (?)	58. Adoration of the Magi Panel Diam. 33 1/8 59. Portrait of a Young Lady Panel 20 1/16 x 13 3/4
Dürer, Albrecht German 1471-1528	60. Hieronymus Holzschuher (a,b) Panel 18 7/8 x 14 1/8 61. Madonna in Prayer Panel 20 7/8 x 16 7/8 62. Madonna with the Siskin Panel 35 7/8 x 30 63. Portrait of a Young Woman Panel 11 1/4 x 8 1/2

Elsheimer, Adam German 1578-1610	64. Landscape with Penitent Magdalen Copper 73/16 x 9 9/16 65. The Holy Family with Angels Copper 14 3/4 x 9 1/2
Elsheimer, Adam (?)	66. Noah's Thank Offering Copper 6 7/8 x 10 3/8 67. Saint Christopher Copper 8 1/4 x 11
Eyck, Jan van Flemish 1386-1441	68. Giovanni Arnolfini Panel 11 3/4 x 8 1/2 69. Madonna and Child in a Church Panel 12 3/16 x 5 1/2 70. Christ Crucified Canvas 16 15/16 x 10 1/4 71. The Man with the Pink Panel 16 1/4 x 12 3/8 72. Baldwin de Lannoy, Knight of the Golden Fleece Panel 10 1/4 x 7 7/8
Fouquet, Jean French 1415/20-1477/81	73. Etienne Chevalier and Saint Stephen Panel 36 5/8 x 33 1/2
French c.1400	74. Coronation of the Virgin Panel Diam. 8 1/16
French c. 1400	75. Christ on the Cross (a) 76. The Man of Sorrows (b) Panel Each: 13 x 10 7/16
Geertgen Tot Sint Jans Dutch c. 1465-c. 1495	77. John the Baptist in the Wilderness Panel 16 1/2 x 11 78. Madonna and Child Panel 31 7/8 x 20 1/2
Giorgione Venetian c. 1478-1510	79. Portrait of a Young Man Canvas 22 3/4 x 17 7/8
Giotto di Bondone Florentine c. 1266-1337	80. Death of the Virgin Panel Center: 29 1/2 Ends: 20, Length 70 1/4

Giovanni di Paolo Sienese c. 1403-1482	81. The Crucifixion Panel 12 5/8 x 9 1/16 82. Admission of Saint Clara to a Cloister (a) Panel 7 5/8 x 11 9/16 83. Saint Clara Aids the Shipwrecked (b) Panel 7 5/8 x 11 9/16
Gossaert, Jan (Mabuse) Flemish 1478-1533/36	84. Christ in the Garden of Gethsemane Panel 33 1/2 x 24 3/4 85. Baudouin de Bourbon Panel 21 1/4 x 15 3/8
Guardi, Francesco Venetian 1712-1793	86. Balloon Ascension on the Giudecca Canvas 27 3/8 x 21 1/8 87. The Piazzetta in Venice Canvas 12 1/16 x 18 88. Piazza San Marco, Venice Canvas22 1/8 x 26 3/4
Hals, Frans Dutch 1580-1666	89. Portrait of a Young Man Canvas 29 7/8 x 24 1/8 90. Portrait of a Young Woman Canvas 29 7/8 x 24 1/8 91. Singing Boy with a Flute Canvas 27 x 21 5/8 92. Tyman Oosdorp Canvas 31 1/2 x 29 1/16 93. The Witch of Haarlem, Malle Bobbe Canvas 31 x 26 1/4 94. The Child-Nurse and her Charge Canvas 35 7/8 x 26 3/4
Hobbema, Meindert Dutch 1638-1709	95. A Road Winding amongst Clumps of Trees and Small Farms Canvas 38 3/8 x 50 3/4
Holbein, Hans, the Younger German 1497-1543	96. Portrait of an Elderly Man Panel 20 1/8 x 14 9/16 97. George Gisze Panel 38 1/2 x 33 7/8 98. Hermann Hillebrandt Wedigh Panel 15 3/8 x 11 3/4

Hooch, Pieter de Dutch 1629-c. 1683	99. The Mother Canvas 37 1/2 x 40 3/8
Hooch, Pieter de (?)	100. The Bugler Canvas 34 1/2 x 37 1/2
Kalf, Willem Dutch 1622-1693	101. Still Life Canvas 26 3/4 x 21 1/2 102. Still Life Canvas 26 1/8 x 20 5/8
Koninck, Philips Dutch 1619-1688	103. Panorama of Holland Canvas 36 3/8 x 66 1/4
La Tour, Georges de French 1600-1652	104. Saint Sebastian Mourned by Saint Irene and her Ladies Canvas 64 1/8 x 51
Leyden, Lucas van Dutch 1494-1533	105. The Chess Players Panel 10 5/8 x 13 3/4 106. Madonna and Child with Angels Panel 29 1/8 x 17 5/16
Lippi, Filippino Florentine 1457-1504	107. Allegory of Music Panel 24 x 20
Lippi, Fra Filippo Florentine c. 1406-1469	108. The Madonna Adoring the Christ Child Panel 51 x 46 3/4
Lorenzetti, Pietro Sienese Mentioned 1306-1348	109. Saint Humilitas Heals a Sick Nun (a) Panel 18 1/8 x 22 1/4 110. Death of Saint Humilitas Panel 16 1/2 x 12 1/4
Lorrain, Claude (Gellee) French c. 1600-1682	111. Italian Coastal Landscape in Early Morning Light Canvas 39 1/4 x 53 11/8
Lotto, Lorenzo Venetian c. 1480-1556	112. Jesus Takes Leave of His Mother Canvas 50 1/8 x 40 1/8
Mainardi, Sebastiano Florentine c. 1460-1513	113. Portrait of a Young Man with a Red Cap Panel 17 x 13

Mantegna, Andrea Paduan 1431-1506	114. Cardinal Lodovico Mezzarota Panel 17 3/8 x 13 115. Presentation in the Temple Canvas 27 x 34
Marmion, Simon French Active 1454-1489	116. Altar of Saint Omer (a) Life of Saint Bertin Panel 22 x 57 7/8 117. Altar of Saint Omer (b) Life of Saint Bertin Panel 22 x 57 7/8
Martini, Simone Sienese 1284-1344	118. The Burial of Christ Panel 9 1/4 x 6 5/8
Masaccio Florentine 1401-1428	119. Adoration of the Magi (a) Panel 8 3/4 x 24 1/4 120. Martyrdom of Saint Peter; Martyrdom of Saint John the Baptist (b) Panel 8 3/4 x 24 1/2 121. Saint Julian Slays His Parents; Saint Nicholas Endows Three Maidens (c) Panel 8 3/4 x 24 3/4 122. The Four Saints Predella (a) An Elderly Carmelite Panel 15 x 4 7/8 123. The Four Saints Predella (b) Saint Augustine Panel 15 x 4 7/8 124. The Four Saints Predella (c) Saint Jerome Panel 15 x 4 7/8 125. The Four Saints Predella (d) A Young Carmelite Panel 15 4 7/8 126. Felicitations at the Birth of a Florentine of a Patrician Family Panel Diam 22
Memling, Hans Flemish c. 1433-1494	127. Madonna and Child Panel 16 15/16 x 12 1/4 128. Madonna and Child Panel 31 7/8 x 21 5/8

Memling, Hans (contd.)	129. Madonna and Child Panel 26 x 18 1/4
Memmi, Lippo Sienese Active 1317-1347	130. Madonna and Child Panel 30 3/8 x 21 5/8
Metsys, Quentin Flemish 1465/66-1530	131. The Mourning Magdalen Panel 13 x 9 1/2
Mostaert, Jan Dutch c.1475-1555/56	132. Portrait of a Man Panel 16 1/2 x 11 3/8
Ouwater, Aelbert van Dutch Active 1430-1460	133. Resurrection of Lazarus Panel 48 x 36 1/4
Palma Vecchio Venetian c.1480-1528	134. Portrait of a Man Panel 29 1/8 x 24 135. A Young Woman Panel 28 3/4 x 22 7/8
Panini, Giovanni Paolo Roman 1691/92-1765	136. Composite View of the Ruins of Rome Canvas 39 1/4 x 53 3/4
Patinir, Joachim Flemish c.1485-1524	137. Rest of the Flight into Egypt Panel 24 3/8 x 30 3/4
Piero di Cosimo Florentine 1462-c. 1521	138. Venus, Mars and Amor Panel 28 3/8 x 71 3/8
Pollaiuolo, Antonio Florentine 1432-1498	139. David with the Head of Goliath Panel 18 1/8 x 13 3/8
Poussin, Nicolas French 1593-1665	140. The Roman Campagna with Saint Matthew and the Angel Canvas 39 3/8 x 53 3/16 141. Jupiter Nourished by the Goat Amalthea Canvas 39 1/2 x 53 1/4
Raphael Umbrian 1483-1520	142. Madonna and Child Panel 20 1/2 x 15 143. Madonna and Child with the Little Saint John Panel Diam. 337/8

Raphael (contd.)	144. Madonna and Child with the Little Saint John Panel 27 1/8 x 19 11/16
Rembrandt Dutch 1606-1669	145. Daniel's Vision Canvas 38 7/8 x 46 3/4 146. Hendrickje Stoffels Canvas 35 x 26 1/2 147. Landscape with a Bridge Panel 11 1/4 x 15 5/8 148. The Man with the Golden Helmet Canvas 26 5/8 x 20 149. Moses Breaking the Tablets of the Law Canvas 66 x 53 3/4 150. Old Man with the Red Cap Canvas 20 1/2 x 15 151. Minerva Panel 23 7/8 x 19 3/8 152. Potiphar's Wife Accuses Joseph Canvas 45 x 35 5/8 153. The Preaching of John the Baptist Canvas on Oak 24 3/8 x 31 1/2 154. Prosperine Panel 32 11/16 x 30 3/4 155. A Rabbi Canvas 44 1/8 x 33 1/8 156. Saskia Panel 28 3/8 x 23 1/4 157. Self Portrait Panel 23 x 18 3/4 158 Susanna and the Elders Panel 29 15/16 x 35 7/8 159. Tobias and the Angel Canvas 34 1/4 x 30 1/8
Rubens, Peter Paul Flemish 1577-1640	160. Andromeda Panel 74 1/8 x 37 161. Isabella Brandt Panel 37 3/4 x 27 9/16 162. Landsacpe with the Shipwreck of Aeneas Canvas 24 1/4 x 39 1/2

Rubens, (contd.)	163. Madonna and Child Enthroned with Saints Panel 31 1/8 x 21 5/8 164. Perseus Frees Andromeda Panel 39 x 54 165. Saint Cecilia Panel 69 3/8 x 54 1/2
Ruisdael, Jacob van Dutch 1628/29-1682	166. Haarlem from the Dunes at Overveen Canvas 21 1/8 x 26 1/4
Sacchi, Andrea (?) Roman 1599-1661	167. Alessandro del Borro (?) Canvas 80 x 7/8 x 48 1/2
Sassetta Sienese c. 1392-1450	168. Episode from the Legend of Saint Francis Panel 18 x 23 1/2 169. The Mass of Saint Anthony Panel 18 1/8 x 12 13/16
Schongauer, Martin German 1445-1491	170. The Nativity Panel 14 3/4 x 11
Sebastiano del Piombo Venetian c. 1485-1547	171. Portrait of a Young Lady of Rome Panel 30 x 23 5/8
Sebastiano del Piombo (?)	172. A Nobleman in the Costume of a Knight of Saint James Canvas 44 7/8 x 36 1/2
Seghers, Hercules Dutch 1589-1645	173. View of Rhenen Panel 16 3/4 x 26 1/4
Signorelli, Luca Umbrian c. 1441-1523	174. Portrait of an Elderly Man Panel 19 11/16 x 12 5/8 175. Saint Catherine of Siena, the Magdalen and Saint Jerome (a) Panel 56 3/4 x 29 1/8 176. Saint Augustine, Saint Anthony of Padua and Saint Catherine of Alexandria Panel 56 3/4 x 29 1/8

Squarcione, Francesco
Paduan 1397-1468

177. Madonna and Child
Panel 31 1/2 x 26 3/8

Steen, Jan
Dutch c. 1626-1679

178. Baptismal Party
Canvas 32 11/16 x 39
179. The Garden of the Inn
Canvas 27 3/8 x 23

Strozzi, Bernardo
Genoese 1581-1644

180. Judith with the Head of Holofernes
Canvas 49 7/8 x 39 1/8

Ter Borch, Gerard
Dutch 1617-1681

181. The Concert
Panel 22 1/2 x 24 3/8
182. Fatherly Advice
Canvas 28 1/4 x 24 3/8

Tiepolo, Giovanni Battista
Venetian 1696-1770

183. Martyrdom of Saint Agatha
Canva 74 x 53 1/4
184. Rinaldo in Armida's Enchanted Garden
Canvas 15 1/2 x 24 1/2
185. Via Crucis
Canvas 21 1/8 x 25 5/8

Tintoretto, Jacopo
Venetian 1518-1594

186. Doge Mocenigo
Canvas 43 1/2 x 38
187. Portrait of a Man with a Long White Beard
Canvas 23 x 17 1/2

Titian,
Venetian c. 1477-1576

188. A Daughter of Roberto Strozzi
Canvas 47 7/8 x 41 1/4
189. Portrait of a Young Man
Canvas 38 1/2 x 29 7/8
190. Self Portrait
Canvas 39 3/8 x 30 3/8
191. Titian's Daughter, Lavinia
Canvas 41 x 32 1/2
192. Venus with the Organ Player
Canvas 47 3/4 x 85 1/4

Tura, Cosimo
Ferrarese c. 1430-1495

193. Saint Christopher
Panel 29 1/2 x 12 5/8
194. Saint Sebastian
Canvas 28 3/4 x 11 13/16

Velazquez de Silva, Diego Spanish 1599-1660	195. Countess Olivares Canvas 48 1/2 x 39 5/8
Velde, Adriaen van de Dutch c. 1636-1672	196. The Farm Canvas on Wood 24 3/4 x 30 3/4
Vermeer, Jan Dutch 1632-1675	197. The Pearl Necklace Canvas 22 1/8 x 18 1/2 198. The Taste of Wine Canvas 26 3/4 x 31
Verrocchio, Andrea del Florentine 1435-1488	199. Madonna and Child Panel 28 3/8 x 20 7/8 200. Madonna and Child Panel 29 1/8 x 18 1/8
Virgo Inter Virgines, Master of the Dutch Active c. 1480-1500	201. Adoration of the Magi Panel 24 3/4 x 18 7/8
Watteau, Antoine French c. 1684-1721	202. The French Comedians Canvas 15 1/8 x 19 1/4 203. The Italian Comedians Canvas 14 9/16 x 18 7/8 204. Outdoor Festival Canvas 45 1/4 x 65 3/4
Westphalian c. 1250-1270	205. Altarpiece: The Trinity with the Virgin and Saint John
Weyden, Rogier van der Flemish 1399/1400-1464	206. Charles the Bold, Duke of Burgundy Panel 19 1/4 x 12 5/8 207. The Nativity (a) Panel 35 7/8 x 35 208. Augustine and the Tiburtine Sibyl (b) Panel 35 7/8 x 15 3/4 209. The Magi (c) Panel 35 7/8 x 15 3/4 210. The Saint John Altar The Life of Saint John Panel Each: 30 3/8 x 18 7/8 211. Portrait of a Young Woman Panel 18 1/2 x 12 5/8
Weyden, Rogier van der (School of)	212. Joys and Sorrows of Mary Panel Each: 27 7/8 x 16 7/8

Witz, Konrad
German c. 1398-1447

213. The Decision on the Redemption of Man
214. The Crucifixion
Canvas 13 3/8 x 10 1/4

List of Paintings from the Nationalgalerie:

Daumier, Honoré
French 1808-1879

215. Don Quixote
Canvas 32 3/8 x 10 1/4

Manet, Edouard
French 1832-1883

216. The Greenhouse
Canvas 45 3/4 x 59 1/2

The attributions of the paintings in this list are taken from the Berlin catalogues.

The increase in the checklist results from the NGA's system of counting polyptypchs.

Appendix III

IIIa Miscellaneous Papers (page 197)

These documents, dated between April 10, 1945 and September 24, 1945, give some evidence of the political background and the debate on restitution and restitution in kind, that led to the decision of the transfer of the "202" paintings to the U.S. in November 1945. All these papers have been classified for many years, their contents were only known as "rumors" by most of the members of the MFA&A. The copies, published here, were found in the microfilmed U.S. files of OMGUS, filmed for the German *Bundesarchiv* in Coblenz and the *Institut für Zeitgeschichte* in Munich in 1977 to 1981. No reference can be given for today's location in the National Archives, Washington D.C. (NARA), because the filming took place before the final cataloguing there. Copies in WIF papers, NGA Washington D.C. (KG).

IIIb Nefertiti (page 208)

Five documents, given here as facsimiles, refer to Egypt's early request for the return of the famous head of Queen Nefertiti. These documents give evidence similar to those in Appendix IIIa of what was happening on a higher level in Military Government in 1945 and 1946. The contents of these papers were not known to most staff members of the US MFA&A at that time.

POLAD 728/11c

TOP SECRET TOP SECRET

SHAEF

STAFF MESSAGE CONTROL

INCOMING MESSAGE

EYES ONLY

WAR

SHAEF FWD 196/20

TOO 101947Z Apr TOR 102314B Apr

TOP SECRET

URGENT

FROM : AGWAR FROM GENERAL MARSHALL

TO : SHAEF FORWARD FOR GENERAL EISENHOWER FOR HIS EYES ONLY

REF NO : W-65929, 10 April 1945

For your information the following memorandum has been received from the State Department and has the approval of the Treasury Department:

"It has come to the Department's attention that American Armed Forces have captured in GERMANY a quantity of gold, foreign currencies and art treasures. Pending final decision as to the ultimate disposition of the foregoing, which will require careful study and probable consultation with our Allies, the State Department hopes that this treasure may be moved to a place of safekeeping in the proposed American Zone of Occupation in GERMANY for the time being and carefully guarded. The Department feels that this temporary solution will be less likely to cause unfortunate political complications".

Please keep me advised on this subject.

DISTRIBUTION:

1. SUPREME COMMANDER
2. CHIEF OF STAFF
3. Gen. McSherry (Personal) Action
4. Mr. Murphy ✓
5.

711.2

COPY NO 47

TOP SECRET

Letter to Eisenhower re capture of gold.

TOP SECRET

URGENT

FROM : AGWAR FROM GENERAL MARSHALL

TO : SHAEF FORWARD FOR GENERAL EISENHOWER FOR HIS EYES ONLY

REF NO: w-69929, 10 April 1945

For your information the following memorandum has been received from the State Department and has the approval of the Treasury Department:

"It has come to the Department's attention that American Armed Forces have captured in GERMANY a quantity of gold, foreign currencies and art treasures. Pending final decision as to the ultimate disposition of the foregoing, which will require careful study and probable consultation with our Allies, the State Department hopes that this treasure may be moved to a place of safekeeping in the proposed American Zone of Occupation in GERMANY for the time being and carefully guarded. The Department feels that this temporary solution will be less likely cause unfortunate political complications".

Please keep me advised on this subject.

DISTRIBUTION:

1. SUPREME COMMANDER

2. CHIEF OF STAFF

3. GEN. McSherry (Personal) Action

4. Mr. Murphy

5.

COPY NO 4

Letter to Eisenhower re capture of gold ... retyped.

U. S. GROUP, CONTROL COUNCIL (GERMANY)
REPARATION, DELIVERIES AND RESTITUTION DIVISION
Monuments, Fine Arts and Archives Branch
APO 742

JNB/ejb

TAS
A

9 August 1945.

SUBJECT: Comments on Document, "Art Objects in US Zone", transmitted by C of S to Col JEFFERSON, RD&R Division, US Group CC, under date 29 July 1945.

TO : Deputy Military Governor, US Group CC (GERMANY)
APO 742, US Army.

I. DISCUSSION

1. The subject document divides all works of art in US Zone into three classes and makes recommendations as to the disposal of each. The following discussion of each class is submitted.

2. Class "A".

a. Quote:

"consisting of works of art taken from the countries overrun by Germany readily identifiable as publicly owned, and works of art taken from private owners of overrun countries by seizure and without compensation."

"It is recommended that all works of art in Class "A" be returned to the country of origin as rapidly as arrangements can be affected, without conditions."

b. Comment:

Reference is made to a Staff Study entitled "Return of Works of Art, Archives, and other cultural Materials in Anticipation of Restitution", dated 17 June 1945.

The action recommended, namely, the immediate return of objects in Class "A", follows substantially the recommendations in the Staff Study, and is approved, subject to technical conditions to be included in receipt.

3. Class "B".

a. Quote:

John Nicolas Brown: "Art Objects in US Zone" (August 9, 1945) "consisting of works of art taken from private collectors in the overrun countries for which some compensation is alleged to have been made to the owner."

"It is recommended that works of art in Class "B" be returned to the countries of origin and that receipts be taken for the amount of compensation alleged to have been paid by the Germans, with these values possibly to be considered as reparations payment to the several countries to which these works of art are returned."

b. Comment:

It is submitted that this question of the ownership of each object is at issue. The author of the subject document states in par. 4., "while there may be some doubt as to the return of all works of art in Class "B" to their original owners, it is believed that the US will desire these works of art to be returned to the country from which they were taken." It would seem, therefore, that before works of art in Class "B" are finally returned that there be an adjudication of title. Merely the fact that some compensation is alleged to have been made to the owners would seem hardly enough to justify action recommended, namely the return to the countries of origin, even with the corollary that this alleged amount of compensation be charged against the reparations account. For instance, if the title, and ownership, is judged to be in a French national, then the object should be returned to the French Government which should give receipt for the amount of compensation involved as laid down in the subject document's recommendations; but if the sale is considered bona fide then the object falls into Class "C". The dealings of the art world were so intricate and so devious that it is submitted that there must be adjudication after evidence and by a suitably set up judicial authority before objects in Class "B", as defined in the Subject document, can safely be returned.

4. <u>Class "C".</u>

a. Quote:

"consisting of works of art placed in the US zone by Germany for safe keeping which are bona fide property of the German nation."

"It is recommended that the works of art in Class "C" be removed to the US as rapidly as arrangements can be affected and distributed among the museums in the US properly equipped to handle these works of art. It is suggested that they be placed on exhibit in the US, but that an announcement be made to the public, to include the German people, that these works of art will be held in trusteeship for return to the German nation when it has re-earned its right to be considered as a nation."

2

b. Comment:

The undersigned strongly protests the action contemplated, ans submits the following arguments against it:

(1) There are no works of art which in a technical and legal sense are the "property of the German nation." The German Museums were not at the Reich level.

(2) The author of the subject document was under a grave misapprehension when he made the statement, contained in the first par. of Section 3, that "neither expert personnel nor satisfactory facilities are available in the US Zone to properly safeguard and handle these priceless works of art." Some of the most competent men in the museum field are serving as MFA&A Specialist Officers, and already the vast majority of the most important and valuable works of art owned in Germany are found in the US Zone are under their care and control. There is therefore no reason to take Class "C" objects to the US simply to keep them from harm. Indeed the shipping and transportation of these objects, most of which are delicate, entail a grave risk and responsibility in itself.

(3) It is manifestly impossible to take all the thousands of objects back to the US "to be inventoried, identified and cared for by our leading museums" as suggested in par. 4 of the subject document. If there is to be a selection, then this identification must be made in Germany. For this purpose there are many European art historians, scholars and technicians available to supplement US Army personnel.

(4) Many objects in the US Zone belong to institutions in other Zones. For instance, pictures found in the mines at SIEGEN, and now safely stored and expertly cared for at MARBURG, both in the US Zone, came from the Museums of COLOGNE, DUSSELDORF and other institutions in the British Zone. Likewise the great treasures found at MERKERS which is now in the Russian Zone, and presently to be placed in the Collecting Point at WIESBADEN, come from the museums in the Russian sector of BERLIN.

(5) The taking of masterpieces of art, regardless of their number, which have been part of GERMANY's national cultural heritage for years past, by the US for distribution among museums in the US under the questionable legal fiction of "trusteeship" seems to the writer, and to his associates in the MFA&A Branch not only immoral but hypocritical. He believes that any such action on the part of the US would be regarded by her allies with distrust and disfavor and would have a seriously adverse effect upon the course of the program of reeducation which the US is attempting to promulgate in Germany itself. For the US to take priceless treasures which all the world would recognize as bona fide property of

the great German museums and transport them 3000 miles, or more, under the guise of taking them "in trusteeship for return to the German nation when it has re-earned its right to be considered as a nation", would be to cast but a thin veil over an act based upon the principles against which we have been fighting. All through the operational phase of MFA&A it was constantly said by our officers in the field that the US Army had established this service in order to preserve and protect works of art and not for the purpose of carrying them off to the USA, as was often accused by our Allies as well as by enemy propaganda. To have the German propaganda turn out to be true would indeed be humiliating.

(6) Many of the objects referred to in Class "C" are church property and on no account should be allowed to be taken to the US without the consent of the ecclesiastical owners.

(7) It is suggested, however, that a series of loan exhibitions could well be arranged; that pending the reerection of suitable museum display facilities in Germany, that the reactivated, de-Nazified German Museum institutions would gladly lend the cream of their less fragile treasures to the US as well as to the formerly occupied countries which have suffered such great artistic losses due to Nazi barbarism, and that in this way the world could enjoy these works of art which perforce must otherwise remain in repositories and collecting points until Germany is rebuilt. But these objects should come to the US as German property and not as taken by some quasi legal act of war.

5. Attention is invited to a memorandum entitled "Suggested Plan for the Restitution of Works of Art taken by Germans from Occupied Territories", dated 27 July 1945, which the undersigned prepared in Berlin before he had seen the subject document and in anticipation of a call for his opinion and advice.

II. ACTION RECOMMENDED.

That since it will be physically impossible to arrange for the transport to the US of any works of art for some time, that no publicity be given to recommendation c. in Section 5 of the subject document, at this time.

John Nicholas Brown
JOHN NICHOLAS BROWN
Adviser on Cultural Matters.

UNITED STATES POLITICAL ADVISER
FOR GERMANY

21 August 1945.

SECRET

MEMORANDUM

TO : Lieutenant General Lucius D. Clay,
Deputy Military Governor, Germany.
Brigadier General C. L. Adcock,
Assistant Chief of Staff, G-5, USFET.
Colonel L. W. Jefferson,
Director, M.F.A. and A. Division, US Group CC.

FROM: Political Adviser.

You may be interested in the following message received from the Department of State:

"The Department of State, while agreeing that the announcement made on the removal of German art to the United States should omit reference to German obligation to make replacement in kind, is disturbed by the view that Germans should not be required to replace looted art not found or destroyed.

"In the past the Department of State has always accepted replacement in kind with respect to restitution of art as distinct from restitution of objects of no unique cultural value. The Department transmitted to Winant on June 5 a draft agreement on restitution of art approved by State-War-Navy Coordinating Committee and the Roberts Commission which provided that "if works of art, books, historic or artistic archives, and other artistic or historic property known to have been looted cannot be found within a period of two years after the unconditional surrender or defeat of Germany, there shall be an obligation on Germany to replace such articles by comparable objects from German collections, public or private." Moreover, replacement in kind will be strongly insisted upon by all countries which lost part of their cultural patrimony to the Germans."

Robert Murphy.

Robert Murphy: Robert Murphy "replacement in kind" (August 31, 1945).

ADDRESS OFFICIAL COMMUNICATIONS TO
THE SECRETARY OF STATE
WASHINGTON, D. C.

DEPARTMENT OF STATE
WASHINGTON

September 14, 1945

SECRET

My dear Mr. Chairman:

As you know, the President approved at the Berlin Conference a proposal by General Clay to transfer works of art of bona fide German ownership to the United States for safekeeping pending their eventual return to Germany.

The National Gallery of Art would seem to be the most appropriate instituion to assume the responsibility for the custody, and to handle the storage and protection, of this art in the United States. I hope, therefore, that the National Gallery can assume these functions. The Department of State is, of course, prepared to support a request by the National Gallery for additional funds necessary to the discharge of this task.

General Clay has been asked to supply information regarding the storage space needed for the art destined for shipment. Since existing facilities for storage and safekeeping in Germany are highly inadequate, I trust that the National Gallery will be able to make prompt arrangements for the reception and storage of this art in the United States so that shipments can commence in the very near future.

Sincerely yours,

Dean Acheson

Acting Secretary

The Honorable Harlan F. Stone,
Chairman, Board of Trustees,
National Gallery of Art,
Washington, D. C.

Dean Acheson: re safekeeping of German-owned art (September 14, 1945).

UNIT AL ADVISER
FOR GERMANY

URGENT 14 September 1945.

MEMORANDUM

TO : Lieutenant General Lucius D. Clay,
Deputy Military Governor, Germany.
Colonel L. W. Jefferson, Director,
R D and R Division, US Group CC.

FROM: Political Adviser.

With reference to our conversation and my memorandum of August 30 regarding the shipment of German art to the United States, the Department of State now telegraphs the text of the proposed announcement as revised and approved by the Department:

"The U. S. Government is removing from Germany to continental United States certain art objects not readily identifiable as looted property with the sole intention of keeping such treasures safe and in trust for the people of Germany or the other rightful owners. The U.S. Government will retain these objects of art in its possession only as long as will be necessary to insure their physical safety or until such time as it may be possible to determine the rightful owners.

"When the appropriate Allied bodies determine the rightful owners or the return of conditions in Germany whereby the safety of these objects can be definitely assured, they will be distributed according to the directives of such Allied groups."

The Department of State adds that it is expected that more detailed announcement will have to be made in Washington in the near future to counter rumors and anticipated criticism concerning the action taken. We will be advised in advance by the Department regarding the date of such an announcement in order to synchronize it with the announcement made in Germany.

Robert Murphy.

Robert Murphy: re safekeeping of German-owned art (September 14, 1945).

C/ 'ER SHEET HEADQUARTERS U.S. GR''P CC

Must remain with attached papers

NUMBER EACH ITEM IN LEFT COLUMN. USE ENTIRE WIDTH OF PAPER.

ITEM No.	TO	FROM	DATE	SUBJECTS Reply to Cable on Removal of German-owned Art. Enter AG File Classification
1	Chief of Staff	Dir RD&R Div	24 Sep /45	The following is submitted as a draft reply to the cable from Mr. McCLOY W-66436 to the Deputy Military GOVERNOR. This cable assigned to O/SS for action.

"In connection with the shipment of German-owned works of art to the United States to prevent their deterioration, subject of your cable W-66436, dated 19 September, it now appears that the bulk of such art objects may be left in suitable repositories and placed in the custody of acceptable German personnel without undue risk of damage or deterioration. A complete check of the repositories in the US Zone is now being made to determine which may suitably be left undisturbed in the custody of German personnel and which should be evacuated either because their contents are loot or because the conditions of storage are unsatisfactory. It is hoped that the rapid restitution of looted art already evacuated to collecting-points will make space available in these for the storage of German-owned art objects which are evacuated from unsatisfactory repositories. Furthermore requests have been received from other zone authorities for the return to their custody of German-owned works of art from museums in their areas which are now stored in the US Zone. It is proposed to return such objects under assurances of proper safe-keeping. This action will not only relieve the US of responsibility for them but also make further storage space available in our collecting-points. When the survey of respositories is completed you will be advised whether and to what extent it appears advisable to evacuate outstanding German-owned works of art to US museums for safekeeping."

L. W. JEFFERSON
Colonel, GSC
Director.

Deliver by hand to Maj Scott, Secy –

" " " " Col Jefferson, Chf, RD&R.

HQ. USGCC FORM NO 9 PAGE No. LIFT HERE. USE OTHER SIDE.

USGCC: re safekeeping of German-owned art (September 24, 1945).

HEADQUARTERS
U.S. GROUP C.C.
A.G. CABLES
INCOMING CLASSIFIED MESSAGE

DATED 181330A

RECD 242005B SEPT
184/24
433

C O N F I D E N T I A L

U R G E N T

FROM : USFET MAIN SIGNED EISENHOWER

TO : US GROUP CC FOR R D & R DIVISION

FOR INFO : ADJ GEN WAR DEPT

REF NO : S-23916 CITE: ETGMC

Subject is removal of German owned cultural art objects to US, reference your CC-16123 dated 13 Sept 1945.

Only available information on cubic footage is on 3 respositories of German owned art evacuated by US Forces to US Zone for safekeeping, namely: 2 from Russian Zone, 17250 cubic feet and 1 from British Zone, 10250 cubic feet. Estimated floor space for storing them, 30,000 square feet. Inasmuch as most of the objects thus evacuated are in unopened crates, their quality is not now determinable. There remain 677 respositories in US Zone still to be investigated as to ownership and cubic content. Many months and much additional museum specialist personnel are required to complete competent estimate. Implementation of restitution program precludes use of present MFA and A personnel for this purpose. This Headquarters requests clarification of policy regarding future evacuation to US of German owned art objects in US Zone but indigenous to British, French and Russian Zones, inasmuch as British and French policy is to reassemble in their original form scattered German collections and to reactivate German Museums.

CC-15123, 13 Sept 45, Originator RD & R

ACTION : RD & R

INFORMATION : O/SS ; Legal
PR ; G (M)
Transport ; AG Records

IN 9554 24 Sept 45 2323 DMB/lm RCP NO: S-23916

C O N F I D E N T I A L

COPY NO 26

The Making Of An Exact Copy Of This Message Is Forbidden

USFET: re safekeeping of German-owned art (September 24, 1945).

DIVISION OF
CENTRAL SERVICES
TELEGRAPH SECTION

DEPARTMENT OF STATE

INCOMING TELEGRAM

INFORMATION
COPY
ACTION MUST BE ENDORSED
ON ACTION COPY

GEM -K
Paraphrase before communicating except to Government Agencies.

1946 FEB 13 AM 9 07

Cairo

DC/L
LIAISON

Dated February 12, 1946

Rec'd 6:01 p.m.

ACTION: ESP
INFO:
S
U
C
A-C
EUR
DC/L
OFD
FC
DC/R

~~RESTRICTED~~

Secretary of State,

Washington.

278, February 12, 7 p.m.

In official note Egyptian Prime Minister requests our govt's assistance with appropriate officials in American zone of occupation in Germany in order expedite return to Egypt of bust of Queen Nefertiti fraudulently taken to Germany in 1913. Prime Minister urgently requests that necessary instructions be given to commanding general or political adviser to deliver bust to representative of Egyptian Govt who will shortly proceed Germany to take delivery of it. Also that this official be given all possible facilities for his return to Egypt.

There is no gesture which would be more deeply appreciated by Egyptian Govt or people than the return to this country of bust of famous Queen Nefertiti. Am sending copies of Prime Minister's note to you and to Murphy.

Repeated to Murphy.

TUCK

JMS

~~RESTRICTED~~

DECLASSIFIED
NND 750168
By NARS, Date 11-22-88

Letter re Nefertiti and Egypt (February 12, 1946).

MEMORANDUM

TO: Mr. Huntington Cairns

FROM: Mr. Lamont Moore

February 14, 1946

It occurred to me in thinking about the Queen Nefertiti case that it might be well for us to consider as follows: let us assume that the buck-slip from the Department of State was really a request for consideration and suggested action. In the event that we do not answer it and the transfer of the sculpture from Germany to Egypt is accomplished, there might be a kick-back which we will not be able to answer, especially if the State Department said "well, we sent you the basic communication". Should we either by telephone or, if you wish, by informal memorandum, state our reactions possibly along the following lines:

1) The bust was taken to Germany long before the Nazis came to power, therefore, existing directives concerning resitution do not apply.

2) It is known that the bust left Egypt without national authorization, an act of so-called "smuggling" or fraudulent passage. Since the bust was purchased, the whole transaction was in no wise different from other transactions some of which brought works of art to American collections. Fraudulent passage cannot be considered looting. Representations by the Egypt should have been made before this date if fraudulent procedure was used in 1913.

3) The piece is to the Berlin Museum what the Winged Victory and Elgin Marbles are to their respective institutions. It has been associated for over a generation with the Berlin Museum by tourists and scholars and it would seem that its return to Egypt at this late date would be principally to satisfy the 'amour propre' of the Egyptians in a Nationalist sense.

4) To return this item to Egypt now would be to follow the Nazi principle of confiscating works of art by pretense or force in order to enlarge their own collections.

From a personal point of view, I should like to follow your recommendation that we consider no immediate action and yet I feel that if the Egyptian authoritier succeed in their plan, we might be faced with similar problems which might not be easily solved once the Nefertiti precedent has been established.

Lm

Letter re Nefertiti and Egypt (February 14, 1946).

File

MEMORANDUM

TO: Mr. Huntington Cairns
Secretary
The Roberts Commission

FROM: Lamont Moore
Assistant Secretary
The Roberts Commission

SUBJECT: LOAN OF THE NEFERTITI TO THE METROPOLITAN MUSEUM

As a result of my telephone conversation with Mr. Taylor of the Metropolitan Museum, he has asked for the Commission's advice on the following:

In connection with their promotion campaign, the Metropolitan Museum is planning to import certain important works of art from European Collections for a big loan exhibit of which the recent Good Shepherd "from the Lateran" is an example. Mr. Taylor was interested in the recent developments concerning the Nefertiti and he has suggested the following plan: Mr. Lansing of the Museum will contact the Egyptian Minister and explain the desire of the Metropolitan to exhibit the Nefertiti for two months. The Egyptian Minister will concur and indicate the approval of the Egyptian Government to the State Department. At the conclusion of the exhibit, Nefertiti will be returned to Egypt.

Mr. Taylor would like your reaction to this idea.

LM.

March 7, 1946

Letter re Nofertiti and Egypt (March 7, 1946).

April 19, 1946

Dear Francis:

I had hoped that by this date current considerations in certain departments would give us a firm basis for approving the loan of the Nefertiti. However, the Commission can only suggest at this time that yo negotiate for the loan through whatever channels you desire, subject to whatever conditions may be imposed by outside authorities This applies particularly to the suggestion that, upon the conclusion of its showing, the Nefertiti be returned to the country of its origin.

Sincerely yours,

Huntington Cairns
Secretary

Mr. Francis H. Taylor
The Metropolitan Museum of Art
Fifth Avenue and 82nd Street
New York 28, New York

Letter re Nefertiti and Egypt (April 19, 1946).

COPY

1

The Secretary of State presents his compliments to the Honorable the Minister of Egypt and has the honor to acknowledge receipt of the note of February 18, 1946, in which are stated the history of the statue of Queen Nefertiti and the request of the Egyptian Government to have this invaluable art object, now in the United States zone of occupation in Germany, returned to the land of its origin.

The Secretary of State fully understands the desire of the Egyptian Government to bring back this statue which has such great significance in the cultural history of Egypt, and has examined with the utmost sympathy the claim advanced in the Legation's note. It must, however, be recalled that the position of the United States as one of the four Occupying Powers who jointly have assumed supreme authority in Germany of necessity precludes unilateral disposition of property found in the United States zone. In so far as this Government has

acted

Letter re Nefertiti and Egypt (May 29, 1946).

-2-

acted with respect to the disposition of art objects found in Germany it has done so either as an agent of the control authority for the restitution of art looted by Germans during the war, in accordance with the United Nations Declaration of January 1943, or as trustee for artistic property in the possession of Germany at the beginning of the war.

On the basis of the latter principle the United States Government has brought from Germany to the National Gallery in Washington, D. C., about two hundred paintings not identifiable as looted property, with the intention of keeping such treasures in trust so long as necessary to insure their physical safety. These paintings will be returned to Germany as soon as conditions warrant, and no attempt will be made to investigate the manner in which Germany acquired them before 1939.

However much the Secretary of State appreciates the wishes of the Egyptian Government, he regretfully feels obliged after long consideration to state that the

present

-3-

present quadripartite military government of Germany, necessarily an agency concerned with specific objectives growing out of the total defeat of Germany, does not appear to be the appropriate authority for dealing with cases of disputed transfer of cultural objects which antedate the war.

In disclaiming the competence of the Allied military government to settle this matter, the Secretary of State does not propose in any way to overlook the merits of the case presented by the Egyptian Government or to pass judgment on the substantive issue. Since he must regard the subject as a juridical question, he earnestly hopes that subsequent to the reestablishment of a competent German Government this case may be brought before the International Court of Justice or other appropriate international agency for settlement.

Department of State,

Washington, May 29, 1946

CE:David Harris
H.C. Vedeler:AMR EUR/M Le NE A-H
5/20/46

863.413/2-1846 CS/H

Appendix IV

William Whobrey is Professor of German Studies and Medieval Studies at the Yale University. The paper **The Obligations of Victory: Walter Farmer and the Wiesbaden Manifesto** was read at a symposium "Preserving Cultural Heritage during Conflict: Legal and Moral Concerns." on November 1, 1997 at Temple University.

The Obligations of Victory: Walter Farmer and the Wiesbaden Manifesto

William Whobrey

Walter Farmer died on the 9th of August this year in Cincinnati, Ohio. Now, your first question might be: who was Walter Farmer, and your second, of what interest is he to me. I would like to take a few minutes today to introduce you to the life of Walter Farmer, especially one critical moment of his life at the end of the Second World War, and finally to discuss what meaning this man has for Civil Affairs soldiers in general and this conference in particular.

First, allow me to describe briefly how it is that I became aware of Walter Farmer's story. It is a story that has only recently begun to be told, a story long forgotten, either through disinterest or perhaps through a special interest. I have a habit af reading the German weekly "Der Spiegel" on a regular basis, and it was here that I happened upon Walter Farmer's obituary. It was here that I read that a CPT Farmer had, after the end of the Second World War, played a major part in the establishment of the central collection point for artwork in Wiesbaden, Germany. I also read about a letter of protest entitled the "Wiesbaden Manifesto." This piqued my interest, and I was determined to look into the story of this former officer who had served in what was then called "Monuments, Fine Arts, and Archives" (MFAA). I was interested as a Civil Affairs officer assigned to the Special Functions team that also had an "Arts and Monuments" section, as a scholar with an interest in German history, both ancient and modern, and as someone who appreciates art. In short, I was hooked.

Walter Farmer's story came to light in the late 80's through the work of Dr. Klaus Goldmann, curator of *Prehistory* at the State Museums of Prussian Culture in Berlin. Dr. Goldmann had, since 1972, conducted research into the subject of lost or stolen art, and in a film project in 1987 had asked for Mr. Farmer's help. But it wasn't until the appearance of Lynn Nicholas's book, *The Rape of Europa,* in 1994 that attention was drawn to the role the US Army had played in rescuing priceless works of art during and after the war. The book sparked international interest in the subject and led, among other things, to the conference entitled "The Spoils of War" sponsored by the Bard College Graduate Center for Studies in the Decorative Arts in January, 1995. The conference brought together many of the original participants in these events, to include Walter Farmer. The proceedings have now been published in a volume by the same name, edited by Elizabeth Simpson, and widely available in various book clubs. Walter Farmer spoke at the conference and, I am told, received a standing ovation. Through this publicity, as well as the work of Dr. Goldmann and others in Germany, Walter Farmer was awarded Germany's highest civilian award, the Grosses Verdienstkreuz or Federal Order of Merit, in February, 1996. In the company of his daughter, Mrs. Margaret Planton, he was praised by the German government as someone who, in the words of Foreign Minister Klaus Kinkel, "stood up for our cultural heritage ... a great son of a great nation." Farmer was again honored by the German masons in May, 1997, and attended several other conferences before his death from cancer this year. I wish to publicly thank Mrs. Planton of Chillicothe, Ohio, for making several articles and notes available to me from Mr. Farmer's personal archives.

We have arrived at the present, but what of the past? This is, after all, the story of CPT Farmer, a young man who served his country during World War II. I would like briefly to recount the events preceding a fateful day in November, 1945.

Born in 1911, Walter Farmer was thirty when the United States entered the war. He had studied architecture and mathematics at Miami University in Oxford, Ohio, graduating in 1935 with BA's in both. With very poor eyesight and at his age, he thought little of the draft. He married in February, 1942, and five weeks later found himself in the Medical Corps as a recruit. After serving as the lSG's assistant, he enrolled in OCS, graduated in January, 1943, and was commissioned a 2LT in the Engineers. In April he joined the 373rd GS Eng. Regt. as the Adjutant and went to England. After the D-Day landings, the regiment was busy repairing bridges in France and Germany. He was awarded a Purple Heart for wounds sustained during one of these actions. In May, 1945, at the end of the war, the regiment ended up in Aschaffenburg, Germany, ready to move to the Far East. An article in "Stars and Stripes" caught CPT Farmer's eye, and he read about the gold and artwork being discovered throughout Germany in caves and salt mines. Having a personal interest in art and architecture, he thought he might be able to contribute to this endeavor. He drove to SHAEF headquarters and requested a transfer to the American Commission for the Protection and Salvage of Artistic and Historic Monuments in War Areas. In June, 1945, he became a Monuments man.

He knew little of the MFAA, only that he, like many others, had seen General Eisenhower's order of May 26th, 1944: "Shortly we will be fighting our way across the continent of Europe in battles designed to preserve our civilization. Inevitably, in the path of our advances will be found historical monuments and cultural centers which symbolize to the world all that we are fighting to preserve. It is the responsibility of every commander to protect and respect these symbols whenever possible." CPT Farmer was an idealist and took these words to heart. They were to prove instrumental in decisions he later made.

He was soon introduced to his new role by other MFAA officers, among them experts and enthusiasts like himself. George Stout and Paul Sachs, professors at Harvard, and Francis Henry Taylor, Director of the Metropolitan Museum of

Art in New York, were at the forefront of the effort to protect and preserve artwork captured in Germany. Given his mission to establish the central collection point for German-owned works of art, he proceeded first to tour the Reichsbank building in Frankfurt, to where masses of crated works of art had been evacuated from the salt mines southwest of Berlin in March, 1945. Space was critical, and other facilities had to be found and prepared to house hundreds of art collections, literally hundreds of thousands of individual works, while providing them the security and environment that would prevent their continued deterioration, having survived the war in damp and dirty conditions. The Landesmuseum in Wiesbaden was still standing, but all 2000 of its windows were broken, there was no heat, and the doors had all been blown off their hinges. CPT Farmer set to work and by August had managed to repair enough space to accept the transfer of art while securing the building with tanks and infantry. Other centers were operating in Munich and Marburg. Along with his translator and secretary, Renate Hobirk, he then had to supervise the cataloguing and storage of thousands of crates from all over the American zone. Expert German museum personnel were brought in to assist in restoration and care of damaged pieces, and works were photographed as well.

And what a treasure it was: the Hungarian crown jewels, the bust of Nefertiti, the Hohenzollern regalia, works by Titian, Botticelli, Lucas Cranach, Rembrandt, and Dürer, along with many others. Officers and officials came from far and wide to view "the loot." CPT Farmer was horrified by one Army colonel who, as a joke, placed the Hungarian crown on his own head.

During the first week of November, the Collection Point was to have a visit from a COL Henry McBride, a liaison to the National Gallery. He was abrupt and wondered why the building was in such bad repair, with puddles of water on the floors. Without a working humidifier, this was the only way to keep wooden panels and Gothic sculpture preserved. This visit was a portent of things to come. On November 6, 1945, a hand-delivered telegram arrived at the CCP, ordering the removal of at least 200 paintings to the United States. The order reads:

> From 7th US Army
> To Office Mil Govt for Stadtkreis Wiesbaden
> BT
>
> Higher headquarters desires that immediate preparations be made for prompt shipment to the UNITEK of a selection of at least two zero zero German works of art of greatest importance X Most of these are now in Art Collecting Point Wiesbaden X Selections will be made by personnel from Headquarters CMA US Forces CMA European theater who will assist in packing and shipment by motor transport to Bremen X

> From CG Seventh Army to Director CMA Office of Military Government for Stadtkreis Wiesbaden CMA REF NO able three three zero two seven X
>
> You will provide sufficient material and personnel X This headquarters is to be informed by telephone of progress and anticipated requirements X Operation to be completed by two zero November X Transportation and military security during transit will be provided by this headquarters X

CPT Farmer was crushed. As he later recalled: "It seemed to me that everything that had been done to demonstrate the integrity of the United States government in the matter of its handling of German cultural properties would be discredited if this shipment took place."

CPT Farmer called a meeting of all 35 MFAA officers for the next day to discuss what could be done. The next day, 32 of 35 arrived, and the result of hours of heated discussion was the so-called "Wiesbaden Manifesto," a letter of protest drafted by Everett Lesley and signed by 24 of those officers present. Three officers agreed in principle but did not sign for fear of their careers, and five wrote separate letters. The letter was turned over to Major Bancel LaFarge, the MFAA representative at higher headquarters.

The protest had no immediate effect. The paintings, 202 of them, were crated and prepared for shipment in ten days. They were picked up, sent by train to Le Havre, then by ship to New York, where they arrived on December 6. From New York they were trucked to the National Gallery in Washington, D.C.

Art continued to arrive in Wiesbaden and in February, 1946, an exhibition was organized by Farmer to show the Germans that much of their cultural heritage remained. Those works that had been stolen by the Nazis after 1933 were returned to their rightful owners, when they could be determined. In March, CPT Farmer returned to the United States to resume a civilian career as an architect. He continued in the Army reserves, retiring with the rank of Colonel.

In the meantime, the "202," as they were called, had sparked controversy in the United States. The "Wiesbaden Manifesto" was first published in January, 1946 in the *College Art Journal* by former MFAA officer Charles Kuhn. In February, the *New York Times, Magazine of Art,* and *Time* discussed the protest. On 9 May, 1946, a further protest was signed by 95 museum officials and academics across the country and sent to President Truman. Controversy over the intentions of the National Gallery escalated. In short, the paintings were exhibited in 1948, but then returned to Germany in 1949. The Wiesbaden CCP was turned over to the Germans that same year, and so, it would seem, our story ends, perhaps a bit of a tempest in a teapot.

But it would be useful to examine more closely the content of the Manifesto and the reasons for its controversial reception. It is not a long document, and I would like to read it in full:

Text see Appendix No IIa, page 147–152.

Some background is necessary to understand the international, national, US military, and personal issues at stake here. First, the establishment of a national and international effort to protect art during and after the war was promulgated in the United States by several agencies, government and private. These agencies often had competing interest and agendas. It is not possible here to discuss these efforts in detail. But it is important to note a few of the conflicting views with regard to what should be done with works of art that came under US and allied control in Germany. Even before December, 1941, groups became active in considering what should be done to protect threatened art, even in the U.S. The concept of restitution-in-kind was advanced by some, to include the Chief Justice of the United States, Harlan Stone. By 1942, Justice Stone recommended to President Roosevelt that, at the time of the Armistice, the Axis powers should replace lost or destroyed art with their own equivalent works of art to be transferred to the invaded countries from Axis museums.

As the war progressed, the War Department put certain suggestions into action. For one, the Civil Affairs Division (CAD) was created under the Secretary of War on March 1, 1943. On the civilian side, the Roberts Commission was established in June, 1943, named after its Chairman, Justice Owen Roberts. This commission was organized at the behest of George Stout, chief of conservation at the Harvard Fogg museum and the country's greatest expert on the techniques of packing and evacuation. Stout and other civilian academics were primarily interested in ensuring that the military would play an active role in the protection of monuments and art as they made their way through Italy, France, and Germany. The CAD and MFAA were instrumental in giving these experts a voice in military operations, and many of them served in uniform. The conflicts between "military necessity" and the well-being of historic artifacts made the work of these men and women, moving with the front-line troops, absolutely critical.

The Soviet Union's policy was clear from the beginning. As they moved through Poland and Germany in 1944 and 45, the Germans were to become the objects of an official policy of retribution. Art work was to be confiscated and evacuated to the east. It was not to be returned, but would represent the spoils of victory in every historic sense. This policy was subject to criticism from the western allies only if a similar policy was not in place. Indeed, the Soviets used the evacuation of the Wiesbaden 202 as justification for their own removal of thousands of pieces of art.

Germany had interests of its own, of course. While not disputing the need to return stolen art to its rightful owners, it wanted to preserve its own patrimony as much as possible. As a nation completely defeated and in ruins, it had little say in the matter and was forced to rely on the goodwill of its conquerors. Although individual Nazis, both high-ranking and not, pushed for a return of their own collections, most were denied and usually ended up in a prison cell for their troubles. In more recent times, especially following the unification of Germany and the collapse of the Soviet Union, efforts have been made to regain that art which was German before the war and still resides in non-German museums, mostly in Russia. With revelations in 1991 that certain treasures, to include Priam's gold from the Trojan city of Troy, believed to have been lost, were in fact being kept in Russian museums, Germany began to push more aggressively for a return of these objects.

The re-emergence of the Wiesbaden Manifesto in the public eye raises certain ethical concerns important to us in Civil Affairs. I would like to close not by presenting a detailed analysis of these arguments but rather by asking questions that might lead us into a discussion of Walter Farmer's actions of November 7, 1945, and the Wiesbaden Manifesto's meaning in terms of military policy and personal obligation. The Manifesto is a statement of conscience. Much has been said about the signators refusal to obey orders and the risk of court martial. I see nothing of the kind in the document. Although the protest was to be sent up the chain of command, there was no refusal to obey the order from higher headquarters, and the 202 were shipped on schedule. The question should be put in terms of what an officer should do when orders are perceived to conflict with previous policy and mission statements and deemed to be harmful to US interests by those who must implement them.

Although the protest never made it up the military chain, it did enter the sphere of public debate. Is it ethical for Army personnel to pursue other avenues, such as the press, in hopes of influencing policy? The MFAA officers were unaware that President Truman and General Clay, the military governor of the American zone, had agreed in the summer of 1945 in principal to return the 202 at a later date. It is probable, however, that further removal of German patrimony was stymied by the public outcry. I believe that this question goes to the heart of military vs. civilian control of policy issues.

Finally, I would like to solicit comment on the Manifesto's meaning for the future. Some have called it a model of an honorable and civilized policy on the preservation of cultural heritage during conflict. The German Foreign Minister, Klaus Kinkel, praised Walter Farmer as a representative of the American people who "were true to their values and ideals." In awarding the Order of Merit, Germany wanted to honor a man who was "a model of civil courage ... and showed how a democrat and citizen of a free nation acts, one who distinguishes between right and wrong, moral rectitude and opportunism."

Appendix V

This Photo Documentation from the files of Walter I. Farmer gives a good insight to the work at the WCCP in 1945 and 1946. The private character of the photos shows better the daily life there than any official press relase.

Two Guards, c: Edith A. Standen, r: Rose Valland

Walter I. Farmer in his office, 1945

Edith A. Standen

Dr. Ferdinand Kutsch

Lore Hengstenberg, Kenneth C. Lindsay

Renate Hobirk

Ernst Holzinger

Walter I. Farmer and "his" Nefertiti

Preparations for the first exhibition in the WCCP, opened 10. February 1946 (l: Kenneth C. Lindsay, c: Ernst Holzinger, r: Wulfhild Schoppa)

Alo Altripp with St. Stephen's Crown

The Hungarian Regalia and three Chalices from the Cathedral of Gniezno (Poland)

Joe Kohlmaier and Edith A. Standen with Lucas Cranach, the Elder: The Fountain of Youth, 1546

Opening of the Exhibition at the Wiesbaden Collecting Point 12. May 1946

Opening of the Exhibition at the Wiesbaden Collecting Point 12. May 1946

Opening of the Exhibition at the Wiesbaden Collecting Point 12 May 1946. (l: Ernst Holzinger, Edith A. Standen, r: Kenneth C. Lindsay and the Princess of Prussia.)

Opening of the Exhibition at the Wiesbaden Collecting Point 12. May 1946. (Theodore A. Heinrich, Prince and Princess of Prussia, Edith A. Standen)

Dr. Holzinger and Captain Farmer examine the condition of a painting of the Nationalgalerie which came uncrated from Frankfurt to these open racks built for them.

Federal Minister for Foreign Affairs Dr. Klaus Kinkel awarding the Grosse Verdienstkreuz to Walter Farmer on 9 February 1996 in Gästehaus Petersberg.

Different cases of the Berlin State Museum in the Wiesbaden Collecting Point 1946.

Polish church treasures found in the Grasleben mine April 1945, later transfered to the Wiesbaden CCP.

Two chalices from the Cathedral of Gniezno (Poland)

The NGA is the likely custodian of art objects removed from Germany for safekeeping near the end of the war and later returned. Director David Finley, Chief Curator John Walker, and Administrator Harry A. McBride (left to right) oversee the transfer

A guard keeps watch over some of the 202 pictures from Germany stored in a NGA vault

When the Berlin paintings go on display without ceremony, visitors swarm to the NGA in unprecedented numbers: nearly one million people in forty days. The so-called "202" exhibit is the first "blockbuster" show (though the sorry term, first coined in wartime to describe a large bomb, is not applied to museum events until decades later)

The NGA's guard force is increased to handle the crush of visitors and the Army sends a detachment of Military Police to help assure security for the "202." The painting at left is Peter Paul Rubens' Saint Cecelia

One Sunday, NGA guards count 67,940 visitors, said to be an alltime high. On another Sunday, Gallery nurses count sixty first-aid cases.
After the exhibition leaves Washington, it tours a dozen cities and is seen by another million people. Thereafter, the Berlin pictures are crated up and returned to Germany, where they land in Bremerhaven

Arrival in Bremerhaven, 1948.

Index

MIX
Papier | Fördert gute Waldnutzung
FSC® C083411

Kolibri 360 GmbH
Ferdinand-Jühlke-Straße 7
99095 Erfurt, Deutschland
produktsicherheit@kolibri360.de